Ninja Foodi Cookbook UK 2023

A Variety of Delicious Recipes for Your Ninja Foodi Pressure Cooker, Easy and Comfortable Newbie Meals

Cindy J. Fortner

All Rights Reserved.

The contents of this book may not be reproduced, copied or transmitted without the direct written permission of the author or publisher. Under no circumstances will the publisher or the author be held responsible or liable for any damage, compensation or pecuniary loss arising directly or indirectly from the information contained in this book.

Legal notice. This book is protected by copyright. It is intended for personal use only. You may not modify, distribute, sell, use, quote or paraphrase any part or content of this book without the consent of the author or publisher.

Notice Of Disclaimer.

Please note that the information in this document is intended for educational and entertainment purposes only. Every effort has been made to provide accurate, up-to-date, reliable and complete information. No warranty of any kind is declared or implied. The reader acknowledges that the author does not engage in the provision of legal, financial, medical or professional advice. The content in this book has been obtained from a variety of sources. Please consult a licensed professional before attempting any of the techniques described in this book. By reading this document, the reader agrees that in no event shall the author be liable for any direct or indirect damages, including but not limited to errors, omissions or inaccuracies, resulting from the use of the information in this document.

CONTENTS

Food Pressure Cooker Basics 7
- FOUR REASONS TO FOODI 7
- Tender Crisp Technology 8
- One Pot Meals 8
- 360 Meals 8
- Frozen to Crispy 9
- CHOOSE THE FOODI FOR YOU 9

Breakfast Recipes 10
- Stuffed Baked Tomatoes 10
- Broccoli, Ham, And Cheddar Frittata 10
- Banana Custard Oatmeal 11
- Breakfast Burritos 11
- Bbq Chicken Sandwiches 11
- Poached Egg Heirloom Tomato 12
- Nutmeg Pumpkin Porridge 12
- Cinnamon Bun Oatmeal 12
- Breakfast Pies 13
- Carrot Cake Muffins 13
- Spinach Turkey Cups 14
- Banana Pancakes 14
- Waffle Bread Pudding With Maple-jam Glaze 14
- Mediterranean Quiche 15
- Cheesecake French Toast 15
- Pumpkin Breakfast Bread 16
- Peaches & Brown Sugar Oatmeal 16
- Soft-boiled Eggs 16
- Chorizo Omelet 16
- Brussels Sprouts Bacon Hash 17
- Almond Quinoa Porridge 17
- Pancetta Hash With Baked Eggs 17
- Cheesy Shakshuka 18
- Blueberry Muffins 18
- Zucchini Pancakes 18
- Bacon & Egg Poppers 19
- Morning Pancakes 19
- Ham & Spinach Breakfast Bake 19
- Pepperoni Omelets 20
- Very Berry Puffs 20
- Glazed Carrots 20
- Spanish Potato And Chorizo Frittata 20
- Cranberry Lemon Quinoa 21
- Walnut Orange Coffee Cake 21
- French Dip Sandwiches 21
- Sweet Bread Pudding 22
- Baked Eggs In Mushrooms 22
- Apricot Oatmeal 22
- Quinoa Protein Bake 23

Snacks, Appetizers & Sides Recipes 23
- Steak And Minty Cheese 23
- Crispy Cheesy Straws 23
- Sweet Potato Skins 24
- Cheesy Chicken Dip 24
- Sweet Potato Gratin 24
- Caramelized Cauliflower With Hazelnuts 25
- Zucchini Egg Tots 25
- Cheesy Stuffed Mushroom 25
- Parmesan Butternut Crisps 26
- Caribbean Chicken Skewers 26
- Parmesan Breadsticks 26
- Herby Fish Skewers 27
- Cheesy Fried Risotto Balls 27
- Seasoned Parsnip Fries 28
- Turkey Scotch Eggs 28
- Cauliflower Gratin 28
- Shallot Pepper Pancakes 29
- Chocolate Chip & Zucchini Snack Bars 29
- Crab Rangoon's 30
- Spicy Turkey Meatballs 30
- Honey Mustard Hot Dogs 30
- Cheesy Cauliflower Tater Tots 31
- Spicy Glazed Pecans 31
- Chicken Bites 31
- Spinach Hummus 32
- Herb Roasted Mixed Nuts 32
- Mushrooms Stuffed With Veggies 32

Bacon Wrapped Scallops 33
Crispy Cheesy Zucchini Bites 33
Beef Chicken Meatloaf 33
Spicy Black Bean Dip 34
Saucy Chicken Wings 34
Mexican Street Corn 34
Brie Spread With Cherries & Pistachios 35
South Of The Border Corn Dip 35
Loaded Potato Skins 35
Garlicky Tomato 36
Cheesy Smashed Sweet Potatoes 36
Potato Samosas 36
Herbed Cauliflower Fritters 37

Poultry Recipes 38

Ginger Orange Chicken Tenders 38
Turkey Enchilada Casserole 38
Sour Cream & Cheese Chicken 38
Jerk Chicken Thighs With Sweet Potato And Banana Mash 39
Chicken Breasts 39
Turkey & Cabbage Enchiladas 39
Honey Garlic Chicken And Okra 40
Turkey Croquettes 40
Spanish Chicken & Olives 41
Italian Turkey & Pasta Soup 41
Chicken And Broccoli 41
Shredded Chicken Salsa 42
Chicken With Bacon And Beans 42
Turkey & Squash Casserole 42
Chicken With Rice And Peas 43
Creamy Tuscan Chicken Pasta 43
Chicken Pot Pie 44
Cajun Chicken & Pasta 44
Crispy Chicken With Carrots And Potatoes 44
Chicken Fajitas With Avocado 45
Buttermilk Chicken Thighs 45
Creamy Chicken Carbonara 45
Chipotle Raspberry Chicken 46
Pizza Stuffed Chicken 46
Chicken Pasta With Pesto Sauce 47
Turkey Green Chili 47

Lime Chicken Chili 48
Chicken Thighs With Thyme Carrot Roast 48
Greek Style Turkey Meatballs 48
Cheesy Basil Stuffed Chicken 49
Hassel Back Chicken 49
Barbeque Chicken Drumettes 49
Spicy Chicken Wings. 50
Southwest Chicken Bake 50
Herb Roasted Drumsticks 50
Tuscany Turkey Soup 51
Braised Chicken With Mushrooms And Brussel Sprouts 51
Speedy Fajitas 52
Korean Barbecued Satay 52
Taiwanese Chicken 52

Beef, Pork & Lamb Recipes 53

Lamb Curry 53
Teriyaki Pork Noodles 53
Beef Mole 53
Smoky Horseradish Spare Ribs 54
Lamb Tagine 54
Beef Tips & Mushrooms 55
Maple Glazed Pork Chops 55
Beef Sirloin Steak 55
Bacon Strips 56
Garlicky Pork Chops 56
Pepper Crusted Tri Tip Roast 56
Creole Dirty Rice 56
Beef Lasagna 57
Beef In Basil Sauce 57
Peppercorn Meatloaf 58
Roasted Pork With Apple Gravy 58
Korean Pork Chops 58
Red Pork And Chickpea Stew 59
Beef & Broccoli Casserole 59
Asian Beef 59
Beef Bulgogi 60
Mexican Pot Roast 60
Chunky Pork Meatloaf With Mashed Potatoes 60
Sour And Sweet Pork 61
Pesto Pork Chops & Asparagus 61

Bacon & Sauerkraut With Apples	61
Corned Cabbage Beef	62
Chorizo Stuffed Yellow Bell Peppers	62
Southern-style Lettuce Wraps	63
Cheesy Ham & Potato Casserole	63
Ham, Ricotta & Zucchini Fritters	63
Hot Dogs With Peppers	64
Zucchini & Beef Lasagna	64
Caribbean Ropa Vieja	64
Pork Sandwiches With Slaw	65
Beef And Bell Pepper With Onion Sauce	65
Pork Chops With Green Beans And Scalloped Potatoes	66
Pork Tenderloin With Ginger And Garlic	66
Beef Bourguignon	67
Short Ribs With Egg Noodles	67

Fish & Seafood Recipes 68

Chili Mint Steamed Snapper	68
Herb Salmon With Barley Haricot Verts	68
Cajun Salmon With Lemon	68
Arroz Con Cod	69
Pistachio Crusted Salmon	69
Citrus Glazed Halibut	69
Paella Señorito	70
Tuna Salad With Potatoes And Asparagus	70
Pistachio Crusted Mahi Mahi	70
Chorizo And Shrimp Boil	71
Sweet & Spicy Shrimp	71
Asian Inspired Halibut	71
Crab Cakes With Spicy Dipping Sauce	72
Baked Cod Casserole	72
Coconut Cilantro Shrimp	72
Stuffed Cod	73
Crab Cakes	73
Spicy Shrimp Pasta With Vodka Sauce	73
Flounder Veggie Soup	74
Haddock With Sanfaina	74
Cajun Shrimp	75
Seafood Gumbo	75
Clam Fritters	75
Lemon Cod Goujons And Rosemary Chips	76

Spiced Red Snapper	76
Mediterranean Cod	77
Low Country Boil	77
Drunken Saffron Mussels	77
Seared Scallops In Asparagus Sauce	78
Crab Alfredo	78
Shrimp And Sausage Paella	78
Shrimp & Sausage Gumbo	79
Italian Flounder	79
Stir Fried Scallops & Veggies	80
Seafood Minestrone	80
Kung Pao Shrimp	80
Mackerel En Papillote With Vegetables	81
Coconut Curried Mussels	81
Tilapia & Tamari Garlic Mushrooms	81
Succotash With Basil Crusted Fish	82

Vegan & Vegetable Recipes 83

Mashed Potatoes With Spinach	83
Cheesy Corn Casserole	83
Veggie Taco Soup	83
Tomato Galette	84
Zucchinis Spinach Fry	84
Hawaiian Tofu	84
Veggie Skewers	85
Rustic Veggie Tart	85
Beets And Carrots	86
Roasted Vegetable Salad	86
Mushroom Risotto With Swiss Chard	86
Pesto With Cheesy Bread	86
Veggie Loaded Pasta	87
Spicy Salmon With Wild Rice	87
Mushroom Poutine	88
Spicy Kimchi And Tofu Fried Rice	88
Balsamic Cabbage With Endives	89
Grilled Cheese	89
Zucchini Quinoa Stuffed Red Peppers	89
Veggie Lasagna	90
Pasta With Roasted Veggies	90
Baked Linguine	91
Veggie And Quinoa Stuffed Peppers	91

- Green Cream Soup 91
- Red Beans And Rice 91
- Asparagus With Feta 92
- Hot & Sour Soup 92
- Italian Spinach & Tomato Soup 92
- Cheesy Squash Tart 93
- Warming Harvest Soup 93
- Pasta Primavera 94
- Cheesy Corn Pudding 94
- Hearty Veggie Soup 94
- Spanish Rice 95
- Southern Pineapple Casserole 95
- Saucy Kale 95
- Radish Apples Salad 96
- Zucchini Rice Gratin 96
- Mushroom Leek Soup With Parmesan Croutons 96
- Pepper And Sweet Potato Skewers 97

Desserts Recipes 97

- Peanut Butter Pie 97
- Sweet And Salty Bars 97
- Raspberry Lemon Cheesecake 98
- Red Velvet Cheesecake 98
- Vanilla Chocolate Spread 99
- Strawberry Crumble 99
- Chocolate Brownie Cake 99
- Fried Oreos 100
- Almond Banana Dessert 100
- Hot Fudge Brownies 100
- Pecan Stuffed Apples 100
- Mixed Berry Cobbler 101
- Poached Peaches 101
- Coconut Milk Crème Caramel 101
- Sweet Potato Pie 101
- Pumpkin Crème Brulee 102
- Chocolate Rice Pudding 102
- Chocolate Soufflé 102
- Chocolate Blackberry Cake 103
- Brownie Bites 103
- Chocolate Peanut Butter And Jelly Puffs 103
- Lemon Cheesecake 104
- Gingerbread 104
- Bacon Blondies 105
- Coconut Cream Dessert Bars 105
- Steamed Lemon Pudding 106
- Spiced Poached Pears 106
- Berry Apple Crisps 106
- Carrot Raisin Cookie Bars 107
- Classic Custard 107
- Yogurt Cheesecake 107
- Coconut Cake 108
- Mocha Cake 108
- Brown Sugar And Butter Bars 108
- Vanilla Pound Cake 109
- Apricots With Honey Sauce 109
- Chocolate Chip Cheesecake 109
- Portuguese Honey Cake 110
- Caramel Pecan Coffee Cake 110
- Mexican Chocolate Walnut Cake 110

RECIPES INDEX 111

Food Pressure Cooker Basics

FOR SO MANY PEOPLE, THERE ARE A FEW UNSPOKEN RULES WHEN it comes to cooking. It needs to be quick, it needs to be tasty, and it needs to be good for you. However, in the constant hustle and bustle of life, too often we sacrifice at least one of these areas to get the job done and move on to the next thing.

Multi-cookers claim to do it all, and slow cookers have long been touted for their versatility and convenience. After all, they do the work for you: just toss ingredients into the pot and come back to a perfectly cooked meal. Pressure cookers take it a step further, making your food incredibly tender, exceptionally fast.

But what about texture? Tender food is great, but no one wants to eat stews and soups every night. We all crave the crispy and crunchy. What are chicken wings without a crispy exterior? Who wants to eat potpie without a flaky crust?

Enter the Ninja Foodi Pressure Cooker, the pressure cooker that crisps—a revolutionary appliance changing the multi-cooker game. With the Foodi Pressure Cooker, you can make quick, healthy, and delicious meals. As a result, you can spend less time cooking and more time doing all of the other things you need to get done.

This chapter will introduce you to the functions and benefits of this revolutionary appliance and help you choose the one that is right for you. Whether you are new to the Foodi or you are a Foodi fanatic, I will break down cooking with the Ninja Foodi Pressure Cooker, giving you the Ninja Test Kitchen tips and tricks, and helping you unleash its full potential. And, of course, I'll introduce you to the recipes and strategies so you can use it every day.

FOUR REASONS TO FOODI

For too long we have settled for convenience over flavor. Opting for takeout over a home-cooked meal or leaning on multi-cookers that don't deliver to answer the question, "What's for dinner?" With the Ninja Foodi Pressure Cooker, you no longer have to settle. Tender Crisp Technology unlocks unlimited possibilities for breakfast, lunch, dinner, dessert, and more.

Tender Crisp Technology

Tender Crisp Technology is quite simple. First, use the pressure function to quickly cook and tenderize food with superheated steam. Then, remove the pressure lid and lower the crisping lid to quickly crisp and caramelize for the perfect finishing touch. With Tender Crisp Technology, you can cook quickly and ensure your food is tender inside and crispy on the outside. I'm talking about Garlic-Herb Roasted Chicken or Crispy Korean-Style Ribs!

One Pot Meals

With the Foodi Pressure Cooker, you can transform boring, one-texture meals into one-pot wonders. Use the pressure function to quickly cook your favorite casseroles, stews, and chilis. Then top with cheese, biscuits, or a crust. Swap the top and use the crisping lid to broil the cheese, bake the biscuits, or crisp the crust. With everything prepared in one pot, your prep time is cut down, and you only have one pot to clean! Make the recipes that have been handed down from generation to generation—but with this unique twist, you can make them in half the time! Try this Cheesy Chicken and Broccoli Casserole or a classic Green Bean Casserole.

360 Meals

Make a delicious, restaurant-inspired meal in one pot. I'm talking a full meal complete with fluffy rice, roasted veggies, and perfectly cooked proteins—each with its own unique texture. Pile grains on the bottom of your cooking pot, add some veggies, pop in the Reversible Rack, and place your proteins on top. Use the recipes throughout the book with the 360 Meal label, or go off book and try your own combination. Some of my favorite 360 Meals include Pork Chops with Green Beans and Scalloped Potatoes and Mustard and Apricot-Glazed Salmon with Smashed Potatoes. Which will you try first?

Frozen to Crispy

Perhaps the most convenient feature of the Ninja Foodi Pressure Cooker is the ability to cook food straight from frozen. There's no need to wait around for food to thaw. Use pressure to quickly defrost and tenderize frozen meat, then lower the crisping lid to sizzle and crisp the outside. No more uneven defrosting using the microwave or waiting hours for your food to defrost on the counter. Check out freezer-to-table recipes like Salmon with Almonds, Cranberries, and Rice and Frozen Chicken and Mozzarella Casserole.

CHOOSE THE FOODI FOR YOU

You asked and we listened! After launching the original Ninja Foodi Pressure Cooker in 2018, we have now expanded our offering.

Whether you are a family of four, empty nesters, a single person, newlyweds, or looking to feed a crowd—there is now a Foodi Pressure Cooker for everyone.

Breakfast Recipes

Stuffed Baked Tomatoes

Servings: 4
Cooking Time: 25 Minutes
Ingredients:
- 4 large tomatoes
- 4 slices turkey bacon, chopped
- ¼ cup green pepper, chopped
- 3 tbsp. mushroom, chopped
- 2 eggs
- 4 egg whites
- 2 tbsp. skim milk
- ¼ tsp salt
- ½ cup cheddar cheese, reduced fat, grated

Directions:
1. Cut off the tops of the tomatoes and scoop out the inside, do not cut the bottom or sides. Set aside.
2. Set cooker to sauté on medium heat. Add bacon and cook until almost crisp.
3. Add the peppers and mushrooms and cook until bacon is crisp and peppers are tender. Spoon into tomatoes.
4. In a medium bowl, whisk together eggs, egg whites, milk, and salt. Pour into tomatoes leaving ¼ inch space at the top.
5. Place tomatoes in the cooking pot and top with cheese. Set to air fryer function on 350°F. Secure the tender-crisp lid and bake 15-20 minutes or until eggs are cooked through. Let rest 5 minutes before serving.

Nutrition Info:
- Calories 165,Total Fat 8g,Total Carbs 9g,Protein 15g,Sodium 483mg.

Broccoli, Ham, And Cheddar Frittata

Servings:6
Cooking Time: 40 Minutes
Ingredients:
- 1 head broccoli, cut into 1-inch florets
- 1 tablespoon canola oil
- Kosher salt
- Freshly ground black pepper
- 12 large eggs
- ¼ cup whole milk
- 1½ cups shredded white Cheddar cheese, divided
- 3 tablespoons unsalted butter
- ½ medium white onion, diced
- 1 cup diced ham

Directions:
1. Place Cook & Crisp Basket in the pot. Close crisping lid. Select AIR CRISP, setting temperature to 390°F, and set time to 5 minutes. Select START/STOP to begin preheating.
2. In a large bowl, toss the broccoli with the oil and season with salt and pepper.
3. Once unit is preheated, open lid and add the broccoli to basket. Close crisping lid.
4. Select AIR CRISP, set temperature to 390°F, and set time to 15 minutes. Select START/STOP to begin.
5. In a separate large bowl, whisk together the eggs, milk, and 1 cup of cheese.
6. After 7 minutes, open lid. Remove basket and shake the broccoli. Return basket to pot and close lid to continue cooking.
7. After 8 minutes, check the broccoli for desired doneness. When cooking is complete, remove broccoli and basket from pot.
8. Select SEAR/SAUTÉ and set to HI. Select START/STOP to begin.
9. After 5 minutes, add the butter. Melt for 1 minute, then add the onion and cook for 3 minutes, stirring occasionally.
10. Add the ham and broccoli and cook, stirring occasionally, for 2 minutes.
11. Add the egg mixture, season with salt and pepper, and stir. Close crisping lid.
12. Select BAKE/ROAST, set temperature to 400°F, and set time to 15 minutes. Select STOP/START to begin.
13. After 5 minutes, open lid and sprinkle the remaining ½ cup of cheese on top. Close lid to continue cooking.
14. When cooking is complete, remove pot from unit and let the frittata sit for 5 to 10 minutes before serving.

Nutrition Info:
- Calories: 404,Total Fat: 30g,Sodium: 671mg,Carbohydrates: 10g,Protein: 27g.

Banana Custard Oatmeal

Servings: 6
Cooking Time: 40 Minutes
Ingredients:
- Butter flavored cooking spray
- 1 2/3 cups vanilla almond milk, unsweetened
- 2 large bananas, mashed
- 1 cup bananas, sliced
- 1 cup steel cut oats
- 1/3 cup maple syrup
- 1/3 cup walnuts, chopped
- 2 eggs, beaten
- 1 tbsp. butter, melted
- 1 ½ tsp cinnamon
- 1 tsp baking powder
- 1 tsp vanilla extract
- ½ tsp nutmeg
- ¼ teaspoon salt
- 2 ½ cups water

Directions:
1. Spray a 1 1/2 –quart baking dish with cooking spray.
2. In a large bowl, combine all ingredients thoroughly. Transfer to prepared baking dish.
3. Pour 1 ½ cups water into the cooking pot and add the trivet. Place dish on the trivet and secure the lid.
4. Select pressure cooking on high and set timer for 40 minutes.
5. When timer goes off, release pressure naturally for 10 minutes, then use quick release. Stir oatmeal well then serve.

Nutrition Info:
- Calories 349,Total Fat 10g,Total Carbs 56g,Protein 10g,Sodium 281mg.

Breakfast Burritos

Servings:4
Cooking Time: 30 Minutes
Ingredients:
- 1 pound ground chorizo
- ½ onion, diced
- ½ red bell pepper, diced
- 1 small jalapeño, minced
- ½ cup canned black beans, rinsed and drained
- Kosher salt
- Freshly ground black pepper
- 6 eggs, beaten
- 4 flour tortillas
- 1 cup shredded Mexican blend cheese
- 1 cup cilantro, minced
- Guacamole, for serving
- Pico de gallo, for serving

Directions:
1. Select SEAR/SAUTÉ and set temperature to MED. Let preheat for 5 minutes.
2. Add the chorizo, breaking up the meat with a silicone spatula until cooked through, 3 to 5 minutes. Add the onions, bell pepper, jalapeño, black beans, and season with salt and pepper. Cook until onions are translucent, about 3 minutes.
3. Add the eggs and cook, stirring frequently, until they have reached your desired consistency. When cooking is complete, transfer the mixture to a large bowl.
4. Lay a tortilla on a flat surface and load with ¼ cup of cheese, ¾ cup of egg mixture, and ¼ cup of cilantro. Roll the burrito by folding the right and left sides over the filling, then roll the tortilla over itself from the bottom forming a tight burrito. Repeat this step three more times with the remaining tortillas, cheese, egg mixture, and cilantro.
5. Place two burritos seam-side down in the Cook & Crisp Basket and place basket in pot. Close crisping lid.
6. Select AIR CRISP, set temperature to 390°F, and set time to 16 minutes. Select START/STOP to begin.
7. After 8 minutes, open lid and remove the burritos from basket. Place the remaining two burritos seam-side down in the basket. Close lid and continue cooking for the remaining 8 minutes.
8. When cooking is complete, let the burritos cool for a few minutes. Serve with the guacamole and pico de gallo.

Nutrition Info:
- Calories: 693,Total Fat: 36g,Sodium: 1732mg,Carbohydrates: 48g,Protein: 44g.

Bbq Chicken Sandwiches

Servings: 4
Cooking Time: 45 Min
Ingredients:
- 4 chicken thighs, boneless and skinless
- 1½ cups iceberg lettuce, shredded /195g
- 2 cups barbecue sauce /500ml
- 1 onion, minced
- 2 garlic cloves, minced
- 4 burger buns
- 2 tbsp minced fresh parsley /30g
- 1 tbsp lemon juice /15ml

- 1 tbsp mayonnaise /15ml
- Salt to taste

Directions:

1. Season the chicken with salt, and transfer into the inner pot. Add in garlic, onion and barbeque sauce. Coat the chicken by turning in the sauce. Seal the pressure lid, choose Pressure, set to High, and set the timer to 15 minutes. Press Start.
2. When ready, do a natural pressure release for 10 minutes. Use two forks to shred the chicken and mix into the sauce. Press Sear/Sauté and let the mixture to simmer for 15 minutes to thicken the sauce, until desired consistency.
3. Meanwhile, using a large bowl, mix the lemon juice, mayonnaise, salt, and parsley; toss lettuce into the mixture to coat.
4. Separate the chicken in equal parts to match the sandwich buns; apply lettuce for topping and complete the sandwiches.

Poached Egg Heirloom Tomato

Servings: 4
Cooking Time: 10 Min

Ingredients:

- 4 large eggs
- 2 large Heirloom ripe tomatoes; halved crosswise
- 4 small slices feta cheese
- 1 cup water /250ml
- 2 tbsp grated Parmesan cheese /30g
- 1 tsp chopped fresh herbs, of your choice /5g
- Salt and black pepper to taste
- Cooking spray

Directions:

1. Pour the water into the Ninja Foodi and fit the reversible rack. Grease the ramekins with the cooking spray and crack each egg into them.
2. Season with salt and pepper. Cover the ramekins with aluminum foil. Place the cups on the trivet. Seal the lid.
3. Select Steam mode for 3 minutes on High pressure. Press Start/Stop. Once the timer goes off, do a quick pressure release. Use a napkin to remove the ramekins onto a flat surface.
4. In serving plates, share the halved tomatoes, feta slices, and toss the eggs in the ramekin over on each tomato half. Sprinkle with salt and pepper, parmesan, and garnish with chopped herbs.

Nutmeg Pumpkin Porridge

Servings: 8
Cooking Time: 5 Hours

Ingredients:

- 1 cup unsweetened almond milk
- 2 pounds pumpkin, peeled and cubed into ½-inch size
- 6-8 drops liquid stevia
- ½ teaspoon ground allspice
- 1 tablespoon ground cinnamon
- 1 teaspoon ground nutmeg
- ¼ teaspoon ground cloves
- ½ cup walnuts, chopped

Directions:

1. In the Ninja Foodi's insert, place ½ cup of almond milk and remaining ingredients and stir to combine.
2. Close the Ninja Foodi's lid with a crisping lid and select "Slow Cooker."
3. Set on "Low" for 4-5 hours.
4. Press the "Start/Stop" button to initiate cooking.
5. Open the Ninja Foodi's lid and stir in the remaining almond milk.
6. With a potato masher, mash the mixture completely.
7. Divide the porridge into serving bowls evenly.
8. Serve warm with the topping of walnuts.

Nutrition Info:

- Calories: 96; Fat: 5.5g; Carbohydrates: 11.2g; Protein: 3.3g

Cinnamon Bun Oatmeal

Servings: 6
Cooking Time: 26 Minutes

Ingredients:

- 1 cup gluten-free steel-cut oats
- 3½ cups water
- ¼ teaspoon sea salt
- 1 teaspoon nutmeg
- 2 teaspoons cinnamon, divided
- ½ cup all-purpose flour
- ½ cup rolled oats
- ⅔ cup brown sugar
- ⅓ cup cold unsalted butter, cut into pieces
- 2 tablespoons granulated sugar
- ¾ cup raisins
- 2 ounces cream cheese, at room temperature
- 2 tablespoons confectioners' sugar

- 1 teaspoon whole milk

Directions:
1. Place the steel-cut oats, water, salt, nutmeg, and 1 teaspoon of cinnamon in the pot. Assemble pressure lid, making sure the pressure release valve is in the SEAL position.
2. Select PRESSURE and set to HI. Set time to 11 minutes. Select START/STOP to begin.
3. In a medium bowl, combine the flour, rolled oats, brown sugar, butter, remaining 1 teaspoon of cinnamon, and granulated sugar until a crumble forms.
4. When pressure cooking is complete, allow pressure to naturally release for 5 minutes. After 5 minutes, quick release any remaining pressure by moving the pressure release valve to the VENT position. Carefully remove lid when unit has finished releasing pressure.
5. Stir the raisins into the oatmeal. Cover and let sit 5 minutes to thicken.
6. Evenly spread the crumble topping over the oatmeal. Close crisping lid.
7. Select AIR CRISP, set temperature to 400°F, and set time to 10 minutes. Select START/STOP to begin.
8. In a small bowl, whisk together the cream cheese, confectioners' sugar, and milk. Add more milk or sugar, as needed, to reach your desired consistency.
9. When crumble topping is browned, cooking is complete. Open lid and serve the oatmeal in individual bowls topped with a swirl of cream cheese topping.

Nutrition Info:
- Calories: 454,Total Fat: 16g,Sodium: 117mg,Carbohydrates: 73g,Protein: 8g.

Breakfast Pies

Servings: 4
Cooking Time: 20 Minutes

Ingredients:
- 1 ½ cup mozzarella cheese, grated
- 2/3 cup almond flour, sifted
- 4 eggs, beaten
- 4 tbsp. butter
- 6 slices bacon, cooked crisp & crumbled

Directions:
1. Select air fryer function and heat cooker to 400°F.
2. In a microwave safe bowl, melt the mozzarella cheese until smooth.
3. Stir in flour until well combined.
4. Roll the dough out between 2 sheets of parchment paper. Use a sharp knife to cut dough into 4 equal rectangles.
5. Heat the butter in a skillet over medium heat. Add the eggs and scramble to desired doneness.
6. Divide eggs evenly between the four pieces of dough, placing them on one side. Top with bacon.
7. Fold dough over filling and seal the edges with a fork. Poke a few holes on the top of the pies.
8. Place the pies in the fryer basket in a single layer. Secure the tender-crisp lid and bake 20 minutes, turning over halfway through. Serve immediately.

Nutrition Info:
- Calories 420,Total Fat 33g,Total Carbs 3g,Protein 28g,Sodium 663mg.

Carrot Cake Muffins

Servings: 12
Cooking Time: 30 Minutes

Ingredients:
- ¾ cup almond flour, sifted
- ½ cup coconut flour
- 1 tsp baking soda
- ½ tsp baking powder
- 1 tsp cinnamon
- ¼ tsp salt
- ¼ tsp cloves
- ¼ tsp nutmeg
- 2 eggs
- ½ cup honey
- 1 tsp vanilla
- ¼ cup coconut milk, unsweetened
- 2 tbsp. coconut oil, melted
- 1 banana, mashed
- 1 ½ cups carrots, grated

Directions:
1. Select the bake function and heat cooker to 350°F. Line 2 6-cup muffin tins with liners.
2. In a medium bowl, combine flours, baking soda, baking powder, cinnamon, salt, cloves, and nutmeg.
3. In a large bowl, beat eggs, honey, vanilla, and milk together until thoroughly combined.
4. Add the melted oil and mix well.
5. Add the banana and beat to combine. Stir in dry ingredients until mixed in. Fold in carrots.
6. Spoon into prepared muffin tins about ¾ full.

7. Place muffin tin, one at a time on the rack in the cooker and secure the tender-crisp lid. Bake 25-30 minutes, or until muffins pass the toothpick test.

Nutrition Info:
- Calories 113,Total Fat 4g,Total Carbs 16g,Protein 1g,Sodium 196mg.

Spinach Turkey Cups

Servings: 4
Cooking Time: 23 Minutes

Ingredients:
- 1 tablespoon unsalted butter
- 1-pound fresh baby spinach
- 4 eggs
- 7 ounces cooked turkey, chopped
- 4 teaspoons unsweetened almond milk
- Black pepper and salt, as required

Directions:
1. Select the "Sauté/Sear" setting of Ninja Foodi and place the butter into the pot.
2. Press the "Start/Stop" button to initiate cooking and heat for about 2-3 minutes.
3. Add the spinach and cook for about 3 minutes or until just wilted.
4. Press the "Start/Stop" button to pause cooking and drain the liquid completely.
5. Transfer the spinach into a suitable and set aside to cool slightly.
6. Set the "Air Crisp Basket" in the Ninja Foodi's insert.
7. Close the Ninja Foodi's lid with a crisping lid and select "Air Crisp."
8. Set its cooking temperature to 355 °F for 5 minutes.
9. Press the "Start/Stop" button to initiate preheating.
10. Divide the spinach into 4 greased ramekins, followed by the turkey.
11. Crack 1 egg into each ramekin and drizzle with almond milk.
12. Sprinkle with black pepper and salt.
13. After preheating, Open the Ninja Foodi's lid.
14. Place the ramekins into the "Air Crisp Basket."
15. Close the Ninja Foodi's lid with a crisping lid and select "Air Crisp."
16. Set its cooking temperature to 355 °F for 20 minutes.
17. Press the "Start/Stop" button to initiate cooking.
18. Open the Ninja Foodi's lid and serve hot.

Nutrition Info:
- Calories: 200; Fat: 10.2g; Carbohydrates: 4.5g; Protein: 23.4g

Banana Pancakes

Servings: 6
Cooking Time: 15 Minutes

Ingredients:
- Butter flavor cooking spray
- 2 bananas
- 3 eggs
- 1 tsp baking powder
- 1 tsp vanilla extract
- ¼ tsp cinnamon

Directions:
1. In a medium bowl, mash bananas. Add remaining ingredients and mix until mostly smooth.
2. Spray the cooking pot and select sauté function on medium.
3. When the cooker is hot, pour 1/8 cup of batter at a time on the bottom. Cook 2 minutes, or until bubbles form on the top. Flip and cook 1 minute more until golden brown. Repeat.

Nutrition Info:
- Calories 74,Total Fat 2g,Total Carbs 10g,Protein 4g,Sodium 37mg.

Waffle Bread Pudding With Maple-jam Glaze

Servings:6
Cooking Time: 25 Minutes

Ingredients:
- 2 whole eggs
- 4 egg yolks
- 1 cup heavy (whipping) cream
- ½ teaspoon ground cinnamon
- ¼ cup granulated sugar
- 1 teaspoon vanilla extract
- 20 waffles, cut in sixths
- 1 cup water
- ⅓ cup desired jam
- raspberry)
- ⅓ cup maple syrup

Directions:
1. In a large mixing bowl, combine the eggs, egg yolks, cream, cinnamon, sugar, and vanilla. Whisk well to combine.

Add the waffle pieces and toss very well to incorporate. The waffles should be completely soaked through with cream sauce, with some extra residual cream sauce at the bottom of the bowl.

2. Place the waffle mixture in the Ninja Multi-Purpose Pan or 8-inch round baking dish. Press down gently to ensure ingredients are well packed into the pan. Cover the pan tightly with plastic wrap.

3. Add the water to the pot. Place the pan on the Reversible Rack and place rack in pot. Assemble pressure lid, making sure the pressure release valve is in the SEAL position.

4. Select PRESSURE and set to HI. Set time to 15 minutes. Select START/STOP to begin.

5. Place the jam and maple syrup in a small bowl and mix well to combine.

6. When pressure cooking is complete, quick release the pressure by moving the pressure release valve to the VENT position. Carefully remove lid when unit has finished releasing pressure.

7. Remove rack from pot, then remove the plastic wrap from the pan. Pour the jam and syrup mixture over top of waffles. Place rack and pan back in pot. Close crisping lid.

8. Select BROIL and set time to 10 minutes. Select START/STOP to begin.

9. When cooking is complete, open lid and remove rack from pot. Serve the bread pudding warm.

Nutrition Info:
- Calories: 640, Total Fat: 30g, Sodium: 765mg, Carbohydrates: 82g, Protein: 12g.

Mediterranean Quiche

Servings: 6
Cooking Time: 45 Minutes

Ingredients:
- Nonstick cooking spray
- 2 cups potatoes, grated
- ¾ cup feta cheese, fat free, crumbled
- 1 tbsp. olive oil
- 1 cup grape tomatoes, halved
- 3 cups baby spinach
- 2 eggs
- 2 egg whites
- ¼ cup skim milk
- ½ tsp salt
- ¼ tsp pepper

Directions:

1. Select bake function and heat to 375°F. Spray an 8-inch round pan with cooking spray.

2. Press the potatoes on the bottom and up sides of the prepared pan. Place in the cooker. Secure the tender-crisp lid and bake 10 minutes.

3. Remove pan from the cooker and sprinkle half the feta cheese over the bottom of the crust.

4. Set cooker to sauté function on medium heat. Add the oil and heat until hot.

5. Add the tomatoes and spinach and cook until spinach has wilted, about 2-3 minutes. Place over the feta cheese.

6. In a medium bowl, whisk together eggs, milk, salt, and pepper. Pour over spinach mixture and top with remaining feta cheese.

7. Place the pan back in the cooking pot and secure the tender-crisp lid. Set temperature to 375°F and bake 30 minutes or until eggs are completely set and starting to brown. Let cool 10 minutes before serving.

Nutrition Info:
- Calories 145, Total Fat 8g, Total Carbs 12g, Protein 7g, Sodium 346mg.

Cheesecake French Toast

Servings: 6
Cooking Time: 50 Minutes

Ingredients:
- Butter flavored cooking spray
- 4 eggs
- ½ cup sugar
- 1 cup milk
- 1 ½ tsp vanilla, divided
- 1/8 tsp salt
- ½ lb. challah bread, cut in 1-inch cubes
- ½ cup strawberries, chopped
- 2 oz. cream cheese, soft
- ¼ cup powdered sugar

Directions:

1. Select bake function and heat the cooker to 350°F. Spray a baking dish with cooking spray.

2. In a large bowl, whisk together eggs, sugar, milk, 1 teaspoon vanilla, and salt until smooth.

3. Add bread and strawberries and fold until the bread is thoroughly coated with the egg mixture.

4. In another bowl, beat cream cheese, powdered sugar, and remaining vanilla until smooth.

5. Place half the bread mixture in the prepared baking dish. Drop half the cheese mixture by teaspoons over bread. Repeat.

6. Carefully place the dish into the cooker and secure the tender-crisp lid. Bake 45-50 minutes, or until golden brown and a toothpick inserted in center comes out clean.

7. Remove the dish and let cool 10 minutes before serving.

Nutrition Info:
- Calories 259,Total Fat 9g,Total Carbs 35g,Protein 9g,Sodium 337mg.

Pumpkin Breakfast Bread

Servings: 14
Cooking Time: 3 Hours

Ingredients:
- Nonstick cooking spray
- 2 cups whole wheat pastry flour
- 1 ½ tsp baking soda
- 2 tsp pumpkin pie spice
- ½ cup coconut oil, melted
- ¾ cup honey
- 2 eggs
- 3 cups pumpkin puree
- 1 tsp. vanilla extract
- 1 banana, mashed
- ½ cup walnuts, chopped & divided

Directions:

1. Spray the cooking pot with cooking spray.

2. In a large bowl, combine flour, baking soda, and pumpkin spice.

3. Make a "well" in the middle of the dry ingredients and add oil, honey, eggs, pumpkin, vanilla, and banana, and ¼ cup of the walnuts. Mix well to thoroughly combine all ingredients.

4. Pour batter into cooking pot and sprinkle remaining walnuts over the top. Place two paper towels over the top of the pot and secure the lid. Select slow cooking function on high. Set timer for 2 hours.

5. When timer goes off check bread, it should pass the toothpick test. If it is not done, continue cooking another 30-60 minutes.

6. When bread is done, transfer to a wire rack to cool.

Nutrition Info:
- Calories 207,Total Fat 9g,Total Carbs 30g,Protein 4g,Sodium 130mg.

Peaches & Brown Sugar Oatmeal

Servings: 8
Cooking Time: 8 Hours

Ingredients:
- Nonstick cooking spray
- 2 cups steel cut oats
- 8 cups water
- 1 tsp cinnamon
- ½ cup brown sugar
- 1 tsp vanilla
- 1 cup peaches, cubed

Directions:

1. Spray cooking pot with cooking spray.

2. Add the oats, water, cinnamon, sugar, and vanilla to the pot, stir to combine.

3. Secure the lid and select slow cooker function on low. Set timer for 8 hours.

4. Stir in peaches and serve.

Nutrition Info:
- Calories 231,Total Fat 3g,Total Carbs 46g,Protein 7g,Sodium 7mg.

Soft-boiled Eggs

Servings: 4
Cooking Time: 15 Min

Ingredients:
- 4 large eggs
- 1 cups water /250ml
- Salt and ground black pepper, to taste.

Directions:

1. To the pressure cooker pot, add water and place a reversible rack. Carefully place eggs on it. Seal the pressure lid, choose Pressure, set to High, and set the timer to 3 minutes. Press Start.

2. When cooking is complete, do a quick pressure release. Allow cooling completely in an ice bath. Peel the eggs and season with salt and pepper before serving.

Chorizo Omelet

Servings: 4
Cooking Time: 30-35 Minutes

Ingredients:
- 3 eggs, whisked
- 3 ounces chorizo, chopped
- 1-ounces Feta cheese, crumbled
- 5 tablespoons almond milk

- ¾ teaspoon chilli flakes
- ¼ teaspoon salt
- 1 green pepper, chopped

Directions:
1. Add listed ingredients to a suitable and mix well.
2. Take an omelette pan and pour the mixture on it.
3. Pre-heat your Ninja Food on "BAKE" mode at a temperature of 320 °F.
4. Transfer pan with omelette mix to your Ninja Foodi and cook for 30 minutes, or until the surface is golden and the egg has set properly.
5. Serve and enjoy.

Nutrition Info:
- Calories: 426; Fat: 38g; Carbohydrates: 7g; Protein: 21g

Brussels Sprouts Bacon Hash

Servings: 4
Cooking Time: 20 Minutes
Ingredients:
- 1/2 lb. brussels sprouts, sliced in half
- 4 slices bacon, chopped
- 1/2 red onion, chopped
- salt, to taste
- black pepper, to taste

Directions:
1. Toss all the ingredients into the Ninja Foodi cooking pot.
2. Secure the Ninja Foodi lid and turn its pressure handle to 'Closed' position.
3. Select mode for 20 minutes at 390 °F.
4. Once done, release the steam naturally then remove the lid.
5. Serve fresh.

Nutrition Info:
- Calories 121; Total Fat 9 g; Total Carbs 13.8 g; Protein 4.3 g

Almond Quinoa Porridge

Servings: 6
Cooking Time: 1 Minute
Ingredients:
- 1¼ cups water
- 1 cup almond milk
- 1½ cups uncooked quinoa, rinsed
- 1 tablespoon choc zero maple syrup
- 1 cinnamon stick
- Pinch of salt

Directions:
1. In the Ninja Foodi's insert, add all ingredients and stir to combine well.
2. Close the Ninja Foodi's lid with the pressure lid and place the pressure valve in the "Seal" position.
3. Select "Pressure" mode and set it to "High" for 1 minute.
4. Press the "Start/Stop" button to initiate cooking.
5. Now turn the pressure valve to "Vent" and do a "Quick" release.
6. Open the Ninja Foodi's lid, and with a fork, fluff the quinoa.
7. Serve warm.

Nutrition Info:
- Calories: 186; Fat: 2.6 g; Carbohydrates: 4.8 g; Protein: 6 g

Pancetta Hash With Baked Eggs

Servings: 4
Cooking Time: 50 Min
Ingredients:
- 6 slices pancetta; chopped
- 2 potatoes, peeled and diced
- 4 eggs
- 1 white onion; diced
- 1 tsp freshly ground black pepper /5g
- 1 tsp garlic powder /5g
- 1 tsp sweet paprika /5g
- 1 tsp salt /5g

Directions:
1. Choose Sear/Sauté, set to Medium High, and choose Start/Stop to preheat the pot for 5 minutes.
2. Once heated, lay the pancetta in the pot, and cook, stirring occasionally; for 5 minutes, or until the pancetta is crispy.
3. Stir in the onion, potatoes, sweet paprika, salt, black pepper, and garlic powder. Close the crisping lid; choose Bake/Roast, set the temperature to 350°F or 177°C, and the time to 25 minutes. Cook until the turnips are soft and golden brown while stirring occasionally.
4. Crack the eggs on top of the hash, close the crisping lid, and choose Bake/Roast. Set the temperature to 350°F or 177°C, and the time to 10 minutes.
5. Cook the eggs and check two or three times until your desired crispiness has been achieved. Serve immediately.

Cheesy Shakshuka

Servings: 4
Cooking Time: 50 Min
Ingredients:
- 1 small red onion; chopped
- 2 cans diced tomatoes with their juice /435ml
- ½ red bell pepper, seeded and chopped
- 1 medium banana pepper, seeded and minced
- 4 eggs
- ⅓ cup crumbled goat cheese /84g
- 2 garlic cloves; chopped
- 2 tbsp fresh cilantro; chopped /30g
- 3 tbsps ghee /45g
- ½ tsp smoked paprika /7.5g
- ½ tsp red chili flakes /2.5g
- ¼ tsp black pepper; freshly ground /1.25g
- 1 tsp salt /5g
- ½ tsp coriander, ground /2.5g

Directions:
1. Choose Sear/Sauté on you Foodi and set on Medium to preheat the inner pot; press Start. Melt the ghee and sauté the onion, bell pepper, banana pepper, and garlic. Season lightly with salt and cook for 2 minutes until the vegetables are fragrant and beginning to soften.
2. Then, stir in the tomatoes, coriander, smoked paprika, red chili flakes, and black pepper. Seal the pressure lid, choose pressure and adjust the pressure to High and the timer to 4 minutes. Press Start to continue cooking.
3. When the timer has read to the end, perform a quick pressure release. Gently crack the eggs onto the tomato sauce in different areas. Seal the pressure lid again, but with the valve set to Vent. Choose Steam and adjust the cook time to 3 minutes. Press Start to cook the eggs.
4. When ready, carefully open the pressure lid. Sprinkle with the shakshuka with goat cheese and cilantro. Dish into a serving platter and serve.

Blueberry Muffins

Servings: 12
Cooking Time: 20 Minutes
Ingredients:
- 2 ½ cups oats
- 1 ½ cups almond milk, unsweetened
- Nonstick cooking spray
- 1 egg, lightly beaten
- 1/3 cup pure maple syrup
- 2 tbsp. coconut oil, melted
- 1 tsp vanilla
- 1 tsp cinnamon
- 1 tsp baking powder
- ¼ tsp salt
- 1 tsp lemon zest, grated
- 1 cup fresh blueberries

Directions:
1. In a large bowl, combine oats and milk. Cover and refrigerate overnight.
2. Select bake function and heat to 375°F. Spray 2 6-cup muffin tins with cooking spray.
3. Stir remaining ingredients into the oat mixture. Spoon into muffin tins.
4. Place the rack in the cooking pot and place muffin tin on it, these will need to be baked in 2 batches.
5. Secure the tender crisp lid and bake 20 minutes or until tops are golden brown. Serve warm.

Nutrition Info:
- Calories 122,Total Fat 4g.Total Carbs 19g,Protein 3g,Sodium 108mg.

Zucchini Pancakes

Servings: 6
Cooking Time: 10 Minutes
Ingredients:
- 1 cup almond milk, unsweetened
- 1 egg
- 2 tbsp. honey
- 1 tbsp. coconut oil, melted
- 1 tsp vanilla
- ½ cup zucchini, grated
- 1 ½ cup oat flour
- 2 tsp cinnamon
- 1 tsp baking powder
- ¼ tsp salt
- Nonstick cooking spray

Directions:
1. In a large bowl, combine milk, egg, honey, oil, vanilla, and zucchini.
2. In a separate bowl, stir together remaining ingredients. Add to zucchini mixture and mix just until combined.
3. Spray the cooking pot with cooking spray. Set to sauté on medium heat.
4. Pour batter, ¼ cup at a time, into cooking pot. Cook 3-4 minutes or until bubble form in the middle. Flip and cook

another 2-3 minutes. Repeat with remaining batter. Serve immediately with your favorite toppings.

Nutrition Info:
- Calories 188, Total Fat 7g, Total Carbs 27g, Protein 6g, Sodium 132mg.

Bacon & Egg Poppers

Servings: 6
Cooking Time: 25 Minutes
Ingredients:
- 12 slices bacon
- 4 jalapeno peppers
- 3 oz. cream cheese, soft
- 8 eggs
- ½ tsp garlic powder
- ½ tsp onion powder
- Salt & pepper, to taste
- Nonstick cooking spray
- ½ cup cheddar cheese, grated

Directions:
1. Select air fryer function and heat cooker to 375°F.
2. Heat a skillet over med-high heat and cook bacon until almost crisp but still pliable. Remove to paper towels to drain and reserve bacon fat for later.
3. Remove the seeds from 3 of the jalapenos and chop them. With the remaining jalapeno, slice into rings.
4. In a large bowl, beat together cream cheese, 1 tablespoon bacon fat, chopped jalapenos, eggs, and seasonings.
5. Spray 2 6-cup muffin tins with cooking spray. Place one slice bacon around the edges of each cup.
6. Pour egg mixture into cups, filling ¾ full then top with cheddar cheese and a jalapeno ring.
7. Place muffin pan, one at a time, in the cooker, secure the tender-crisp lid and bake 20-25 minutes, or until eggs are cooked. Repeat with other pan and serve immediately.

Nutrition Info:
- Calories 399, Total Fat 34g, Total Carbs 3g, Protein 19g, Sodium 666mg.

Morning Pancakes

Servings: 4
Cooking Time: 10 Minutes
Ingredients:
- 2 cups cream cheese
- 2 cups almond flour
- 6 large whole eggs
- 1/4 teaspoon salt
- 2 tablespoons butter
- ¼ teaspoon ground ginger
- ½ teaspoon cinnamon powder

Directions:
1. Take a large bowl and add cream cheese, eggs, 1 tablespoon butter. Blend on high until creamy.
2. Slow add flour and keep beating.
3. Add salt, ginger, cinnamon.
4. Keep beating until fully mixed.
5. Select "Sauté" mode on your Ninja Foodi and grease stainless steel insert.
6. Add butter and heat it up.
7. Add ½ cup batter and cook for 2-3 minutes, flip and cook the other side.
8. Repeat with the remaining batter. Enjoy.

Nutrition Info:
- Calories: 432; Fat: 40g; Carbohydrates: 3g; Protein: 14g

Ham & Spinach Breakfast Bake

Servings: 6
Cooking Time: 30 Minutes
Ingredients:
- Nonstick cooking spray
- 10 eggs
- 1 cup spinach, chopped
- 1 cup ham, chopped
- 1 cup red peppers, chopped
- 1 cup onion, chopped
- 1 tsp garlic powder
- ½ tsp onion powder
- ¼ tsp salt
- ¼ tsp pepper
- 1 cup Swiss cheese, grated

Directions:
1. Select the bake function and heat cooker to 350°F. Spray the cooking pot with cooking spray.
2. In a large bowl, whisk eggs together.
3. Add remaining ingredients and mix well.
4. Pour into cooking pot and secure the tender-crisp lid. Cook 25-30 minutes, or until eggs are set and top has started to brown.
5. Let cool 5 minutes before serving.

Nutrition Info:

- Calories 287, Total Fat 18g, Total Carbs 7g, Protein 23g, Sodium 629mg.

Pepperoni Omelets

Servings: 4
Cooking Time: 5 Minutes
Ingredients:
- 4 tablespoons heavy cream
- 15 pepperoni slices
- 2 tablespoons butter
- Black pepper and salt to taste
- 6 whole eggs

Directions:
1. Take a suitable and whisk in eggs, cream, pepperoni slices, salt, and pepper.
2. Set your Ninja Foodi to "Sauté" mode and add butter and egg mix.
3. Sauté for 3 minutes, flip.
4. Lock and secure the Ninja Foodi's lid and Air Crisp for 2 minutes at 350 °F.
5. Transfer to a serving plate and enjoy.

Nutrition Info:
- Calories: 141; Fat: 11g; Carbohydrates: 0.6g; Protein: 9g

Very Berry Puffs

Servings: 3
Cooking Time: 20 Min
Ingredients:
- 3 pastry dough sheets
- 2 cups cream cheese /260g
- 1 tbsp honey /15ml
- 2 tbsp mashed raspberries /30g
- 2 tbsp mashed strawberries /30g
- ¼ tsp vanilla extract /1.25ml

Directions:
1. Divide the cream cheese between the dough sheets and spread it evenly. In a small bowl, combine the berries, honey, and vanilla. Divide the mixture between the pastry sheets. Pinch the ends of the sheets, to form puff.
2. You can seal them by brushing some water onto the edges, or even better, use egg wash. Lay the puffs into a lined baking dish.
3. Place the dish into the Ninja Foodi, close the crisping lid and cook for 15 minutes on Air Crisp mode at 370 °F or 188°C. Once the timer beeps, check the puffs to ensure they're puffed and golden. Serve warm.

Glazed Carrots

Servings: 4
Cooking Time: 4 Minutes
Ingredients:
- 2 pounds carrots, washed, peeled and sliced
- Pepper, to taste
- 1 cup of water
- 1 tablespoon butter
- 1 tablespoon choc zero maple syrup

Directions:
1. Add carrots, water to the Instant Pot.
2. Lock and secure the Ninja Foodi's lid, then cook on "HIGH" pressure for 4 minutes.
3. Quick-release Pressure.
4. Strain carrots.
5. Add butter, maple syrup to the warm mix, stir it gently.
6. Transfer strained carrots back to the pot and stir.
7. Coat well with maple syrup.
8. Sprinkle a bit of pepper and serve.
9. Enjoy.

Nutrition Info:
- Calories: 358; Fat: 12g; Carbohydrates: 20g; Protein: 2g

Spanish Potato And Chorizo Frittata

Servings: 4
Cooking Time: 20 Minutes
Ingredients:
- 4 eggs
- 1 cup milk
- Sea salt
- Freshly ground black pepper
- 1 potato, diced
- ½ cup frozen corn
- 1 chorizo sausage, diced
- 8 ounces feta cheese, crumbled
- 1 cup water

Directions:
1. In a medium bowl, whisk together the eggs and milk. Season with salt and pepper.
2. Place the potato, corn, and chorizo in the Multi-Purpose Pan or an 8-inch baking pan. Pour the egg mixture and feta cheese over top. Cover the pan with aluminum foil and place on the Reversible Rack. Make sure it's in the lower position.

3. Pour the water into the pot. Assemble pressure lid, making sure the pressure release valve is in the SEAL position.
4. Select PRESSURE and set to HI. Set time to 20 minutes. Select START/STOP to begin.
5. When pressure cooking is complete, quick release the pressure by moving the pressure release valve to the VENT position. Carefully remove lid when unit has finished releasing pressure.
6. Remove the pan from pot and place it on a cooling rack for 5 minutes, then serve.

Nutrition Info:
- Calories: 361,Total Fat: 24g,Sodium: 972mg,Carbohydrates: 17g,Protein: 21g.

Cranberry Lemon Quinoa

Servings: 6
Cooking Time: 20 Minutes
Ingredients:
- 16 oz. quinoa
- 4 ½ cups water
- ½ cup brown sugar, packed
- 1 tsp lemon extract
- ½ tsp salt
- ½ cup cranberries, dried

Directions:
1. Add all ingredients, except the cranberries, to the cooker and stir to mix.
2. Secure the lid and select pressure cooking on high. Set timer for 20 minutes.
3. When timer goes off, use natural release for 10 minutes. Then use quick release and remove the lid.
4. Stir in cranberries and serve.

Nutrition Info:
- Calories 284,Total Fat 4g,Total Carbs 56g,Protein 8g,Sodium 152mg.

Walnut Orange Coffee Cake

Servings: 8
Cooking Time: 25 Minutes
Ingredients:
- Butter flavor cooking spray
- 1 cup Stevia
- 1/4 cup butter, unsalted, soft
- 1 egg
- 2 tsp orange zest, grated
- ½ tsp vanilla
- 1/8 tsp cinnamon
- 2 cups whole wheat flour
- 1 tsp baking soda
- ½ cup orange juice, fresh squeezed
- ½ cup water
- ½ cup walnuts, chopped

Directions:
1. Select bake function and heat cooker to 350°F. Spray a 7-inch round pan with cooking spray.
2. In a medium bowl, beat Stevia and butter until smooth.
3. Add egg, zest, vanilla, and cinnamon and mix until combined.
4. In a separate bowl, combine dry ingredients. Add to butter mixture and mix until thoroughly combined. Stir in nuts.
5. Spread batter in prepared pan and place in the cooker. Secure the tender-crisp lid and bakke 20-25 minutes, or until it passes the toothpick test.
6. Let cool in pan 10 minutes, then invert onto wire rack. Serve warm.

Nutrition Info:
- Calories 203,Total Fat 10g,Total Carbs 53g,Protein 6g,Sodium 170mg.

French Dip Sandwiches

Servings: 8
Cooking Time: 1 Hr 35 Min
Ingredients:
- 2 ½ pounds beef roast /1125g
- 2 tbsp olive oil /30ml
- 1 onion; chopped
- 4 garlic cloves; sliced
- ½ cup dry red wine /125ml
- 2 cups beef broth stock /500ml
- 1 tsp dried oregano /5g
- 16 slices Fontina cheese
- 8 split hoagie rolls

Directions:
1. Generously apply pepper and salt to the beef for seasoning. Warm oil on Sear/Sauté and brown the beef for 2 to 3 minutes per side. Set aside on a plate.
2. Add onions and cook for 3 minutes, until translucent. Mix in garlic and cook for one a minute until soft.
3. To the Foodi, add red wine to deglaze. Scrape the cooking surface to remove any browned sections of the food

using a wooden spoon's flat edge; mix in beef broth and take back the juices and beef to your pressure cooker. Over the meat, scatter some oregano.

4. Seal the pressure lid, choose Pressure, set to High, and set the timer to 50 minutes; press Start. Release pressure naturally for around 10 minutes. Transfer the beef to a cutting board and slice.

5. Roll the sliced beef and add a topping of onions. Each sandwich should be topped with 2 slices fontina cheese.

6. Place the sandwiches in the pot, close the crisping lid and select Air Crisp. Adjust the temperature to 360°F or 183°C and the time to 3 minutes. Press Start. When cooking is complete, the cheese should be cheese melt.

Sweet Bread Pudding

Servings: 3
Cooking Time: 45 Min
Ingredients:
- 8 slices of bread
- 2 eggs
- ¼ cup sugar /32.5g
- ¼ cup honey /62.5ml
- 1 cup milk /250ml
- ½ cup buttermilk /125ml
- 4 tbsp raisins /60g
- 2 tbsp chopped hazelnuts /30g
- 2 tbsp butter, softened /30g
- ½ tsp vanilla extract /2.5ml
- Cinnamon for garnish

Directions:
1. Beat the eggs along with the buttermilk, honey, milk, vanilla, sugar, and butter. Stir in raisins and hazelnuts. Cut the bread into cubes and place it in a bowl.
2. Pour the milk mixture over the bread. Let soak for about 10 minutes. Close the crisping lid and cook the bread pudding for 25 minutes on Roast mode. Leave the dessert to cool for 5 minutes, then invert onto a plate and sprinkle with cinnamon to serve.

Baked Eggs In Mushrooms

Servings: 4
Cooking Time: 15 Minutes
Ingredients:
- 4 large Portobello mushrooms, rinse & remove stems
- 4 eggs
- 1 ½ tbsp. extra virgin olive oil
- ½ tsp salt, divided
- ½ tsp black pepper, divided

Directions:
1. Set to bake function on 450°F.
2. Rub mushrooms with oil and half the salt and pepper. Place on a small baking sheet, cap side down.
3. Carefully crack an egg into each mushroom and season with remaining salt and pepper.
4. Place sheet in the cooker and secure the tender-crisp lid. Bake 12-15 minutes, or until whites of the eggs are cooked through. Serve immediately.

Nutrition Info:
- Calories 122,Total Fat 10g,Total Carbs 2g,Protein 7g,Sodium 363mg.

Apricot Oatmeal

Servings: 8
Cooking Time: 8 Hours
Ingredients:
- 2 cups steel-cut oats
- 1/3 cup dried apricots, chopped
- ½ cup dried cherries
- 1 teaspoon ground cinnamon
- 4 cups milk
- 4 cups water
- ¼ teaspoon liquid stevia

Directions:
1. In the Ninja Foodi's insert, place all ingredients and stir to combine.
2. Close the Ninja Foodi's lid with a crisping lid and select "Slow Cooker."
3. Set on "Low" for 6-8 hours.
4. Press the "Start/Stop" button to initiate cooking.
5. Open the Ninja Foodi's lid and serve warm.

Nutrition Info:
- Calories: 148; Fat: 3.5g; Carbohydrates: 4.2 g; Protein: 5.9 g

Quinoa Protein Bake

Servings: 4
Cooking Time: 30 Minutes
Ingredients:
- Nonstick cooking spray
- 1 cup white quinoa, cooked
- 3 egg whites, lightly beaten
- ½ tsp salt
- ¼ cup red bell pepper, chopped
- ¼ cup spinach, chopped
- ½ cup mozzarella cheese, grated

Directions:
1. Spray the cooking pot with cooking spray.
2. In a large bowl, combine all ingredients thoroughly. Pour into pot.
3. Add the tender-crisp lid and select air fry on 350°F. Bake 25-30 minutes until lightly browned on top and eggs are completely set.
4. Let cool a few minutes before serving.

Nutrition Info:
- Calories 191,Total Fat 3g,Total Carbs 28g,Protein 13g,Sodium 441mg.

Snacks, Appetizers & Sides Recipes

Steak And Minty Cheese

Servings: 4
Cooking Time: 15 Min
Ingredients:
- 2 New York strip steaks
- 8 oz. halloumi cheese /240g
- 12 kalamata olives
- Juice and zest of 1 lemon
- Olive oil
- 2 tbsp chopped parsley /30g
- 2 tbsp chopped mint /30g
- Salt and pepper, to taste

Directions:
1. Season the steaks with salt and pepper, and gently brush with olive oil. Place into the Ninja Foodi, close the crisping lid and cook for 6 minutes (for medium rare) on Air Crisp mode at 350 °F or 177°C. When ready, remove to a plate and set aside.
2. Drizzle the cheese with olive oil and place it in the Ninja Foodi; cook for 4 minutes.
3. Remove to a serving platter and serve with sliced steaks and olives, sprinkled with herbs, and lemon zest and juice.

Crispy Cheesy Straws

Servings: 8
Cooking Time: 45 Min
Ingredients:
- 2 cups cauliflower florets, steamed /260g
- 5 oz. cheddar cheese /150g
- 3 ½ oz. oats /105g
- 1 egg
- 1 red onion; diced
- 1 tsp mustard /5g
- Salt and pepper, to taste

Directions:
1. Add the oats in a food processor and process until they resemble breadcrumbs. Place the steamed florets in a cheesecloth and squeeze out the excess liquid.
2. Put the florets in a large bowl, and add the rest of the ingredients to the bowl.
3. Mix well with your hands, to combine the ingredients thoroughly.
4. Take a little bit of the mixture and twist it into a straw. Place in the lined Ninja Foodi basket; repeat with the rest of the mixture.
5. Close the crisping lid and cook for 10 minutes on Air Crisp mode at 350 °F or 177°C. After 5 minutes, turn them over and cook for an additional 10 minutes.

Sweet Potato Skins

Servings: 4
Cooking Time: 20 Minutes
Ingredients:
- 2 sweet potatoes, baked & halved lengthwise
- 1 tsp olive oil
- 2 cloves garlic, diced fine
- 1 tbsp. fresh lime juice
- 2 cups baby spinach
- ½ cup chicken, cooked & shredded
- 1 tsp oregano
- 1 tsp cumin
- 2 tsp chili powder
- ½ cup mozzarella cheese, grated
- ¼ cup cilantro, chopped

Directions:
1. Scoop out the center of the potatoes, leaving some on the side to help keep the shape.
2. Set the cooker to sauté on med-high heat and add the oil.
3. Once the oil is hot, add garlic, lime juice, and spinach. Cook 2-3 minutes until spinach is wilted.
4. In a large bowl, mash the sweet potato centers until almost smooth.
5. Stir in chicken, oregano, cumin, and chili powder. Stir in spinach until combined.
6. Place the rack in the cooking pot and top with parchment paper.
7. Spoon the potato mixture into the skins and top with cheese. Place on the rack.
8. Add the tender-crisp lid and set to bake on 400°F. Bake 15-20 minutes until cheese is melted and lightly browned. Let cool slightly then cut each skin in 4 pieces and serve garnished with cilantro.

Nutrition Info:
- Calories 132,Total Fat 2g,Total Carbs 20g,Protein 9g,Sodium 155mg.

Cheesy Chicken Dip

Servings: 6
Cooking Time: 2 Hours
Ingredients:
- 1 lb. cheddar cheese, cubed
- 2 cups chicken, cooked & shredded
- 4 oz. cream cheese, cubed
- 1 cup tomatoes, diced
- 1 cup black beans, drained & rinsed
- ½ cup black olives, pitted & sliced
- 1 jalapeno, seeded & diced
- 2 tbsp. taco seasoning

Directions:
1. Place all ingredients in the cooking pot and stir to mix.
2. Add the lid and set to slow cooking on low heat. Set timer for 2 hours. Let dip cook, stirring occasionally until hot and bubbly and the cheese has melted.
3. Stir well then transfer to a serving dish and serve warm.

Nutrition Info:
- Calories 507,Total Fat 35g,Total Carbs 12g,Protein 35g,Sodium 1022mg.

Sweet Potato Gratin

Servings:6
Cooking Time: 15 Minutes
Ingredients:
- 2 tablespoons unsalted butter
- 3 tablespoons all-purpose flour
- 2 cups heavy (whipping) cream, warmed in microwave
- 2 teaspoons kosher salt
- 1 teaspoon pumpkin pie spice
- ¼ cup water
- 3 large sweet potatoes, peeled and cut in half, then cut into half-moons ¼-inch thick
- 1¼ cups shredded Cheddar cheese, divided
- ½ cup chopped walnuts or pecans, or slivered almonds

Directions:
1. Select SEAR/SAUTÉ and set to MD:HI. Select START/STOP to begin. Let preheat for 5 minutes.
2. Add the butter. Once melted, add the flour and stir together until a thick paste forms, about 1 minute. (The combination of butter and flour is called a roux). Continue cooking the roux for 2 minutes, stirring frequently with a rubber-coated whisk. Slowly add the warm cream while continuously whisking so there are no lumps, about 3 minutes. The cream should be thickened.
3. Add the salt and pumpkin pie spice and whisk to incorporate. Whisk in the water and let the mixture simmer for 3 minutes.
4. Place the potatoes in the pot. Assemble pressure lid, making sure the pressure release valve is in the SEAL position.
5. Select PRESSURE and set to LO. Set time to 1 minute. Select START/STOP to begin.
6. When pressure cooking is complete, quick release pressure by moving the pressure release valve to the VENT

position. Carefully remove lid when unit has finished releasing pressure.

7. Add ¼ cup of cheese and stir gently to incorporate, being careful not to break up the cooked potatoes. Ensure mixture is flat, then cover top with remaining 1 cup of cheese. Sprinkle the nuts over the cheese. Close crisping lid.

8. Select BROIL and set time to 5 minutes. Select START/STOP to begin.

9. When cooking is complete, open lid and let the gratin cool for 10 minutes before serving.

Nutrition Info:
- Calories: 536,Total Fat: 47g,Sodium: 409mg,Carbohydrates: 20g,Protein: 10g.

Caramelized Cauliflower With Hazelnuts

Servings: 4
Cooking Time: 15 Minutes
Ingredients:
- 1 head cauliflower, cut in ½-inch thick slices
- 2 cups cold water
- 2 tbsp. olive oil
- 1 tbsp. honey
- ½ tsp fresh lemon juice
- ½ tsp salt
- ¼ tsp pepper
- 1 tbsp. fresh sage, chopped
- 1 tbsp. hazelnuts, toasted & chopped
- ¼ cup parmesan cheese, reduced fat

Directions:
1. Remove any core from the cauliflower slices. Lay them in a single layer in the cooking pot.
2. Add enough water to come halfway up the sides of the cauliflower. Add oil, honey, lemon, salt, and pepper.
3. Set cooker to sauté on high. Cover and cook cauliflower until the water has evaporated, about 6-8 minutes. When it begins to brown reduce heat to low.
4. Once water has evaporated, flip cauliflower over and cook another 5 minutes, or until bottom is golden brown.
5. Transfer to serving plates and top with sage, hazelnuts, and parmesan cheese. Serve.

Nutrition Info:
- Calories 112,Total Fat 8g,Total Carbs 9g,Protein 3g,Sodium 407mg.

Zucchini Egg Tots

Servings: 8
Cooking Time: 9 Minutes
Ingredients:
- 2 medium zucchinis
- 1 egg
- 1 teaspoon salt
- ½ teaspoon baking soda
- 1 teaspoon lemon juice
- 1 teaspoon basil
- 1 tablespoon oregano
- ⅓ cup oatmeal flour
- 1 tablespoon olive oil
- 1 teaspoon minced garlic
- 1 tablespoon butter

Directions:
1. Wash the zucchini and grate it. Beat the egg in a suitable mixing bowl and blend it using a whisk.
2. Add the baking soda, lemon juice, basil, oregano, and flour to the egg mixture.
3. Stir it carefully until smooth. Combine the grated zucchini and egg mixture together.
4. Knead the dough until smooth. Mix olive oil with minced garlic together.
5. Set the Ninja Foodi's insert to" Sauté" mode.
6. Add butter and transfer the mixture to the Ninja Foodi's insert. Melt the mixture.
7. Make the small tots from the zucchini dough and place them in the melted butter mixture.
8. Sauté the dish for 3 minutes on each side.
9. Once the zucchini tots are cooked, remove them from the Ninja Foodi's insert and serve.

Nutrition Info:
- Calories: 64; Fat: 4.4g; Carbohydrates: 4.35g; Protein: 2g

Cheesy Stuffed Mushroom

Servings: 7
Cooking Time: 7 Minutes
Ingredients:
- 12 ounces Parmesan cheese
- 7 mushroom caps
- 2 teaspoons minced garlic
- ¼ sour cream
- 1 teaspoon butter
- 1 teaspoon ground white pepper

- 2 teaspoons oregano

Directions:
1. Mix the minced garlic, sour cream, ground white pepper, and oregano, and stir the mixture.
2. Add grated parmesan to the minced garlic mixture.
3. Blend the mixture until smooth.
4. Stuff the mushrooms with the cheese mixture and place the dish in the Ninja Foodi's insert.
5. Set the Ninja Foodi's insert to "Pressure" mode, add butter, and close the Ninja Foodi's lid.
6. Cook the dish for 7 minutes.
7. Once done, remove it from the Ninja Foodi's insert, let it rest briefly, and serve.

Nutrition Info:
- Calories: 203; Fat: 7.6g; Carbohydrates: 8.35g; Protein: 8g

Parmesan Butternut Crisps

Servings: 4
Cooking Time: 20 Minutes

Ingredients:
- 1 butternut squash, peeled, seeded & halved lengthwise
- 1 ½ tsp salt
- ½ tsp fresh rosemary, chopped
- 1/8 tsp cayenne pepper
- 2 tbsp. extra-virgin olive oil
- ¼ cup parmesan cheese, reduced fat

Directions:
1. Bring a large pot of water to a boil.
2. Cut the squash in 1/8-1/4-inch thick slices. When water is boiling, add squash and boil 1-2 minutes. Drain and rinse in cold water. Pat dry.
3. Place the rack in the cooking pot and line with parchment paper.
4. In a small bowl, combine salt, rosemary, and cayenne pepper.
5. Place the squash in a large bowl, sprinkle the spice mixture and oil over the top and toss well to coat.
6. Lay slices in a single layer on the parchment paper, these will need to be cooked in batches, and sprinkle with parmesan.
7. Add the tender-crisp lid, set to air fry on 350°F. Bake the chips 15-20 minutes or until golden brown. Store in an airtight container.

Nutrition Info:
- Calories 108,Total Fat 8g,Total Carbs 8g,Protein 2g,Sodium 971mg.

Caribbean Chicken Skewers

Servings: 8
Cooking Time: 30 Minutes

Ingredients:
- 2 tsp jerk seasoning
- 1 lime, juiced
- 1 tbsp. extra virgin olive oil
- 1 lb. chicken, boneless, skinless & cut in 1-inch cubes
- 1 red onion, cut in 1-inch pieces
- 1 cup cherry tomatoes
- 1 cup fresh pineapple, cut in 1-inch cubes
- 1 very ripe plantain, peel on, sliced
- ½ tsp salt
- ½ tsp pepper
- Nonstick cooking spray

Directions:
1. If using wood skewers, soak them in water for 30 minutes.
2. In a large bowl, combine jerk seasoning, lime juice, and olive oil.
3. Add the chicken, onions, and tomatoes and toss to coat. Cover and refrigerate 20 minutes.
4. Thread skewers with chicken, onion, tomatoes, pineapple, and plantains, leaving a little space at both ends. Sprinkle skewers with salt and pepper.
5. Lightly spray the rack with cooking spray and place in the cooking pot. Place the skewers on top.
6. Add the tender-crisp lid and set to air fry on 400°F. Cook skewers 25-30 minutes until chicken is cooked through. Baste with marinade and turn over halfway through cooking time. Serve.

Nutrition Info:
- Calories 127,Total Fat 3g,Total Carbs 11g,Protein 13g,Sodium 173mg.

Parmesan Breadsticks

Servings: 8
Cooking Time: 10 Minutes

Ingredients:
- 1 teaspoon baking powder
- ½ teaspoon Erythritol
- ½ teaspoon salt
- 1 cup of warm water
- 2 cups almond flour
- 5 ounces Parmesan
- 1 tablespoon olive oil

- 1 teaspoon onion powder
- 1 teaspoon basil

Directions:
1. Combine the baking powder, Erythritol, and warm water in a mixing bowl.
2. Stir the mixture well. Add the almond flour, onion powder, salt, and basil.
3. Knead the dough until smooth. Separate dough into 10 pieces and make the long logs.
4. Twist the logs in braids. Grate the Parmesan cheese.
5. Place the twisted logs in the Ninja Foodi's insert.
6. Sprinkle the grated Parmesan cheese and olive oil, and close the Ninja Foodi's lid.
7. Cook the breadsticks at the "Pressure" mode for 10 minutes.
8. Release the pressure and remove the lid.
9. Leave the breadsticks for 10 minutes to rest.
10. Serve the breadsticks immediately or keep them in a sealed container.

Nutrition Info:
- Calories: 242; Fat: 18.9g; Carbohydrates: 2.7g; Protein: 11.7g

Herby Fish Skewers

Servings: 4
Cooking Time: 75 Min

Ingredients:
- 1 pound cod loin, boneless, skinless; cubed /450g
- 2 garlic cloves, grated
- 1 lemon, juiced and zested
- 1 lemon, cut in wedges to serve
- 3 tbsp olive oil /45ml
- 1 tsp dill; chopped /5g
- 1 tsp parsley; chopped /5g
- Salt to taste

Directions:
1. In a bowl, combine the olive oil, garlic, dill, parsley, salt, and lemon juice. Stir in the cod and place in the fridge to marinate for 1 hour. Thread the cod pieces onto halved skewers.
2. Arrange into the oiled Ninja Foodi basket; close the crisping lid and cook for 10 minutes at 390 °F or 199°C. Flip them over halfway through cooking. When ready, remove to a serving platter, scatter lemon zest and serve with wedges.

Cheesy Fried Risotto Balls

Servings: 6
Cooking Time: 45 Minutes

Ingredients:
- ½ cup extra-virgin olive oil, plus 1 tablespoon
- 1 small yellow onion, diced
- 2 garlic cloves, minced
- 5 cups vegetable broth
- ½ cup white wine
- 2 cups arborio rice
- ½ cup shredded mozzarella cheese
- ½ cup shredded fontina cheese
- ½ cup grated Parmesan cheese, plus more for garnish
- 2 tablespoons chopped fresh parsley
- 1 teaspoon sea salt
- 1 teaspoon freshly ground black pepper
- 2 cups fresh bread crumbs
- 2 large eggs

Directions:
1. Select SEAR/SAUTÉ and set to MD:HI. Select START/STOP to begin. Allow the pot to preheat for 5 minutes.
2. Add 1 tablespoon of oil and the onion to the preheated pot. Cook until soft and translucent, stirring occasionally. Add the garlic and cook for 1 minute.
3. Add the broth, wine, and rice to the pot; stir to incorporate. Assemble the pressure lid, making sure the pressure release valve is in the SEAL position.
4. Select PRESSURE and set to HI. Set the time to 7 minutes. Press START/STOP to begin.
5. When pressure cooking is complete, allow pressure to naturally release for 10 minutes. After 10 minutes, quick release any remaining pressure by turning the pressure release valve to the VENT position. Carefully remove the lid when the unit has finished releasing pressure.
6. Add the mozzarella, fontina, and Parmesan cheeses, the parsley, salt, and pepper. Stir vigorously until the rice begins to thicken. Transfer the risotto to a large mixing bowl and let cool.
7. Meanwhile, clean the pot. In a medium mixing bowl, stir together the bread crumbs and the remaining ½ cup of olive oil. In a separate mixing bowl, lightly beat the eggs.
8. Divide the risotto into 12 equal portions and form each one into a ball. Dip each risotto ball in the beaten eggs, then coat in the breadcrumb mixture.

9. Arrange half of the risotto balls in the Cook & Crisp Basket in a single layer.

10. Close the crisping lid. Select AIR CRISP, set the temperature to 400°F, and set the time to 10 minutes. Select START/STOP to begin.

11. Repeat steps 9 and 10 to cook the remaining risotto balls.

Nutrition Info:
- Calories: 722, Total Fat: 33g, Sodium: 1160mg, Carbohydrates: 81g, Protein: 23g.

Seasoned Parsnip Fries

Servings: 4
Cooking Time: 15 Minutes
Ingredients:
- Nonstick cooking spray
- 1 lb. parsnips, cut in shoestrings 3" x ¼"
- 1 ½ tsp fresh thyme, chopped
- ½ tsp garlic powder
- ¼ tsp salt
- 1/8 tsp pepper

Directions:
1. Spray the fryer basket with cooking spray. Line a baking sheet with parchment paper.
2. Place the parsnip fries on the baking sheet and spray with cooking spray. Toss the fries and spray again.
3. Sprinkle the seasonings over fries and toss to coat well. Place fries in the basket, don't over crowd them. Place the basket in the cooker.
4. Add the tender crisp lid and set to air fry on 450°F. Cook fries, in batches, about 15 minutes or until golden brown, turning over halfway through cooking time. Serve.

Nutrition Info:
- Calories 118, Total Fat 4g, Total Carbs 21g, Protein 1g, Sodium 157mg.

Turkey Scotch Eggs

Servings: 6
Cooking Time: 20 Min
Ingredients:
- 10 oz. ground turkey /300g
- 4 eggs, soft boiled, peeled
- 2 garlic cloves, minced
- 2 eggs, lightly beaten
- 1 white onion; chopped
- ½ cup flour /65g
- ½ cup breadcrumbs /65g
- 1 tsp dried mixed herbs /5g
- Salt and pepper to taste
- Cooking spray

Directions:
1. Mix together the onion, garlic, salt, and pepper. Shape into 4 balls. Wrap the turkey mixture around each egg, and ensure the eggs are well covered.
2. Dust each egg ball in flour, then dip in the beaten eggs and finally roll in the crumbs, until coated. Spray with cooking spray.
3. Lay the eggs into your Ninja Foodi's basket. Set the temperature to 390 °F or 199°C, close the crisping lid and cook for 15 minutes. After 8 minutes, turn the eggs. Slice in half and serve warm.

Cauliflower Gratin

Servings: 6
Cooking Time: 28 Minutes
Ingredients:
- 2 cups water
- 1 large head cauliflower, cut into 1-inch florets
- 3 tablespoons unsalted butter
- 3 tablespoons all-purpose flour
- 1½ cups whole milk
- 1 cup heavy (whipping) cream
- 2 tablespoons capers, drained
- 1 tablespoon fresh thyme
- Kosher salt
- Freshly ground black pepper
- ¾ cup shredded Swiss cheese
- ¼ cup grated Parmesan cheese

Directions:
1. Pour the water in the pot. Place the Reversible Rack in the lower position in the pot. Place the cauliflower on the rack. Assemble pressure lid, making sure the pressure release valve is in the SEAL position.
2. Select PRESSURE and set to HI. Set time to 5 minutes. Select START/STOP to begin.
3. When pressure cooking is complete, quick release the pressure by turning the pressure release valve to the VENT position. Carefully remove lid when the unit has finished releasing pressure.
4. Remove rack and place the cauliflower in the Ninja Multi-Purpose Pan or 8-inch baking dish. Drain the water from the pot and wipe it dry. Reinsert pot into base.
5. Select SEAR/SAUTÉ and set temperature to HI. Select START/STOP to begin. Let preheat for 5 minutes.

6. Add the butter. Once melted, add the onion and cook 3 minutes. Add the flour and cook, stirring constantly, 1 minute.
7. Add the milk, cream, capers, and thyme. Season with salt and pepper. Bring to a boil and cook, about 4 minutes.
8. Pour the sauce over the cauliflower. Place the pan onto the Reversible Rack, making sure the rack is in the lower position. Place the rack with pan in the pot. Close crisping lid.
9. Select BAKE/ROAST, set temperature to 400°F, and set time to 20 minutes. Select START/STOP to begin.
10. After 15 minutes, open lid and sprinkle the cauliflower with the Swiss and Parmesan cheeses. Close lid and continue cooking.
11. Once cooking is complete, open lid. Let the gratin sit for 10 minutes before serving.

Nutrition Info:
- Calories: 341,Total Fat: 27g,Sodium: 263mg,Carbohydrates: 16g,Protein: 11g.

Shallot Pepper Pancakes

Servings: 8
Cooking Time: 15 Minutes
Ingredients:
- 8 ounces shallot, chopped
- 2 tablespoons chives, chopped
- 1 red onion, chopped
- 1 cup coconut flour
- 2 egg
- ¼ cup sour cream
- 1 teaspoon baking soda
- 1 tablespoon lemon juice
- 1 teaspoon salt
- 1 teaspoon cilantro, chopped
- ½ teaspoon basil
- 1 tablespoon olive oil
- 1 bell pepper, chopped

Directions:
1. Chop the shallot and chives and combine them into a mixing bowl.
2. Whisk the eggs in a another bowl and add baking soda and lemon juice.
3. Stir the mixture and add the cream, salt, cilantro, basil, and coconut flour.
4. Blend the mixture well until smooth.
5. Add the vegetables to the egg mixture.
6. Stir it to the batter that forms. Set the Ninja Foodi's insert to" Sauté" mode.
7. Pour the olive oil in the Ninja Foodi's insert and preheat it.
8. Ladle the batter and cook the pancakes for 2 minutes on each side.
9. Keep the pancakes under aluminium foil to keep them warm until all the pancakes are cooked.
10. Serve the pancakes while warm.

Nutrition Info:
- Calories: 138; Fat: 6g; Carbohydrates: 7.6g; Protein: 4.7g

Chocolate Chip & Zucchini Snack Bars

Servings: 12
Cooking Time: 30 Minutes
Ingredients:
- Nonstick cooking spray
- 1 ¼ cup oat flour
- ¼ cup + 2 tbsp. coconut flour
- ¼ cup oats
- 1 ½ tsp baking powder
- ½ tsp baking soda
- ½ tsp cinnamon
- ¼ tsp salt
- 2 bananas, mashed
- 1 cup zucchini, grated
- ½ cup almond milk, unsweetened
- ¼ cup applesauce, unsweetened
- 2 tsp vanilla
- ¾ cup chocolate chips, sugar free

Directions:
1. Set to air fryer on 350°F. Lightly spray an 8-inch square baking pan with cooking spray.
2. In a large bowl, combine both flours, oats, baking powder, baking soda, cinnamon, and salt.
3. In a medium bowl, whisk together bananas, zucchini, milk, applesauce, and vanilla. Add to dry ingredients and mix just until combined.
4. Fold in chocolate chips and pour into prepared pan.
5. Add the rack to the cooking pot and place the pan on it. Add the tender-crisp lid and bake 30-35 minutes or until toothpick inserted in center comes out clean.
6. Let cool in pan 10 minutes then cut into 12 bars.

7. Preheat oven to 350F. Lightly grease a 9×9 baking pan with cooking spray or oil.

Nutrition Info:
- Calories 194,Total Fat 7g,Total Carbs 27g,Protein 5g,Sodium 168mg.

Crab Rangoon's

Servings: 15
Cooking Time: 20 Minutes
Ingredients:
- Nonstick cooking spray
- 8 oz. cream cheese, reduced fat, soft
- 1 tsp garlic powder
- 2 cups crab meat, chopped
- ¼ cup green onion, sliced thin
- 30 wonton wrappers

Directions:
1. Lightly spray the fryer basket with cooking spray.
2. In a medium bowl, beat cream cheese and garlic powder until smooth.
3. Stir in crab and onions and mix well.
4. Spoon a teaspoon of crab mixture in the center of each wrapper. Lightly brush edges with water and fold in half. Press edges to seal and lay in a single layer of the basket.
5. Add the tender-crisp lid and set to air fry on 350°F. Bake 15-20 minutes until crisp and golden brown, turning over halfway through cooking time. Serve immediately.

Nutrition Info:
- Calories 236,Total Fat 3g,Total Carbs 15g,Protein 11g,Sodium 416mg.

Spicy Turkey Meatballs

Servings: 8
Cooking Time: 15 Minutes
Ingredients:
- 1 lb. lean ground turkey
- 1 onion, chopped fine
- ¼ cup shredded wheat cereal, crushed
- 2 egg whites
- ½ tsp garlic powder
- ½ tsp salt
- ¼ tsp pepper
- Nonstick cooking spray
- ¼ cup jalapeno pepper jelly

Directions:
1. In a large bowl, combine all ingredients, except pepper jelly, and mix well. Form into 24 1-inch meatballs.
2. Lightly spray the fryer basket with cooking spray. Place meatballs in a single layer in the basket, these will need to be cooked in batches.
3. Add the basket to the cooking pot and secure the tender crisp lid. Set to air fry on 400°F. Cook meatballs 12-15 minutes, until no longer pink inside, turning halfway through cooking time.
4. Place the pepper jelly in a medium, microwave safe bowl. Microwave in 30 second intervals until the jelly is melted.
5. Toss cooked meatballs in the melted pepper jelly and serve immediately.
6. In a medium bowl, combine the turkey, onion, cereal, egg whites, garlic powder, salt, and black pepper. Shape into 24 one-inch meatballs.

Nutrition Info:
- Calories 113,Total Fat 5g,Total Carbs 6g,Protein 12g,Sodium 199mg.

Honey Mustard Hot Dogs

Servings: 4
Cooking Time: 22 Min
Ingredients:
- 20 Hot Dogs, cut into 4 pieces
- ¼ cup honey /62.5ml
- ¼ cup red wine vinegar /62.5ml
- ½ cup tomato puree /125ml
- ¼ cup water /62.5ml
- 1½ tsp soy sauce /7.5ml
- 1 tsp Dijon mustard /5g
- Salt and black pepper to taste

Directions:
1. Add the tomato puree, red wine vinegar, honey, soy sauce, Dijon mustard, salt, and black pepper in a medium bowl. Mix them with a spoon.
2. Put sausage weenies in the crisp basket, and close the crisping lid. Select Air Crisp mode. Set the temperature to 370 °F or 188°C and the timer to 4 minutes. Press Start/Stop. At the 2-minute mark, turn the sausages.
3. Once ready, open the lid and pour the sweet sauce over the sausage weenies.
4. Close the pressure lid, secure the pressure valve, and select Pressure mode on High for 3 minutes. Press Start/Stop. Once the timer has ended, do a quick pressure release. Serve and enjoy.

Cheesy Cauliflower Tater Tots

Servings: 10
Cooking Time: 35 Min
Ingredients:
- 2 lb. cauliflower florets, steamed /900g
- 5 oz. cheddar cheese /150g
- 1 egg, beaten
- 1 onion; diced
- 1 cup breadcrumbs /130g
- 1 tsp chopped chives /5g
- 1 tsp garlic powder /5g
- 1 tsp chopped parsley /5g
- 1 tsp chopped oregano /5g
- Salt and pepper, to taste

Directions:
1. Mash the cauliflower and place it in a large bowl. Add the onion, parsley, oregano, chives, garlic powder, salt, and pepper, and cheddar cheese. Mix with hands until thoroughly combined.
2. Form 12 balls out of the mixture. Line a baking sheet with paper. Dip half of the tater tots into the egg and then coat with breadcrumbs.
3. Arrange them on the baking sheet, close the crisping lid and cook in the Ninja Foodi at 350 °F or 177°C for 15 minutes on Air Crisp mode. Repeat with the other half.

Spicy Glazed Pecans

Servings: 12
Cooking Time: 30 Minutes
Ingredients:
- Nonstick cooking spray
- 6 cups pecan halves
- 6 tbsp. butter, melted
- ¼ cup Worcestershire sauce
- 2 tbsp. hot sauce
- 1 tbsp. soy sauce
- 1 tbsp. hot curry powder
- 1 tbsp. chili powder

Directions:
1. Lightly spray the fryer basket with cooking spray.
2. In a large bowl, combine all ingredients and toss well to coat the pecans.
3. Add half the mixture to the fryer basket and place in the cooking pot. Add the tender-crisp lid and set to air fry on 250°F. Cook 20 minutes. Shake the basket and cook 10 minutes more.
4. Transfer cooked nuts to a baking sheet lined with parchment paper and spread out to cool. Repeat with remaining nut mixture. Serve warm or room temperature.

Nutrition Info:
- Calories 402,Total Fat 41g,Total Carbs 9g,Protein 5g,Sodium 220mg.

Chicken Bites

Servings:4
Cooking Time: 8 Minutes
Ingredients:
- ½ cup Italian seasoned bread crumbs
- 2 tablespoons grated Parmesan cheese
- ¼ teaspoon sea salt
- ¼ teaspoon freshly ground black pepper
- 1 boneless, skinless chicken breast, cut into 1-inch pieces
- ½ cup unsalted butter, melted
- Cooking spray

Directions:
1. Place Cook & Crisp Basket in pot. Close crisping lid. Select AIR CRISP, set temperature to 390°F, and set time to 5 minutes. Select START/STOP to begin preheating.
2. In a medium bowl, combine the bread crumbs, Parmesan cheese, salt, and pepper. In a separate medium bowl, toss the chicken in the butter until well coated. Move a few of the chicken pieces to the breadcrumb mixture and coat. Repeat until all the chicken is coated.
3. Once unit is preheated, open lid and place the chicken bites in the basket in a single layer. Coat well with cooking spray. Close lid.
4. Select AIR CRISP, set temperature to 390°F, and set time to 8 minutes. Select START/STOP to begin.
5. After 4 minutes, open lid, then lift basket and flip the chicken bites with silicone-tipped tongs. Coat well with cooking spray. Lower basket back into pot and close lid to continue cooking.
6. After 4 minutes, check for desired crispness. Cooking is complete when the internal temperature of the chicken reads at least 165°F on a food thermometer.

Nutrition Info:
- Calories: 279,Total Fat: 25g,Sodium: 246mg,Carbohydrates: 5g,Protein: 10g.

Spinach Hummus

Servings: 12
Cooking Time: 1 Hr 10 Min
Ingredients:
- 2 cups spinach; chopped /260g
- ½ cup tahini /65g
- 2 cups dried chickpeas /260g
- 8 cups water /2000ml
- 5 garlic cloves, crushed
- 5 tbsp grapeseed oil /75ml
- 2 tsp salt; divided /10g
- 5 tbsp lemon juice /75ml

Directions:
1. In the pressure cooker, mix 2 tbsp oil, water, 1 tsp or 5g salt, and chickpeas. Seal the pressure lid, choose Pressure, set to High, and set the timer to 35 minutes. Press Start. When ready, release the pressure quickly. In a small bowl, reserve ½ cup of the cooking liquid and drain chickpeas.
2. Mix half the reserved cooking liquid and chickpeas in a food processor and puree until no large chickpeas remain; add remaining cooking liquid, spinach, lemon juice, remaining tsp salt, garlic, and tahini.
3. Process hummus for 8 minutes until smooth. Stir in the remaining 3 tbsp or 45ml of olive oil before serving.

Herb Roasted Mixed Nuts

Servings: 12
Cooking Time: 15 Minutes
Ingredients:
- ½ cup pecan halves
- ½ cup raw cashews
- ½ cup walnut halves
- ½ cup hazelnuts
- ½ cup Brazil nuts
- ½ cup raw almonds
- 1 tbsp. fresh rosemary, chopped
- 1 tbsp. fresh thyme, chopped
- ½ tbsp. fresh parsley, chopped
- 1 tsp garlic granules
- ½ tsp paprika
- ½ tsp salt
- ¼ tsp pepper
- ½ tbsp. olive oil

Directions:
1. Combine all ingredients in a large bowl and toss to coat thoroughly.
2. Pour the nuts in the fryer basket and place in the cooking pot. Add the tender-crisp lid and select air fry on 375°F. Cook 10 minutes, then stir the nuts around.
3. Cook another 5-10 minutes, stirring every few minutes and checking to make sure they don't burn. Serve warm.

Nutrition Info:
- Calories 229,Total Fat 21g,Total Carbs 7g,Protein 5g,Sodium 99mg.

Mushrooms Stuffed With Veggies

Servings: 6
Cooking Time: 25 Minutes
Ingredients:
- 12 large mushrooms, washed
- 1 tbsp. olive oil
- 1 zucchini, grated
- ½ onion, chopped fine
- ½ red bell pepper, chopped fine
- ¼ cup bread crumbs
- ½ tsp garlic powder
- ¼ tsp salt
- ¼ tsp pepper

Directions:
1. Remove stems from mushroom and finely chop them.
2. Add oil to the cooking pot and set to sauté on medium heat.
3. Once oil is hot, add mushroom stems, zucchini, onion, and bell pepper. Cook, stirring occasionally, about 5 minutes or until vegetables are tender.
4. Stir in bread crumbs, garlic powder, salt, and pepper. Transfer mixture to a bowl.
5. Place the rack in the cooking pot and top with parchment paper.
6. Stuff each mushroom cap with vegetable mixture and place on the parchment.
7. Add the tender-crisp lid and set to air fry on 350°F. Bake 15-20 minutes or until mushrooms are tender. Serve immediately.

Nutrition Info:
- Calories 56,Total Fat 3g,Total Carbs 6g,Protein 2g,Sodium 134mg.

Bacon Wrapped Scallops

Servings: 8
Cooking Time: 10 Minutes
Ingredients:
- 1/3 cup ketchup
- 2 tbsp. vinegar
- 1 tbsp. brown sugar
- ¼ tsp hot pepper sauce
- 13 slices turkey bacon, cut in half
- 1 lb. scallops, rinse & pat dry
- Nonstick cooking spray

Directions:
1. In a large bowl, whisk together ketchup, vinegar, brown sugar, and hot pepper sauce until smooth.
2. Wrap each scallop with a piece of bacon and use a toothpick to secure. Add to the sauce and toss to coat. Cover and refrigerate 20 minutes.
3. Place the rack in the cooking pot. Spray a small baking sheet with cooking spray. Working in batches, place scallops in a single layer on the tray and place on the rack.
4. Add the tender-crisp lid and set to air fry on 450°F. Cook scallops 4-5 minutes, then flip over and cook another 4-5 minutes or until cooked through. Serve immediately.

Nutrition Info:
- Calories 100, Total Fat 2g, Total Carbs 6g, Protein 13g, Sodium 525mg.

Crispy Cheesy Zucchini Bites

Servings: 6
Cooking Time: 10 Minutes
Ingredients:
- 2 zucchini, cut in 3/4-inch thick slices
- Nonstick cooking spray
- ½ cup panko bread crumbs
- 1 tbsp. parmesan cheese
- 1 tbsp. lite mayonnaise
- ½ tsp garlic powder
- ½ tsp onion powder
- ¼ tsp seasoned salt
- ¼ tsp pepper

Directions:
1. Pour enough water to cover the bottom of the cooking pot about 1 inch. Set to sauté on high heat and bring to a boil.
2. Add zucchini, reduce heat to low and simmer 3-5 minutes or just until tender. Drain and pat dry with paper towels.
3. Lightly spray the fryer basket with cooking spray and place it in the cooking pot.
4. In a small bowl, stir together bread crumbs, cheese, garlic powder, onion powder, salt, and pepper.
5. Spread one side of each zucchini slice with mayonnaise and place in a single layer in the basket. Sprinkle crumb mixture over top of each slice.
6. Add tender-crisp lid and set to air fry on 450°F. Bake 3-5 minutes, or until golden brown. Serve immediately.

Nutrition Info:
- Calories 48, Total Fat 1g, Total Carbs 7g, Protein 1g, Sodium 196mg.

Beef Chicken Meatloaf

Servings: 9
Cooking Time: 40 Minutes
Ingredients:
- 2 cups ground beef
- 1 cup ground chicken
- 2 eggs
- 1 tablespoon salt
- 1 teaspoon black pepper
- ½ teaspoon paprika
- 1 tablespoon butter
- 1 teaspoon cilantro, chopped
- 1 tablespoon basil
- ¼ cup fresh dill, chopped

Directions:
1. Combine the ground chicken and ground beef together in a mixing bowl.
2. Add egg, salt, black pepper, paprika, butter, and cilantro.
3. Add the basil and dill and add it to the ground meat mixture and stir using your hands.
4. Place the meat mixture on aluminium foil, shape into a loaf and wrap it.
5. Place it in the Ninja Foodi's insert. Close the Ninja Foodi's lid and cook the dish in the" Sauté" mode for 40 minutes.
6. Once done, remove the meatloaf from the Ninja Foodi's insert and let it rest.
7. Remove from the foil, slice it, and serve.

Nutrition Info:
- Calories: 173; Fat: 11.5g; Carbohydrates: 0.81g; Protein: 16g

Spicy Black Bean Dip

Servings: 12
Cooking Time: 20 Minutes
Ingredients:
- 2 16 oz. cans black beans, rinsed & drained, divided
- 1 cup salsa, divided
- 1 tsp olive oil
- ¾ onion, diced fine
- 1 red bell pepper, diced fine
- 3 cloves garlic, diced fine
- 1 tbsp. cilantro
- 2 tsp cumin
- ¼ tsp salt
- ¼ cup cheddar cheese, reduced fat, grated
- 1 tomato, chopped

Directions:
1. Add 1 can beans and ¼ cup salsa to a food processor or blender. Pulse until smooth.
2. Set cooker to sauté on medium heat. Add oil and let it get hot.
3. Add the onion, pepper, and garlic and cook, stirring occasionally, 5-7 minutes, or until vegetables are tender.
4. Add the pureed bean mixture along with remaining ingredients except cheese and tomatoes, mix well. Reduce heat to low and bring to a simmer. Let cook 5 minutes, stirring frequently.
5. Transfer dip to serving bowl and top with cheese and tomato. Serve immediately.

Nutrition Info:
- Calories 100, Total Fat 2g, Total Carbs 16g, Protein 6g, Sodium 511mg.

Saucy Chicken Wings

Servings: 6
Cooking Time: 35 Minutes
Ingredients:
- 1-pound chicken wings
- 1 teaspoon black pepper
- 1 teaspoon tomato paste
- 1 tablespoon garlic, minced
- ⅓ teaspoon soy sauce
- 3 tablespoons olive oil
- 1 teaspoon red pepper
- 1 teaspoon cilantro, chopped
- 1 tablespoon tomato sauce

Directions:
1. Combine the black pepper, red pepper, and cilantro together in a mixing bowl and stir the mixture.
2. Place the chicken wings in a separate bowl and sprinkle the meat with the black pepper mixture.
3. Add tomato paste, minced garlic, soy sauce, and tomato sauce.
4. Coat the chicken completely using your hands.
5. Transfer the meat to the Ninja Foodi's insert.
6. Close the Ninja Foodi's lid and cook the dish in the "Sauté" mode for 35 minutes.
7. Once done, remove the dish from the Ninja Foodi's insert.
8. Serve the chicken wings hot.

Nutrition Info:
- Calories: 165; Fat: 9.5g; Carbohydrates: 2.02g; Protein: 17g

Mexican Street Corn

Servings: 3
Cooking Time: 14 Minutes
Ingredients:
- 3 ears corn, husked, rinsed, and dried
- Olive oil spray
- ¼ cup sour cream
- ¼ cup mayonnaise
- ¼ cup crumbled cotija cheese, plus more for garnish
- 1 teaspoon freshly squeezed lime juice
- ½ teaspoon garlic powder
- ¼ teaspoon chili powder, plus more as needed
- Fresh cilantro leaves, for garnish
- ½ teaspoon salt
- ½ teaspoon freshly ground black pepper

Directions:
1. Select AIR CRISP, set the temperature to 400°F, and set the time to 5 minutes to preheat. Select START/STOP to begin.
2. Lightly mist the corn with olive oil and place the corn in the Cook & Crisp Basket. Close the crisping lid.
3. Select AIR CRISP, set the temperature to 400°F, and set the time to 12 minutes. Select START/STOP to begin. After 7 minutes, flip the corn. Close the crisping lid and cook for 5 minutes more.
4. While the corn cooks, in a small bowl, stir together the sour cream, mayonnaise, cotija cheese, lime juice, garlic powder, and chili powder until blended.

5. When cooking is complete, carefully remove the corn and brush or spoon the sauce onto it. Sprinkle with cilantro, cotija cheese, and more chili powder.
6. If desired, return the corn to the basket. Close the crisping lid. Select BROIL and set the time for 2 minutes. Select START/STOP to begin.
7. Serve hot, seasoned with salt and pepper, as needed.

Nutrition Info:
- Calories: 280,Total Fat: 15g,Sodium: 701mg,Carbohydrates: 35g,Protein: 7g.

Brie Spread With Cherries & Pistachios

Servings: 10
Cooking Time: 3 Hours

Ingredients:
- ½ cup dried cherries, chopped
- ¼ cup cherry preserves
- 1 tbsp. Cognac
- 2 8 oz. wheels Brie cheese
- ½ cup pistachio nuts, toasted & chopped

Directions:
1. In a small bowl, combine cherries, preserves, and cognac, mix well.
2. Place on wheel of Brie in the cooking pot. Pour half the cherry mixture over the top. Repeat layers one more time.
3. Add the lid and select slow cooking function on low heat. Set timer for 3 hours.
4. Cook until cheese is soft, but not melted. Transfer to a serving plate and sprinkle with toasted pistachios. Serve warm.

Nutrition Info:
- Calories 224,Total Fat 15g,Total Carbs 10g,Protein 11g,Sodium 290mg.

South Of The Border Corn Dip

Servings: 8
Cooking Time: 2 Hours

Ingredients:
- 33 oz. corn with chilies
- 10 oz. tomatoes & green chilies, diced
- 8 oz. cream cheese, cubed
- ½ cup cheddar cheese, grated
- ¼ cup green onions, chopped
- ½ tsp garlic, diced fine
- ½ tsp chili powder

Directions:
1. Place all ingredients in the cooking pot and stir to mix.
2. Add the lid and set to slow cooking function on low heat. Set timer for 2 hours. Stir occasionally.
3. Dip is done when all the cheese is melted and it's bubbly. Stir well, then transfer to serving bowl and serve warm.

Nutrition Info:
- Calories 225,Total Fat 13g,Total Carbs 24g,Protein 7g,Sodium 710mg.

Loaded Potato Skins

Servings:4
Cooking Time: 45 Minutes

Ingredients:
- 2 large Russet potatoes, cleaned
- 1 tablespoon extra-virgin olive oil
- Kosher salt
- Freshly ground black pepper
- ¾ cup shredded sharp Cheddar cheese
- 3 tablespoons unsalted butter
- ¼ cup milk
- ¼ cup sour cream, plus more for serving
- 1 bunch chives, sliced
- 4 slices of ham, cubed

Directions:
1. Using a fork, poke holes in each potato. Rub each potato with the olive oil and season the skin with salt and pepper. Place the potatoes on the Reversible Rack in the lower position and place in the pot. Close the crisping lid.
2. Select AIR CRISP, set temperature to 390°F, and set time to 35 minutes. Select START/STOP to begin.
3. When cooking is complete, open lid and use tongs to transfer the potatoes to a cutting board.
4. Cut the potatoes in half lengthwise. Using a spoon, scoop out the flesh into a large bowl, leaving about ¼ inch of flesh on the skins. Set aside.
5. Sprinkle the hollowed-out potato skins with ¼ cup of cheese and place them back in the pot on the rack. Close crisping lid.
6. Select BROIL and set time to 5 minutes. Select START/STOP to begin.
7. Add the butter, milk, and sour cream to the bowl with the flesh. Season with salt and pepper and mash together. Use a spatula to fold in ¼ cup of cheese, one-quarter of the chives, and ham into the potato mixture.

8. When cooking is complete, open lid. Using tongs, carefully transfer the potato skins to the cutting board. Evenly distribute the mashed potato mixture into each potato skin and top with the remaining ¼ cup of cheese. Return the loaded potato skins to the rack. Close crisping lid.
9. Select BROIL and set time to 5 minutes. Select START/STOP to begin.
10. When cooking is complete, open lid. Carefully remove the potatoes. Cut them in half and garnish with the remaining chives. Serve with additional sour cream, if desired.

Nutrition Info:
- Calories: 402, Total Fat: 24g, Sodium: 561mg, Carbohydrates: 32g, Protein: 14g.

Garlicky Tomato

Servings: 5
Cooking Time: 5 Minutes
Ingredients:
- 5 tomatoes
- ¼ cup chives, chopped
- ⅓ cup garlic clove, minced
- ½ teaspoon salt
- ½ teaspoon black pepper
- 1 tablespoon olive oil
- 7 ounces Parmesan cheese

Directions:
1. Wash the tomatoes and slice them into thick slices.
2. Place the sliced tomatoes in the Ninja Foodi's insert.
3. Combine the grated cheese and minced garlic and stir the mixture.
4. Sprinkle the tomato slices with chives, black pepper, and salt.
5. Then sprinkle the sliced tomatoes with the cheese mixture.
6. Close the Ninja Foodi's lid and cook the dish in the "Pressure" mode for 5 minutes.
7. Once done, remove the tomatoes carefully and serve.

Nutrition Info:
- Calories: 224; Fat: 14g; Carbohydrates: 12.55g; Protein: 13g

Cheesy Smashed Sweet Potatoes

Servings: 4
Cooking Time: 70 Min
Ingredients:
- 2 slices bacon, cooked and crumbled
- 12 ounces baby sweet potatoes /360g
- ¼ cup shredded Monterey Jack cheese /32.5g
- ¼ cup sour cream /62.5ml
- 1 tbsp chopped scallions /15g
- 1 tsp melted butter /5ml
- Salt to taste

Directions:
1. Put the Crisping Basket in the pot and close the crisping lid. Choose Air Crisp, set the temperature to 350°F or 177°C, and the time to 5 minutes. Press Start/Stop to begin preheating.
2. Meanwhile, toss the sweet potatoes with the melted butter until evenly coated. Once the pot and basket have preheated, open the lid and add the sweet potatoes to the basket. Close the lid, Choose Air Crisp, set the temperature to 350°F or 177°C, and set the time to 30 minutes; press Start.
3. After 15 minutes, open the lid, pull out the basket and shake the sweet potatoes. Return the basket to the pot and close the lid to continue cooking. When ended, check the sweet potatoes for your desired crispiness, which should also be fork tender.
4. Take out the sweet potatoes from the basket and use a large spoon to crush the soft potatoes just to split lightly. Top with the cheese, sour cream, bacon, and scallions, and season with salt.

Potato Samosas

Servings: 4
Cooking Time: 31 Minutes
Ingredients:
- 2 tablespoons canola oil
- 4 cups Russet potatoes, peeled and cut into ½-inch cubes
- 1 small yellow onion, diced
- 1 cup frozen peas
- 1½ teaspoons kosher salt
- 2½ teaspoons curry powder
- 1 cup vegetable stock
- 1 (½ package) frozen puff pastry sheet, thawed
- 1 egg beaten with 1 teaspoon water

Directions:
1. Select SEAR/SAUTÉ and set temperature to HI. Select START/STOP to begin. Let preheat for 5 minutes.
2. Add the oil and let heat for 1 minute. Add the potatoes, onions, and peas and cook, stirring frequently, about 10 minutes. Add the salt and curry powder and stir to coat the

vegetables with it. Add the vegetable stock. Assemble pressure lid, making sure the pressure release valve is in the SEAL position.

3. Select PRESSURE and set to LO. Set time to 1 minute. Select START/STOP to begin.

4. When pressure cooking is complete, quick release the pressure by turning the pressure release valve to the VENT position. Carefully remove the lid when the unit has finished releasing pressure.

5. Transfer the potato mixture to a medium bowl. Let fully cool, about 15 minutes.

6. Lay out the puff pastry sheet on a cutting board. Using a rolling pin, roll out the sheet into a 12-by-10-inch rectangle. Cut it in 4 strips lengthwise, then cut the strips into thirds for a total of 12 squares.

7. Place 2 tablespoons of potato mixture in center of a pastry square. Brush the egg wash onto edges, and then fold one corner to another to create a triangle. Use a fork to seal edges together. Repeat with the remaining potato mixture and pastry squares.

8. Insert Cook & Crisp Basket into unit. Close crisping lid. Select AIR CRISP, set temperature to 390°F, and set time to 20 minutes. Select START/STOP to begin. Let preheat for 5 minutes.

9. Once unit has preheated, working in batches, place 3 samosas in the basket. Close lid to begin cooking.

10. After 5 minutes, open lid and use silicone-tipped tongs to remove the samosas. Repeat with the remaining batches of samosas.

11. Once all samosas are cooked, serve immediately.

Nutrition Info:
- Calories: 449,Total Fat: 24g,Sodium: 639mg,Carbohydrates: 53g,Protein: 10g.

Herbed Cauliflower Fritters

Servings: 7
Cooking Time: 13 Minutes

Ingredients:
- 1-pound cauliflower
- 1 medium white onion
- 1 teaspoon salt
- ½ teaspoon ground white pepper
- 1 tablespoon sour cream
- 1 teaspoon turmeric
- ½ cup dill, chopped
- 1 teaspoon thyme
- 3 tablespoons almond flour
- 1 egg
- 2 tablespoons butter

Directions:
1. Wash the cauliflower and separate it into the florets.
2. Chop the florets and place them in a blender.
3. Peel the onion and dice it. Add the diced onion to a blender and blend the mixture.
4. When you get the smooth texture, add salt, ground white pepper, sour cream, turmeric, dill, thyme, and almond flour.
5. Add egg blend the mixture well until a smooth dough form.
6. Remove the cauliflower dough from a blender and form the medium balls.
7. Flatten the balls a little. Set the Ninja Foodi's insert to" Sauté" mode.
8. Add the butter to the Ninja Foodi's insert and melt it.
9. Add the cauliflower fritters in the Ninja Foodi's insert, and sauté them for 6 minutes.
10. Flip them once. Cook the dish in" Sauté" stew mode for 7 minutes.
11. Once done, remove the fritters from the Ninja Foodi's insert.
12. Serve immediately.

Nutrition Info:
- Calories: 143; Fat: 10.6g; Carbohydrates: 9.9g; Protein: 5.6g

Poultry Recipes

Ginger Orange Chicken Tenders

Servings: 4
Cooking Time: 25 Minutes
Ingredients:
- Nonstick cooking spray
- 1 ½ lbs. chicken tenders
- 1 cup orange juice
- 2 tsp tamari, low sodium
- ½ tsp ginger
- 11 oz. mandarin oranges, drained

Directions:
1. Spray the fryer basket with cooking spray.
2. Place chicken in a single layer in the basket, these may need to be cooked in batches.
3. Add the tender-crisp lid and set to air fry on 350°F. Cook 10 minutes, turning over halfway through cooking time.
4. Add all the tenders to the cooking pot.
5. In a small bowl, whisk together orange juice, soy sauce, and ginger. Pour over chicken and stir to coat all the pieces.
6. Set to sauté on medium heat. Cover and cook chicken, stirring occasionally, about 10 minutes.
7. Add the orange slices and cook another 5 minutes. Serve.

Nutrition Info:
- Calories 259,Total Fat 5g,Total Carbs 17g,Protein 36g,Sodium 210mg.

Turkey Enchilada Casserole

Servings: 6
Cooking Time: 70 Min
Ingredients:
- 1 pound boneless; skinless turkey breasts /450g
- 2 cups shredded Monterey Jack cheese; divided /260g
- 2 cups enchilada sauce /500ml
- 1 yellow onion; diced
- 2 garlic cloves; minced
- 1 can pinto beans, drained and rinsed /450g
- 1 bag frozen corn /480g
- 8 tortillas, each cut into 8 pieces
- 1 tbsp butter /15g
- ¼ tsp salt /1.25g
- ¼ tsp freshly ground black pepper /1.25g

Directions:
1. Choose Sear/Sauté on the pot and set to Medium High. Choose Start/Stop to preheat the pot. Melt the butter and cook the onion for 3 minutes, stirring occasionally. Stir in the garlic and cook until fragrant, about 1 minute more.
2. Put the turkey and enchilada sauce in the pot, and season with salt and black pepper. Stir to combine. Seal the pressure lid, choose Pressure, set to High, and set the time to 15 minutes. Choose Start/Stop.
3. When done cooking, perform a quick pressure release and carefully open the lid. Shred the turkey with two long forks while being careful not to burn your hands. Mix in the pinto beans, tortilla pieces, corn, and half of the cheese to the pot. Sprinkle the remaining cheese evenly on top of the casserole.
4. Close the crisping lid. Choose Broil and set the time to 5 minutes. Press Start/Stop to begin broiling. When ready, allow the casserole to sit for 5 minutes before serving.

Sour Cream & Cheese Chicken

Servings: 8
Cooking Time: 25 Minutes
Ingredients:
- Nonstick cooking spray
- 1 cup sour cream
- 2 tsp garlic powder
- 1 tsp seasoned salt
- ½ tsp pepper
- 1 ½ cups parmesan cheese, divided
- 3 lbs. chicken breasts, boneless

Directions:
1. Spray the cooking pot with cooking spray.
2. In a medium bowl, combine sour cream, garlic powder, seasoned salt, pepper, and 1 cup parmesan cheese, mix well.
3. Place the chicken in the cooking pot. Spread the sour cream mixture over the top and sprinkle with remaining parmesan cheese.
4. Add the tender-crisp lid and set to bake on 375°F. Bake chicken 25-30 minutes until cooked through.
5. Set cooker to broil and cook another 2-3 minutes until top is lightly browned. Serve immediately.

Nutrition Info:

- Calories 377, Total Fat 21g, Total Carbs 3g, Protein 41g, Sodium 737mg.

Jerk Chicken Thighs With Sweet Potato And Banana Mash

Servings: 6
Cooking Time: 20 Minutes
Ingredients:
- 4 boneless, skin-on chicken thighs
- ½ cup spicy jerk marinade
- 3 large sweet potatoes, peeled and cut into 1-inch cubes
- ½ cup unsweetened full-fat coconut milk
- Kosher salt
- Freshly ground black pepper
- 2 bananas, peeled and quartered
- 2 tablespoons agave nectar

Directions:
1. Place the chicken thighs and jerk marinade in a container, rubbing the marinade all over the chicken. Cover the container with plastic wrap and marinate 15 minutes.
2. Place the sweet potatoes, coconut milk, salt, and pepper in the pot. Place Reversible Rack in pot, making sure it is in the higher position. Place the chicken skin-side up on the rack, leaving space between the pieces. Assemble pressure lid, making sure the pressure release valve is in the SEAL position.
3. Select PRESSURE and set to HI. Set time to 4 minutes. Select START/STOP to begin.
4. When pressure cooking is complete, quick release the pressure by turning the pressure release valve to the VENT position. Carefully remove lid when unit has finished releasing pressure.
5. Place the bananas in the spaces between chicken thighs. Close crisping lid.
6. Select BROIL and set time to 15 minutes. Select START/STOP to begin.
7. After 10 minutes, remove the bananas and set aside. Turn over the chicken thighs. Close lid and continue cooking.
8. When cooking is complete, remove rack and chicken and let rest 5 to 10 minutes. Add the roasted bananas and agave nectar and mash them along with the sweet potatoes. Once rested, serve the chicken and sweet potato and banana mash.

Nutrition Info:

- Calories: 397, Total Fat: 22g, Sodium: 709mg, Carbohydrates: 35g, Protein: 20g.

Chicken Breasts

Servings: 4
Cooking Time: 15 Min
Ingredients:
- 4 boneless; skinless chicken breasts
- 1/4 cup dry white wine /62.5ml
- 1 cup water /250ml
- ½ tsp marjoram /2.5g
- ½ tsp sage /2.5g
- ½ tsp rosemary /2.5g
- ½ tsp mint /2.5g
- ½ tsp salt /2.5g

Directions:
1. Sprinkle salt over the chicken and set in the pot of the Foodi. Mix in mint, rosemary, marjoram, and sage. Pour wine and water around the chicken.
2. Seal the pressure lid, choose Pressure, set to High, and set the timer to 6 minutes. Press Start. Release the pressure naturally for 10 minutes.

Turkey & Cabbage Enchiladas

Servings: 4
Cooking Time: 30 Minutes
Ingredients:
- Nonstick cooking spray
- 8 large cabbage leaves
- 1 tbsp. olive oil
- ½ cup onion, chopped
- ½ red bell pepper, chopped
- 3 cloves garlic, chopped fine
- 2 tsp cumin
- 1 tbsp. chili powder
- 1 tsp salt
- ¼ tsp crushed red pepper flakes
- 2 cups turkey, cooked & shredded
- 1 cup enchilada sauce, sugar free
- ½ cup cheddar cheese, fat free, grated

Directions:
1. Spray a small baking dish with cooking spray.
2. Bring a large pot of water to boil. Add cabbage leaves and cook 30 seconds. Transfer leaves to paper towel lined surface and pat dry.

3. Add the oil to the cooking pot and set to sauté on medium heat.

4. Add the onion, bell pepper, and garlic and cook, stirring occasionally, until onions are translucent, about 5 minutes.

5. Stir in cumin, chili powder, salt, red pepper flakes, and turkey. Cook just until heat through. Transfer mixture to a bowl.

6. Add the rack to the cooking pot.

7. Lay cabbage leaves on work surface. Divide turkey mixture evenly between leaves. Fold in the sides and roll up. Place in the prepared dish, seam side down. Pour the enchilada sauce over the top and sprinkle with cheese.

8. Place dish on the rack and add the tender-crisp lid. Set to bake on 400°F. Cook enchiladas 15-20 minutes until cheese is melted and bubbly. Let rest 5 minutes before serving.

Nutrition Info:
- Calories 289, Total Fat 12g, Total Carbs 4g, Protein 32g, Sodium 735mg.

Honey Garlic Chicken And Okra

Servings: 4
Cooking Time: 25 Min
Ingredients:
- 4 boneless; skinless chicken breasts; sliced
- 4 spring onions, thinly sliced
- 6 garlic cloves, grated
- ⅓ cup honey /84ml
- 1 cup rice, rinsed /130g
- ¼ cup tomato puree /62.5ml
- ½ cup soy sauce /125ml
- 2 cups water /500ml
- 2 cups frozen okra /260g
- 1 tbsp cornstarch /15g
- 2 tbsp rice vinegar /30ml
- 1 tbsp olive oil /15ml
- 1 tbsp water /15ml
- 2 tsp toasted sesame seeds /10g
- ½ tsp salt /2.5g

Directions:
1. In the inner pot of the Foodi, mix garlic, tomato puree, vinegar, soy sauce, ginger, honey, and oil; toss in chicken to coat. In an ovenproof bowl, mix water, salt and rice. Set the reversible rack on top of chicken. Lower the bowl onto the reversible rack.

2. Seal the pressure lid, choose Pressure, set to High, and set the timer to 10 minutes; press Start. Release pressure naturally for 5 minutes, release the remaining pressure quickly.

3. Use a fork to fluff the rice. Lay okra onto the rice. Allow the okra steam in the residual heat for 3 minutes. Take the trivet and bowl from the pot. Set the chicken to a plate.

4. Press Sear/Sauté. In a small bowl, mix 1 tbsp of water and cornstarch until smooth; stir into the sauce and cook for 3 to 4 minutes until thickened.

5. Divide the rice, chicken, and okra between 4 bowls. Drizzle sauce over each portion; garnish with spring onions and sesame seeds.

Turkey Croquettes

Servings: 10
Cooking Time: 20 Minutes
Ingredients:
- Nonstick cooking spray
- 2 ½ cups turkey, cooked
- 1 stalk celery, chopped
- 2 green onions, chopped
- ½ cup cauliflower, cooked
- ½ cup broccoli, cooked
- 1 cup stuffing, cooked
- 1 cup cracker crumbs
- 1 egg, lightly beaten
- 1/8 tsp salt
- 1/8 tsp pepper
- 1 cup French fried onions, crushed

Directions:
1. Spray the fryer basket with cooking spray.

2. Add the turkey, celery, onion, cauliflower, and broccoli to a food processor and pulse until finely chopped. Transfer to a large bowl.

3. Stir in stuffing and 1 cup of the cracker crumbs until combined.

4. Add the egg, salt and pepper and stir to combine. Form into 10 patties.

5. Place the crushed fried onions in a shallow dish. Coat patties on both sides in the onions and place in the basket. Lightly spray the tops with cooking spray.

6. Add the tender-crisp lid and set to air fry on 375°F. Cook 5-7 minutes until golden brown. Flip over and spray with cooking spray again, cook another 5-7 minutes. Serve immediately.

Nutrition Info:

- Calories 133, Total Fat 4g, Total Carbs 16g, Protein 9g, Sodium 449mg.

Spanish Chicken & Olives

Servings: 4
Cooking Time: 50 Minutes
Ingredients:
- ¼ cup extra virgin olive oil
- ¼ cup red wine vinegar
- 2 tsp fresh oregano, chopped
- 1 tsp salt
- ½ tsp garlic powder
- 1/8 tsp pepper
- 3 bay leaves
- ½ cup golden raisins
- ¼ cup green olives, pitted & halved
- 3 lbs. chicken
- ½ cup dry white wine
- 2 tbsp. brown sugar

Directions:
1. In a medium bowl, whisk together oil, vinegar, oregano, salt, garlic powder, pepper, bay leaves, raisins, and olives.
2. Prick the chicken with a fork all over and add to marinade, turning to coat. Cover and refrigerate several hours or overnight.
3. Transfer the chicken to the cooking pot. Whisk the wine and brown sugar into the marinade and pour over the top.
4. Add the tender-crisp lid and set to bake on 350 °F. Bake 45-50 minutes, basting occasionally, until chicken is cooked through. Discard bay leaves before serving.

Nutrition Info:
- Calories 143, Total Fat 5g, Total Carbs 6g, Protein 16g, Sodium 208mg.

Italian Turkey & Pasta Soup

Servings: 8
Cooking Time: 10 Minutes
Ingredients:
- 1 lb. ground turkey sausage
- 1 onion, chopped fine
- 5 cloves garlic, chopped fine
- 1 green bell pepper, chopped fine
- 1 tbsp. Italian seasoning
- 2 15 oz. cans tomatoes, diced
- 2 8 oz. cans tomato sauce
- 4 cups chicken broth, low sodium
- 3 cups whole wheat pasta
- ¼ cup parmesan cheese
- ¼ cup mozzarella cheese, grated

Directions:
1. Add the sausage, onions, and garlic to the cooking pot. Set to sauté on med-high and cook, breaking sausage up, until meat is no longer pink and onions are translucent. Drain off excess fat.
2. Stir in bell pepper, Italian seasoning, tomatoes, tomato sauce, broth, and pasta, mix well.
3. Add the lid and set to pressure cook on high. Set the timer for 5 minutes. Once the timer goes off, use the natural release for 5-10 minutes, then quick release to remove the pressure.
4. Stir the soup and ladle into bowls. Serve garnished with parmesan and mozzarella cheeses.

Nutrition Info:
- Calories 294, Total Fat 8g, Total Carbs 37g, Protein 22g, Sodium 841mg.

Chicken And Broccoli

Servings: 4
Cooking Time: 20 Minutes
Ingredients:
- 3 pounds boneless chicken, cut into thin strips
- 1 tablespoon olive oil
- 1 yellow onion, peeled and chopped
- 1/2 cup beef stock
- 1-pound broccoli florets
- 2 teaspoons toasted sesame oil
- 2 tablespoons arrowroot
- For Marinade
- 1 cup coconut aminos
- 1 tablespoon sesame oil
- 2 tablespoons fish sauce
- 5 garlic cloves, peeled and minced
- 3 red peppers, dried and crushed
- 1/2 teaspoon Chinese five-spice powder
- Toasted sesame seeds, for serving

Directions:
1. Take a suitable and mix in coconut aminos, fish sauce, 1 tablespoon sesame oil, garlic, five-spice powder, crushed red pepper and stir.
2. Stir in chicken strips to the bowl and toss to coat.
3. Keep it on the side for 10 minutes.

4. Select "Sauté" mode on your Ninja Foodi and stir in oil, let it heat up, add onion and stir cook for 4 minutes.
5. Stir in chicken and marinade, stir cook for 2 minutes.
6. Add stock and stir.
7. Lock the pressure lid of Ninja Foodi and cook on "HIGH" pressure for 5 minutes.
8. Release pressure naturally over 10 minutes.
9. Mix arrowroot with 1/4 cup liquid from the pot and gently pour the mixture back to the pot and stir.
10. Place a steamer basket in the Ninja Foodi's pot and stir in broccoli to the steamer rack, Lock and secure the Ninja Foodi's lid.
11. Then cook on "HIGH" pressure mode for 3 minutes more, quick-release pressure.
12. Divide the dish between plates and serve with broccoli, toasted sesame seeds and enjoy.

Nutrition Info:
- Calories: 433; Fat: 27g; Carbohydrates: 8g; Protein: 20g

Shredded Chicken Salsa

Servings: 4
Cooking Time: 20 Minutes

Ingredients:
- 1-pound chicken breast, boneless
- ¾ teaspoon cumin
- ½ teaspoon salt
- Pinch of oregano
- Pepper to taste
- 1 cup chunky salsa

Directions:
1. Season chicken with spices and add to Ninja Foodi.
2. Cover with salsa and lock lid, cook on "HIGH" pressure for 20 minutes.
3. Quick-release pressure.
4. Add chicken to a platter and shred the chicken.
5. Serve and enjoy.

Nutrition Info:
- Calories: 125; Fat: 3g; Carbohydrates: 2g; Protein: 22g

Chicken With Bacon And Beans

Servings: 4
Cooking Time: 45 Min

Ingredients:
- 4 boneless; skinless chicken thighs
- 4 garlic cloves; minced
- 15 ounces red kidney beans, drained and rinsed /450g
- 4 slices bacon, crumbled
- 1 can whole tomatoes /435g
- 1 red bell pepper; chopped
- 1 onion; diced
- 1 cup shredded Monterey Jack cheese /130g
- 1 cup sliced red onion /130g
- ¼ cup chopped cilantro /32.5g
- 1 cup chicken broth /250ml
- 1 tbsp tomato paste /15ml
- 1 tbsp olive oil /15ml
- 1 tbsp oregano /15g
- 1 tbsp ground cumin/15g
- 1 tsp chili powder /5g
- ½ tsp cayenne pepper /2.5g
- 1 tsp salt /5g
- 1 cup cooked corn /130g

Directions:
1. Warm oil on Sear/Sauté. Sear the chicken for 3 minutes for each side until browned. Set the chicken on a plate. In the same oil, fry bacon until crispy, about 5 minutes and set aside.
2. Add in onions and cook for 2 to 3 minutes until fragrant. Stir in garlic, oregano, cayenne pepper, cumin, tomato paste, bell pepper, and chili powder and cook for 30 more seconds. Pour the chicken broth, salt, and tomatoes and bring to a boil. Press Start/Stop.
3. Take back the chicken and bacon to the pot and ensure it is submerged in the braising liquid. Seal the pressure lid, choose Pressure, set to High, and set the timer to 15 minutes. Press Start. When ready, release the pressure quickly.
4. Pour the kidney beans in the cooker, press Sear/Sauté and bring the liquid to a boil; cook for 10 minutes. Serve topped with shredded cheese and chopped cilantro.

Turkey & Squash Casserole

Servings: 8
Cooking Time: 55 Minutes

Ingredients:
- 2 tsp olive oil
- 1 onion, chopped
- 1 lb. zucchini, sliced ¼-inch thick
- 1 lb. yellow squash, sliced ¼-inch thick
- 14 ½ oz. tomatoes, diced
- ¼ cup fresh basil, chopped
- 1 tsp garlic powder
- 10 ¾ oz. cream of chicken soup, low sodium

- 1 cup sour cream, fat free
- 1 cup sharp cheddar cheese, reduced fat, grated
- 4 cups turkey, cooked & chopped
- ½ tsp black pepper
- 2 tbsp. whole wheat bread crumbs

Directions:

1. Add the oil to the cooking pot and set to sauté on med-high heat.
2. Add the onion, zucchini, and yellow squash and cook until soft, about 10 minutes.
3. Transfer to a large bowl and stir in tomatoes, basil, and garlic powder.
4. In a medium bowl, combine soup, sour cream, cheese, turkey, and pepper, mix well.
5. Spread half the vegetable mixture on the bottom of the pot. Top with half the chicken mixture. Repeat. Sprinkle the bread crumbs over the top.
6. Add the tender-crisp lid and set to bake on 350°F. Bake 45 minutes or until hot and bubbly. Serve.

Nutrition Info:
- Calories 219,Total Fat 5g,Total Carbs 18g,Protein 25g,Sodium 469mg.

Chicken With Rice And Peas

Servings: 4
Cooking Time: 30 Min

Ingredients:
- 4 boneless; skinless chicken breasts; sliced
- 1 onion; chopped
- 1 celery stalk; diced
- 1 garlic clove; minced
- 2 cups chicken broth; divided /500ml
- 1 cup long grain rice /130g
- 1 cup frozen green peas /130g
- 1 tbsp oil olive /15ml
- 1 tbsp tomato puree /15ml
- ½ tsp paprika /2.5g
- ¼ tsp dried oregano/1.25g
- ¼ tsp dried thyme /1.25g
- ⅛ tsp cayenne pepper /0.625g
- ⅛ tsp ground white pepper /0.625g
- Salt to taste

Directions:

1. Season chicken with garlic powder, oregano, white pepper, thyme, paprika, cayenne pepper, and salt. Warm the oil on Sear/Sauté. Add in onion and cook for 4 minutes until fragrant. Mix in tomato puree to coat.
2. Add ¼ cup or 65ml chicken stock into the Foodi to deglaze the pan, scrape the pan's bottom to get rid of browned bits of food. Mix in celery, rice, and the seasoned chicken. Add in the remaining broth to the chicken mixture.
3. Seal the pressure lid, choose Pressure, set to High, and set the timer to 8 minutes. Press Start. Once ready, do a quick release. Mix in green peas, cover with the lid and let sit for 5 minutes. Serve warm.

Creamy Tuscan Chicken Pasta

Servings:8
Cooking Time: 6 Minutes

Ingredients:
- 32 ounces chicken stock
- 1 jar oil-packed sun-dried tomatoes, drained
- 2 teaspoons Italian seasoning
- 3 garlic cloves, minced
- 1 pound chicken breast, cubed
- 1 box penne pasta
- 4 cups spinach
- 1 package cream cheese, cubed
- 1 cup shredded Parmesan cheese
- Kosher salt
- Freshly ground black pepper

Directions:

1. Place the chicken stock, sun-dried tomatoes, Italian seasoning, garlic, chicken breast, and pasta and stir. Assemble pressure lid, making sure the pressure release valve is in the SEAL position.
2. Select PRESSURE and set to HI. Set time to 6 minutes. Select START/STOP to begin.
3. When pressure cooking is complete, quick release the pressure by turning the pressure release valve to the VENT position. Carefully remove lid when unit has finished releasing pressure.
4. Add the spinach and stir, allowing it to wilt with the residual heat. Add the cream cheese, Parmesan cheese, salt and pepper and stir until melted. Serve.

Nutrition Info:
- Calories: 429,Total Fat: 21g,Sodium: 567mg,Carbohydrates: 32g,Protein: 29g.

Chicken Pot Pie

Servings: 8
Cooking Time: 25 Minutes
Ingredients:
- Nonstick cooking spray
- 1 tbsp. light butter
- ½ cup onion, chopped
- 8 oz. mushrooms, chopped
- 1 ½ cup frozen mixed vegetables, thawed
- 3 cups chicken, cooked & chopped
- ½ tsp thyme
- ½ tsp salt
- ¼ tsp pepper
- 1 cup chicken broth, low sodium
- ½ cup evaporated milk, fat free
- 2 tbsp. flour
- 4 slices refrigerated crescent rolls, low fat

Directions:
1. Spray an 8-inch deep dish pie plate with cooking spray.
2. Add the butter to the cooking pot and set to sauté on med-high to melt.
3. Add onions and mushrooms and cook 3-5 minutes until they start to soften. Add vegetables, chicken, thyme, salt, and pepper and stir to mix. Bring to a simmer and cook 5-6 minutes.
4. In a small bowl, whisk together milk and flour until smooth. Stir into the chicken mixture and cook 3-5 minutes until thickened. Pour into prepared pie plate.
5. Add the rack to the cooking pot. Arrange slices of dough on top of the chicken mixture with widest part of dough on the outside edge.
6. Place the pie on the rack and add the tender-crisp lid. Set to bake on 375°F. Bake 20-25 minutes until crust is golden brown and filling is hot and bubbly. Serve.

Nutrition Info:
- Calories 203,Total Fat 6g,Total Carbs 17g,Protein 21g,Sodium 197mg.

Cajun Chicken & Pasta

Servings: 8
Cooking Time: 20 Minutes
Ingredients:
- 2 tsp olive oil
- ½ cup onion, chopped fine
- ¼ cup red bell pepper, chopped fine
- ¼ cup green bell pepper, chopped fine
- 3 cloves garlic, chopped fine
- 1 cup Andouille sausage, cut in 1-inch pieces
- 1 tbsp. Cajun seasoning
- 2 cup chicken, cooked & shredded
- 16 oz. whole wheat penne pasta, cooked
- 1 ½ cups skim milk
- ½ cup parmesan cheese, low fat
- 1 tbsp. cornstarch
- ¼ cup chicken broth, low sodium

Directions:
1. Add the oil to the cooking pot and set to sauté on med-high heat.
2. Add the onion, peppers, and garlic and cook until they soften.
3. Add the sausage and cook 5 minutes, until heated through, stirring occasionally.
4. Add the Cajun seasoning and chicken and cook, stirring occasionally until heated through.
5. Stir in the pasta and milk and bring to a simmer. Cook 5 minutes.
6. In a small bowl, whisk together cornstarch and broth until smooth. Add to the pot and cook, stirring until sauce thickens.
7. Stir in parmesan cheese and serve.

Nutrition Info:
- Calories 359,Total Fat 10g,Total Carbs 42g,Protein 23g,Sodium 457mg.

Crispy Chicken With Carrots And Potatoes

Servings: 4
Cooking Time: 35 Min
Ingredients:
- 4 bone-in skin-on chicken thighs
- 1 pound potatoes, quartered /450g
- 2 carrots; sliced into rounds
- 2 dashes hot sauce
- ¼ cup chicken stock /62.5ml
- 2 tbsp melted butter /30ml
- 1 tbsp olive oil /15ml
- 1 tsp dried oregano /5g
- ½ tsp dry mustard /2.5g
- ½ tsp garlic powder /2.5g
- ¼ tsp sweet paprika /1.25g
- ½ tsp salt /2.5g

- 2 tsp Worcestershire sauce /10ml
- 2 tsp turmeric powder /10g

Directions:

1. Season the chicken on both sides with salt. In a small bowl, mix the melted butter, Worcestershire sauce, turmeric, oregano, dry mustard, garlic powder, sweet paprika, and hot sauce to be properly combined and stir in the chicken stock.

2. On your Foodi, choose Sear/Sauté and adjust to Medium-High. Press Start to preheat the inner pot. Heat olive oil and add the chicken thighs and fry for 4 to 5 minutes or until browned. Turn and briefly sear the other side, about 1 minute. Remove from the pot.

3. Add the potatoes and carrots to the pot and stir to coat with the fat. Pour in about half of the spicy sauce and mix to coat. Put the chicken thighs on top and drizzle with the remaining sauce.

4. Seal the pressure lid, choose pressure; adjust the pressure to High and the cook time to 3 minutes; press Start. After cooking, do a quick pressure release, and carefully open the lid.

5. Transfer the chicken to the reversible rack. Use a spoon to gently move the potatoes and carrots aside and fetch some of the sauce over the chicken. Mix the potatoes and carrots back into the sauce and carefully set the rack in the pot.

6. Close the crisping lid and Choose Bake/Roast; adjust the temperature to 375°F or 191°C and the cook time to 16 minutes. Press Start to begin crisping the chicken. When done cooking, open the lid and transfer the potatoes, carrots and chicken to a serving platter, drizzling with any remaining sauce.

Chicken Fajitas With Avocado

Servings: 4
Cooking Time: 30 Min

Ingredients:

- 4 chicken breasts, boneless and skinless
- 1 can diced tomatoes /720g
- 3 bell peppers, julienned
- 1 shallot; chopped
- 4 garlic cloves; minced
- 4 flour tortillas
- 1 avocado; sliced
- 1 taco seasoning
- 2 tbsp cilantro; chopped /30g
- 1 tbsp olive oil /15ml
- Juice of 1 lemon
- salt and pepper to taste

Directions:

1. In a bowl, mix taco seasoning and chicken until evenly coated. Warm oil on Sear/Sauté. Sear chicken for 2 minutes per side until browned. To the chicken, add tomatoes, shallot, lemon juice, garlic, and bell peppers; season with pepper and salt.

2. Seal the pressure lid, choose Pressure, set to High, and set the timer to 4 minutes. Press Start. When ready, release the pressure quickly.

3. Move the bell peppers and chicken to tortillas. Add avocado slices and serve.

Buttermilk Chicken Thighs

Servings: 6
Cooking Time: 4 Hours 40 Min

Ingredients:

- 1 ½ lb. chicken thighs /675g
- 2 cups buttermilk /500ml
- 2 cups flour /260g
- 1 tbsp paprika /15g
- 1 tbsp baking powder /15g
- 2 tsp black pepper /10g
- 1 tsp cayenne pepper /5g
- 3 tsp salt divided /15g

Directions:

1. Rinse and pat dry the chicken thighs. Place the chicken thighs in a bowl. Add cayenne pepper, 2 tsp or 10g salt, black pepper, and buttermilk, and stir to coat well.

2. Refrigerate for 4 hours. Preheat the Foodi to 350 °F or 177°C. In another bowl, mix the flour, paprika, 1 tsp or 5g salt, and baking powder.

3. Dredge half of the chicken thighs, one at a time, in the flour, and then place on a lined dish. Close the crisping lid and cook for 18 minutes on Air Crisp mode, flipping once halfway through. Repeat with the other batch.

Creamy Chicken Carbonara

Servings: 4
Cooking Time: 15 Minutes

Ingredients:

- 4 strips bacon, chopped
- 1 medium onion, diced
- 1½ pounds chicken breast, cut into ¾ inch-cubes
- 6 garlic cloves, minced
- 2 cups chicken stock
- 8 ounces dry spaghetti, with noodles broken in half

- 2 cups freshly grated Parmesan cheese, plus more for serving
- 2 eggs
- Sea salt
- Freshly ground black pepper

Directions:
1. Select SEAR/SAUTÉ and set to HI. Select START/STOP to begin. Let preheat for 5 minutes.
2. Add the bacon and cook, stirring frequently, for about 6 minutes, or until crispy. Using a slotted spoon, transfer the bacon to a paper towel-lined plate to drain. Leave any bacon fat in the pot.
3. Add the onion, chicken, and garlic and sauté for 2 minutes, until the onions start to become translucent and the garlic is fragrant.
4. Add the chicken stock and spaghetti noodles. Assemble pressure lid, making sure the pressure release valve is in the SEAL position.
5. Select PRESSURE and set to HI. Set time to 6 minutes. Select START/STOP to begin.
6. When pressure cooking is complete, allow pressure to naturally release for 5 minutes. After 5 minutes, quick release remaining pressure by moving the pressure release valve to the VENT position. Carefully remove lid when unit has finished releasing pressure.
7. Add the cheese and stir to fully combine. Close the crisping lid, leaving the unit off, to keep the heat inside and allow the cheese to melt.
8. Whisk the eggs until full beaten.
9. Open lid, select SEAR/SAUTÉ, and set to LO. Select START/STOP to begin. Add the eggs and stir gently to incorporate, taking care to ensure the eggs are not scrambling while you work toward your desired sauce consistency. If your pot gets too warm, turn unit off.
10. Add the bacon back to the pot and season with salt and pepper. Stir to combine. Serve, adding more cheese as desired.

Nutrition Info:
- Calories: 732,Total Fat: 28g,Sodium: 1518mg,Carbohydrates: 47g,Protein: 70g.

Chipotle Raspberry Chicken

Servings: 8
Cooking Time: 6 Hours
Ingredients:
- Nonstick cooking spray
- 2 lbs. chicken breasts, boneless & skinless
- 1 cup raspberry preserves, sugar free
- 2 tbsp. chipotle in adobo sauce
- 2 tbsp. fresh lime juice
- ½ tsp cumin

Directions:
1. Spray the cooking pot with cooking spray and add the chicken.
2. In a medium bowl, combine remaining ingredients. Pour over chicken.
3. Add the lid and set to slow cook on low. Cook 6 hours or until chicken is tender. Stir well before serving.

Nutrition Info:
- Calories 168,Total Fat 4g,Total Carbs 8g,Protein 26g,Sodium 144mg.

Pizza Stuffed Chicken

Servings: 4
Cooking Time: 20 Minutes
Ingredients:
- Nonstick cooking spray
- 2 chicken breasts, boneless & skinless
- 2 tbsp. parmesan cheese, divided
- ½ tsp oregano
- 12 slices turkey pepperoni
- ½ cup mozzarella cheese, grated, divided
- 3 tbsp. whole-wheat bread crumbs
- 4 tbsp. marinara sauce, low sodium

Directions:
1. Place the rack in the cooking pot. Spray the fryer basket with cooking spray.
2. Cut each breast in half horizontally. Place between 2 sheets of plastic wrap and pound out to ¼-inch thick.
3. Sprinkle 1 tablespoon of parmesan and the oregano over chicken. Top each cutlet with 3 slices of pepperoni and 1 tablespoon mozzarella. Roll up.
4. In a shallow dish, combine bread crumbs and remaining parmesan, mix well. Coat chicken rolls in bread crumbs and place, seam side down, in the fryer basket. Lightly spray with cooking spray.
5. Add the tender-crisp lid and set to air fry on 400 °F. Cook 15 minutes.
6. Open the lid and top each chicken roll with 1 tablespoon marinara sauce and remaining mozzarella. Cook 5-7 minutes until chicken is cooked through and cheese is melted. Serve immediately.

Nutrition Info:

- Calories 268, Total Fat 8g, Total Carbs 7g, Protein 41g, Sodium 800mg.

Chicken Pasta With Pesto Sauce

Servings: 8
Cooking Time: 30 Min
Ingredients:
- 4 chicken breast, boneless, skinless; cubed
- 8 oz. macaroni pasta /240g
- 1 garlic clove; minced
- 1/4 cup Asiago cheese, grated /32.5g
- 2 cups fresh collard greens, trimmed /260g
- ¼ cup cream cheese, at room temperature /32.5g
- 1 cup cherry tomatoes, halved /130g
- ½ cup basil pesto sauce /125ml
- 3½ cups water /875ml
- 1 tbsp butter /15g
- 1 tbsp salt; divided/15g
- 1 tsp freshly ground black pepper to taste /5g
- Freshly chopped basil for garnish

Directions:
1. To the inner steel pot of the Foodi, add water, chicken, 2 tsp salt, butter, and macaroni, and stir well to mix and be submerged in water.
2. Seal the pressure lid, choose Pressure, set to High, and set the timer to 2 minutes. Press Start. When ready, release the pressure quickly. Press Start/Stop, open the lid, get rid of ¼ cup water from the pot.
3. Set on Sear/Sauté. Into the pot, mix in collard greens, pesto sauce, garlic, remaining 1 tsp o 5g salt, cream cheese, tomatoes, and black pepper. Cook, for 1 to 2 minutes as you stir, until sauce is creamy.
4. Place the pasta into serving plates; top with asiago cheese and basil before serving.

Turkey Green Chili

Servings: 8
Cooking Time: 4 Hours
Ingredients:
- Nonstick cooking spray
- 2 poblano chilies
- 1 ½ lbs. fresh green tomatillos
- 5 cloves garlic, peel on
- 3 cloves garlic, chopped fine
- 1 jalapeno, seeded & chopped
- 1 bunch of cilantro, chopped
- 2 tsp salt, divided
- 2 tbsp. lime juice
- 1/8 tsp sugar
- 3 lbs. turkey thighs
- 2 tbsp. extra virgin olive oil
- 3 cups onion, chopped
- 1 teaspoon cumin
- 2 ½ cups chicken broth, low sodium
- 1 tsp chipotle powder
- 2 tbsp. fresh oregano, chopped
- 2 bay leaves
- 1/8 tsp ground cloves

Directions:
1. Lightly spray the fryer basket with cooking spray.
2. Place the poblano's in the basket. Add the tender-crisp lid and set to broil. Cook chilies until they have charred on all sides, turning every couple of minutes. Transfer to a paper bag, close and let the chilies sit for 5 minutes.
3. After 5 minutes, remove the charred skin, stems and seeds from the chilies.
4. Place the tomatillos, cut side down, in the fryer basket along with the garlic cloves. Add the tender-crisp lid and broil 5-7 minutes until nicely browned. Let cool to the touch then remove the garlic peel.
5. Place the tomatillos, garlic, jalapeno, poblanos, cilantro, 1 teaspoon salt, lime juice, and sugar in a blender. Process on low to start, then increase the speed until mixture is smooth.
6. Season the turkey with salt and pepper.
7. Add the oil to the cooking pot and set to sear on med-high. Add the turkey, in batches, and sear until lightly browned on all sides. Transfer to a plate.
8. Add the onions and cumin and cook, stirring to scrape up any brown bits on the bottom of the pot, until onions are translucent. Add the chopped garlic and cook 30 seconds more.
9. Add the tomatillo sauce, broth, chipotle powder, oregano, bay leaves, 1 teaspoon salt, ½ teaspoon pepper, and clove to the pot and stir to mix. Add the turkey and turn to coat well.
10. Add the lid and set to slow cook on high. Cook 3-4 hours or until turkey starts to fall off the bone. Transfer turkey to a work surface and remove the skin and bones. Chop the meat and return it to the pot. Serve, this is delicious on its own or makes a great filling for burritos.

Nutrition Info:

- Calories 97, Total Fat 5g, Total Carbs 3g, Protein 9g, Sodium 337mg.

Lime Chicken Chili

Servings: 6
Cooking Time: 23 Minutes
Ingredients:
- ¼ cup cooking wine Keto-Friendly
- ½ cup chicken broth
- 1 onion, diced
- 1 teaspoon salt
- ½ teaspoon paprika
- 5 garlic cloves, minced
- 1 tablespoon lime juice
- ¼ cup butter
- 2 pounds chicken thighs
- 1 teaspoon dried parsley
- 3 green chillies, chopped

Directions:
1. Set your Ninja-Foodi to Sauté mode and stir in onion and garlic.
2. Sauté for 3 minutes, add remaining ingredients.
3. Lock and secure the Ninja Foodi's lid and cook on "Medium-High" pressure for 20 minutes.
4. Release pressure naturally over 10 minutes.
5. Serve and enjoy.

Nutrition Info:
- Calories: 282; Fat: 15g; Carbohydrates: 6g; Protein: 27g

Chicken Thighs With Thyme Carrot Roast

Servings: 4
Cooking Time: 50 Min
Ingredients:
- 4 bone-in, skin-on chicken thighs
- 1 ½ cups chicken broth /375ml
- 1 cup basmati rice /130g
- 2 carrots; chopped
- 2 tbsp melted butter /30ml
- 2 tsp chopped fresh thyme /10g
- 2 tsp chicken seasoning /10g
- 1 tsp salt; divided /5g

Directions:
1. Pour the chicken broth and rice in the pot. Then, put the reversible rack in the pot. Arrange the chicken thighs on the rack, skin side up, and arrange the carrots around the chicken.
2. Put the pressure lid together and lock in the Seal position. Choose Pressure, set to High, and the time to 2 minutes. Choose Start/Stop to begin cooking the chicken.
3. When done cooking, perform a quick pressure release, and carefully open the lid. Brush the carrots and chicken with the melted butter. Season the chicken with the chicken seasoning and half of the salt. Also, season the carrots with the thyme and remaining salt.
4. Close the crisping lid; choose Broil and set the time to 10 minutes. Choose Start/Stop to begin crisping. When done cooking, check for your desired crispiness, and the turn the Foodi off. Spoon the rice into serving plates, and serve the chicken and carrots over the rice.

Greek Style Turkey Meatballs

Servings: 6
Cooking Time: 30 Min
Ingredients:
- 1 pound ground turkey /450g
- 1 carrot; minced
- ½ celery stalk; minced
- 1 onion; minced and divided
- 1 egg, lightly beaten
- 3 cups tomato puree /750ml
- 2 cups water /500ml
- ½ cup plain bread crumbs /65g
- ⅓ cup feta cheese, crumbled /44g
- 1 tbsp olive oil /15ml
- 2 tsp salt; divided /10g
- ½ tsp dried oregano /2.5g
- ¼ tsp ground black pepper /1.25g

Directions:
1. In a mixing bowl, thoroughly combine half the onion, oregano, ground turkey, salt, bread crumbs, pepper, and egg and stir until everything is well incorporated.
2. Heat oil on Sear/Sauté, and cook celery, remaining onion, and carrot for 5 minutes until soft. Pour in water, and tomato puree. Adjust the seasonings as necessary.
3. Roll the mixture into meatballs, and drop into the sauce. Seal the pressure lid, choose Pressure, set to High, and set the timer to 5 minutes. Press Start. Allow the cooker to cool and release pressure naturally for 20 minutes. Serve topped with feta cheese.

Cheesy Basil Stuffed Chicken

Servings: 4
Cooking Time: 25 Minutes
Ingredients:
- 4 chicken breasts, boneless & skinless
- 1 tsp garlic powder, divided
- ¼ tsp pepper
- 2 slices Swiss cheese, cut in half
- 12 basil leaves
- 1 tbsp. olive oil
- ¼ cup onion, chopped fine
- ½ cup cherry tomatoes, halved
- 1 tbsp. fresh parsley, chopped
- ½ cup chicken broth, low sodium

Directions:
1. Place chicken between 2 sheets of plastic wrap and pound out to ¼-inch thick.
2. Sprinkle chicken with ½ teaspoon garlic powder and pepper. Place half a slice of cheese on each piece of chicken. Top with 3 basil leaves and roll up, secure with a toothpick.
3. Add oil to the cooking pot and set to sauté on medium heat.
4. Add onion, tomatoes, remaining garlic powder, and parsley. Cook 5 minutes, stirring occasionally.
5. Add broth and cook 1 minute more.
6. Add the chicken to the sauce and turn to coat well, spoon some sauce over the top. Add the tender-crisp lid and set to bake on 350°F. Bake 20-25 minutes until chicken is no longer pink. Serve.

Nutrition Info:
- Calories 215, Total Fat 9g, Total Carbs 2g, Protein 29g, Sodium 175mg.

Hassel Back Chicken

Servings: 4
Cooking Time: 60 Minutes
Ingredients:
- 4 tablespoons butter
- Black pepper and salt to taste
- 2 cups fresh mozzarella cheese, sliced
- 8 large chicken breasts
- 4 large Roma tomatoes, sliced

Directions:
1. Make few deep slits in chicken breasts, season with black pepper and salt.
2. Stuff mozzarella cheese slices and tomatoes in chicken slits.
3. Grease Ninja Foodi pot with butter and set stuffed chicken breasts.
4. Lock and secure the Ninja Foodi's lid and "Bake/Roast" for 1 hour at 365 °F.
5. Serve and enjoy.

Nutrition Info:
- Calories: 278; Fat: 15g; Carbohydrates: 3.8g; Protein: 15g

Barbeque Chicken Drumettes

Servings: 4
Cooking Time: 30 Min
Ingredients:
- 2 lb. chicken drumettes, bone in and skin in /900g
- 1 stick butter; sliced in 5 pieces
- ½ cup chicken broth /125ml
- BBQ sauce to taste
- ½ tbsp cumin powder /7.5g
- ½ tsp onion powder /2.5g
- ¼ tsp Cayenne powder/1.25g
- ½ tsp dry mustard /2.5g
- ½ tsp sweet paprika /2.5g
- Salt and pepper, to taste
- Cooking spray

Directions:
1. Pour the chicken broth into the inner pot of Foodi P and insert the reversible rack. In a zipper bag, pour in dry mustard, cumin powder, onion powder, cayenne powder, salt, and pepper.
2. Add the chicken, close the bag and shake to coat the chicken well with the spices. You can toss the chicken in the spices in batches too.
3. Then, remove the chicken from the bag and place on the rack. Spread the butter slices on the drumsticks. Close the lid, secure the pressure valve, and select Pressure mode on High pressure for 10 minutes. Press Start/Stop.
4. Once the timer has ended, do a quick pressure release, and open the lid. Remove the chicken onto a clean flat surface like a cutting board and brush them with the barbecue sauce using the brush. Return to the rack and close the crisping lid. Cook for 10 minutes at 400 °F or 205°C on Air Crisp mode.

Spicy Chicken Wings.

Servings: 2
Cooking Time: 25 Min
Ingredients:
- 10 chicken wings
- ½ tbsp honey /15ml
- 2 tbsp hot chili sauce /30ml
- ½ tbsp lime juice /7.5ml
- ½ tsp kosher salt /2.5g
- ½ tsp black pepper /2.5g

Directions:
1. Mix the lime juice, honey, and chili sauce. Toss the mixture over the chicken wings.
2. Put the wings in the fryer's basket, close the crisping lid and cook for 25 minutes on Air Crisp mode at 350 °F or 177°C. Shake the basket every 5 minutes.

Southwest Chicken Bake

Servings: 8
Cooking Time: 20 Minutes
Ingredients:
- 1 tablespoon extra-virgin olive oil
- 2 boneless, skinless chicken breasts, cut into 1-inch cubes
- ½ red onion, diced
- ½ red bell pepper, diced
- 1 cup white rice
- 1 can fire-roasted tomatoes with chiles
- 1 can black beans, rinsed and drained
- 1 can corn, rinsed
- 1 packet taco seasoning
- 2 cups chicken broth
- Kosher salt
- Freshly ground black pepper
- 2 cups shredded Cheddar cheese

Directions:
1. Select SEAR/SAUTÉ and set to MD:HI. Select START/STOP to begin. Let preheat for 5 minutes.
2. Place the olive oil and chicken into the pot and cook, stirring occasionally, until the chicken is cooked through, 2 to 3 minutes. Add the onion and bell pepper and cook until softened, about 2 minutes.
3. Add the rice, tomatoes, beans, corn, taco seasoning, broth, salt, and pepper and stir. Assemble pressure lid, making sure the pressure release valve is in the SEAL position.
4. Select PRESSURE and set to HI. Set time to 7 minutes. Select START/STOP to begin.
5. When complete, quick release the pressure by turning the pressure release valve to the VENT position. Carefully remove lid when unit has finished releasing pressure.
6. Add the cheese on top of the mixture. Close crisping lid.
7. Select BROIL and set time to 8 minutes. Select START/STOP to begin.
8. When cooking is complete, serve along with your choice of toppings, such as chopped cilantro, diced avocado, diced fresh tomatoes, sour cream, and sliced scallions.

Nutrition Info:
- Calories: 333, Total Fat: 17g, Sodium: 630mg, Carbohydrates: 27g, Protein: 25g.

Herb Roasted Drumsticks

Servings: 3
Cooking Time: 40 Minutes
Ingredients:
- Nonstick cooking spray
- 1 tsp paprika
- ¼ tsp salt
- ½ tsp garlic powder
- ¼ tsp onion powder
- ¼ tsp dried thyme
- ¼ tsp pepper
- 6 chicken drumsticks, skin removed, rinsed & patted dry
- ½ tbsp. butter, melted

Directions:
1. Place the rack in the cooking pot and spray it with cooking spray.
2. In a small bowl, combine spices, mix well.
3. Place chicken on the rack and sprinkle evenly over chicken. Drizzle with melted butter.
4. Add the tender-crisp lid and set to roast on 375°F. Bake 35-40 minutes until juices run clear. Serve.

Nutrition Info:
- Calories 319, Total Fat 12g, Total Carbs 0g, Protein 50g, Sodium 505mg.

Tuscany Turkey Soup

Servings: 4
Cooking Time: 40 Min
Ingredients:
- 1 pound hot turkey sausage /450g
- 4 Italian bread slices
- 3 celery stalks; chopped
- 3 garlic cloves; chopped
- 1 can cannellini beans, rinsed /450g
- 9 ounces refrigerated tortellini /270g
- 1 Parmesan cheese rind
- 1 red onion; chopped
- ½ cup dry white wine /125ml
- 4 cups chicken broth /1000ml
- 2 cups chopped spinach /260g
- ½ cup grated Parmesan cheese /130g
- 2 tbsp melted butter /30ml
- 2 tbsp olive oil /30ml
- ½ tsp fennel seeds /2.5g
- 1 tsp salt /5g
- Cooking spray

Directions:
1. On the Foodi, choose Sear/Sauté and adjust to Medium. Press Start to preheat the inner pot. Heat olive oil and cook the sausage for 4 minutes, while stirring occasionally until golden brown.
2. Stir in the celery, garlic, and onion, season with the salt and cook for 2 to 3 minutes, stirring occasionally. Pour in the wine and bring the mixture to a boil until the wine reduces by half. Scrape the bottom of the pot to let off any browned bits. Add the chicken stock, fennel seeds, tortellini, Parmesan rind, cannellini beans, and spinach.
3. Lock the pressure lid into place and to seal. Select Pressure; adjust the pressure to High and the cook time to 5 minutes; press Start. Brush the butter on the bread slices, and sprinkle with half of the cheese. Once the timer is over, perform a natural pressure release for 5 minutes.
4. Grease the reversible rack with cooking spray and fix in the upper position of the pot. Lay the bread slices on the rack.
5. Close the crisping lid and Choose Broil. Adjust the cook time to 5 minutes; press Start.
6. When the bread has browned and crisp, transfer from the rack to a cutting board and let cool for a couple of minutes. Cut the slices into cubes.
7. Ladle the soup into bowls and sprinkle with the remaining cheese. Share the croutons among the bowls and serve.

Braised Chicken With Mushrooms And Brussel Sprouts

Servings: 4
Cooking Time: 40 Min
Ingredients:
- 4 chicken thighs, bone-in skin-on
- ½ small onion; sliced
- ¼ cup heavy cream /62.5ml
- 1 cup frozen halved Brussel sprouts; thawed /130g
- ½ cup dry white wine /125ml
- ⅓ cup chicken stock /188ml
- 1 cup sautéed Mushrooms /130g
- 1 bay leaf
- 1 tbsp olive oil /15ml
- 1 tsp salt or to taste; divided /5g
- ¼ tsp dried rosemary /1.25g
- Freshly ground black pepper

Directions:
1. Season the chicken on both sides with half of the salt. On your pot, Choose Sear/Sauté and adjust to Medium-High. Press Start to preheat the inner pot.
2. Heat olive oil and add the chicken thighs. Fry for 4 to 5 minutes or until browned. Turn and lightly sear the other side, about 1 minute. Use tongs to remove the chicken into a plate and spoon out any thick coating of oil in the pot.
3. Sauté the onion in the pot and season with the remaining salt. Cook for about 2 minutes to soften and just beginning to brown for 2 minutes. Stir in the white wine and bring to a boil for 2 to 3 minutes or until reduced by about half.
4. Mix in the chicken stock, brussel sprouts, bay leaf, rosemary, and several grinds of black pepper. Arrange the chicken thighs on top with skin-side up.
5. Seal the pressure lid, choose Pressure; adjust the pressure to High and the cook time to 5 minutes. Press Start to begin cooking.
6. When the timer is over, perform a quick pressure release and carefully open the lid. Remove the bay leaf. Remove the chicken onto the reversible rack, and stir the mushrooms into the sauce. Carefully set the rack in the upper position of the pot.

7. Close the crisping lid and Choose Bake/Roast; adjust the temperature to 375°F or 191°C and the cook time to 12 minutes. Press Start to commence browning.

8. When ready, open the lid and transfer the chicken to a platter. Stir the heavy cream into the sauce and adjust the taste with salt and pepper. Spoon the sauce and vegetables around the chicken and serve.

Speedy Fajitas

Servings: 4
Cooking Time: 15 Minutes
Ingredients:
- Nonstick cooking spray
- 1 clove garlic, chopped fine
- 1 cup onion, sliced
- 1 green bell pepper, cut in strips
- 1 red bell pepper, cut in strips
- 2 chicken breasts, boneless, skinless & cut in strips
- 2 tsp fajita seasoning
- 4 low-carb whole wheat tortillas, warmed

Directions:
1. Spray the cooking pot with cooking spray and set to sauté on medium heat.
2. Add garlic, onion, and bell peppers and cook until tender, about 6-8 minutes. Transfer to a plate.
3. Add the chicken and fajita seasoning and cook until no longer pink, about 5-7 minutes.
4. Return the vegetables to the pot and cook, stirring, 2-4 minutes until heated through.
5. Spoon onto serving plates and serve with tortillas and your favorite toppings.

Nutrition Info:
- Calories 180,Total Fat 5g,Total Carbs 26g,Protein 21g,Sodium 574mg.

Korean Barbecued Satay

Servings: 4
Cooking Time: 4h 15 Min
Ingredients:
- 1 lb. boneless; skinless chicken tenders /450g
- ½ cup pineapple juice /125ml
- ½ cup soy sauce /125ml
- ⅓ cup sesame oil /84ml
- 4 scallions; chopped
- 1 pinch black pepper
- 4 cloves garlic; chopped
- 2 tsp sesame seeds, toasted /10g
- 1 tsp fresh ginger, grated /5g

Directions:
1. Skew each tender and trim any excess fat. Mix the other ingredients in one large bowl. Add the skewered chicken and place in the fridge for 4 to 24 hours.
2. Preheat the Foodi to 370 For 188°C. Using a paper towel, pat the chicken dry. Fry for 10 minutes on Air Crisp mode.

Taiwanese Chicken

Servings: 4
Cooking Time: 10 Minutes
Ingredients:
- 6 dried red chilis
- ¼ cup sesame oil
- 2 tablespoons ginger
- ¼ cup garlic, minced
- ¼ cup red wine vinegar
- ¼ cup coconut aminos
- Salt, to taste
- 1.2 teaspoon xanthan gum for the finish
- ¼ cup Thai basil, chopped

Directions:
1. Select "Sauté" mode on your Ninja Foodi and add ginger, chilis, garlic and Sauté for 2 minutes.
2. Add remaining ingredients.
3. Lock and secure the Ninja Foodi's lid, then cook on "HIGH" pressure for 10 minutes.
4. Quick-release pressure.
5. Serve and enjoy.

Nutrition Info:
- Calories: 307; Fat: 15g; Carbohydrates: 7g; Protein: 31g

Beef, Pork & Lamb Recipes

Lamb Curry

Servings: 6
Cooking Time: 6 Hours
Ingredients:
- ¼ cup flour
- 2 lbs. lamb shoulder, cubed
- ½ tsp salt
- ½ tsp pepper
- 2 tbsp. olive oil
- 1 onion, chopped
- 2 cloves garlic, chopped fine
- 2-inch piece fresh ginger, peeled, grated
- 1 hot red chili, chopped fine
- ¼ cup Indian madras curry paste
- 1 ¼ cups light coconut milk
- ¾ cups vegetable broth, low sodium
- 1 cinnamon stick
- 1 bay leaf
- 2 tbsp. cilantro, chopped

Directions:
1. Place flour in a large Ziploc bag. Season lamb with salt and pepper and add to the flour. Seal and turn to coat.
2. Add oil to the cooking pot and set to sauté on med-high. Cook lamb, in batches until browned on the outside. Transfer to a bowl.
3. Add onion, garlic, and ginger to the pot. Cook, stirring frequently, 4-5 minutes until tender.
4. Stir in chili and curry paste and cook 1 minute more. Add the milk and broth and bring to a boil.
5. Return the lamb to the pot along with the cinnamon stick and bay leaf. Add the lid and set to slow cook on low. Cook 6 hours or until lamb is tender. Discard the bay leaf and cinnamon stick. Serve over hot cooked rice garnished with cilantro.

Nutrition Info:
- Calories 407,Total Fat 25g,Total Carbs 13g,Protein 33g,Sodium 373mg.

Teriyaki Pork Noodles

Servings: 4
Cooking Time: 60 Min
Ingredients:
- 1 pork tenderloin, trimmed and cut into 1-inch pieces
- 1 pound green beans, trimmed /450g
- 1 cup teriyaki sauce /250ml
- 8 ounces egg noodles /240g
- 1 tbsp olive oil /15ml
- ¼ tsp salt /1.25g
- ¼ tsp black pepper /1.25g
- Cooking spray
- Sesame seeds, for garnish

Directions:
1. Pour the egg noodles and cover with enough water in the pot. Seal the pressure lid, choose Pressure, set to High, and set the time to 2 minutes. Choose Start/Stop.
2. In a large bowl, toss the green beans with the olive oil, salt, and black pepper. In another bowl, toss the pork with the teriyaki sauce. When the egg noodles are ready, perform a quick pressure release, and carefully open the lid.
3. Fix the reversible rack in the upper position of the pot, which will be over the egg noodles. Oil the rack with cooking spray and place the pork in the rack. Also, lay the green beans around the pork.
4. Close the crisping lid. Choose Broil and set the time to 12 minutes. Press Start/Stop to begin cooking the pork and vegetables.
5. When done cooking, check for your desired crispiness and take the rack out of the pot. Serve the pork and green beans over the drained egg noodles and garnish with sesame seeds.

Beef Mole

Servings: 8
Cooking Time: 8 Hours
Ingredients:
- 2 lbs. beef stew meat, cut in 1-inch cubes
- 3 tsp salt, divided
- 2 tbsp. olive oil
- 2 onions, chopped fine
- 4 cloves garlic, chopped fine
- 1 chili, seeded & chopped fine
- 3 tsp chili powder
- 1 tsp ancho chili powder
- 2 tsp oregano
- 2 tsp cumin

- 1 tsp paprika
- 1 lb. dried red beans, soaked in water overnight, drained
- 5 cups water
- 2 cups beer
- 2 15 oz. tomatoes, crushed
- 1 tbsp. brown sugar
- 2 oz. unsweetened chocolate, chopped
- 1 bay leaf
- 3 tbsp. lime juice

Directions:

1. Place the beef in a large Ziploc bag with 1 ½ teaspoons salt, seal and rub gently to massage the salt into the meat. Refrigerate overnight.
2. Add the oil to the cooking pot and set to sauté on med-high heat.
3. Working in batches, add the beef and cook until deep brown on all sides. Transfer to a bowl.
4. Add the onions to the pot and cook about 5 minutes or until softened. Stir in garlic, chilies, remaining salt, chili powders, oregano, cumin, and paprika and cook 1 minute more.
5. Stir in beans, water, beer, tomatoes, brown sugar, and chocolate and mix well. Stir in the beef and add the bay leaf.
6. Add the lid and set to slow cook on low. Cook 8 hours or until beef is tender. Stir in lime juice and serve.

Nutrition Info:

- Calories 127, Total Fat 8g, Total Carbs 7g, Protein 7g, Sodium 310mg.

Smoky Horseradish Spare Ribs

Servings: 4
Cooking Time: 55 Min
Ingredients:

- 1 spare rack ribs
- 1 cup smoky horseradish sauce /250ml
- 1 tsp salt /5g

Directions:

1. Season all sides of the rack with salt and cut into 3 pieces. Cut the rack into 3 pieces. Pour 1 cup of water into the Foodi's inner pot. Fix the reversible rack in the pot in the lower position and put the ribs on top, bone-side down.
2. Seal the pressure lid, choose Pressure; adjust the pressure to High and the cook time to 18 minutes. Press Start. After cooking, perform a quick pressure release and carefully open the lid.
3. Take out the rack with ribs and pour out the water from the pot. Return the inner pot to the base. Set the reversible rack and ribs in the pot in the lower position. Close the crisping lid and Choose Air Crisp; adjust the temperature to 400°F or 205°C and the cook time to 20 minutes. Press Start.
4. After 10 minutes, open the lid and turn the ribs. Lightly baste the bony side of the ribs with the smoky horseradish sauce and close the lid to cook further. After 4 minutes, open the lid and turn the ribs again. Baste the meat side with the remaining sauce and close the lid to cook until the ribs are done.

Lamb Tagine

Servings: 8
Cooking Time: 55 Minutes
Ingredients:

- 1 cup couscous
- 2 cups water
- 3 tablespoons extra-virgin olive oil, divided
- 2 yellow onions, diced
- 3 garlic cloves, minced
- 2 pounds lamb stew meat, cut into 1- to 2-inch cubes
- 1 cup dried apricots, sliced
- 2 cups chicken stock
- 2 tablespoons ras el hanout seasoning
- 1 can chickpeas, drained
- Kosher salt
- Freshly ground black pepper
- 1 cup toasted almonds, for garnish

Directions:

1. Place the couscous in the pot and pour in the water. Assemble pressure lid, making sure the pressure release valve is in the SEAL position.
2. Select PRESSURE and set to HI. Set time to 5 minutes. Select START/STOP to begin.
3. When pressure cooking is complete, quick release the pressure by turning the pressure release valve to the VENT position. Carefully remove lid when unit has finished releasing pressure.
4. Stir 1 tablespoon of oil into the couscous, then transfer the couscous to a bowl.
5. Select SEAR/SAUTÉ and set to MD:HI. Select START/STOP to begin. Let preheat for 3 minutes
6. Add the remaining 2 tablespoons of oil, onion, garlic, and lamb. Sauté for 7 to 10 minutes, stirring frequently.
7. Add the apricots, chicken stock, and ras el hanout. Stir to combine. Assemble pressure lid, making sure the pressure release valve is in the SEAL position.

8. Select PRESSURE and set to HI. Set time to 30 minutes. Select START/STOP to begin.
9. When pressure cooking is complete, quick release the pressure by turning the pressure release valve to the VENT position. Carefully remove lid when unit has finished releasing pressure.
10. Stir in the chickpeas.
11. Select SEAR/SAUTÉ and set to MD:LO. Select START/STOP to begin. Let the mixture simmer for 10 minutes. Season with salt and pepper.
12. When cooking is complete, ladle the tagine over the couscous. Garnish with the toasted almonds.

Nutrition Info:
- Calories: 596,Total Fat: 21g,Sodium: 354mg,Carbohydrates: 65g,Protein: 39g.

Beef Tips & Mushrooms

Servings: 8
Cooking Time: 5 Hours

Ingredients:
- 2 tbsp. olive oil
- 3 lbs. beef stew meat
- Salt & pepper, to taste
- 3 cups beef broth, low sodium
- 1 pkg. dry onion soup mix
- 1 tbsp. Worcestershire sauce
- 1 onion chopped
- 2 cups mushrooms, sliced
- 3 cloves garlic, chopped fine
- ¼ cup water
- 3 tbsp. cornstarch

Directions:
1. Add the oil to the cooking pot and set to sauté on med-high heat.
2. Season the beef with salt and pepper. Add to the pot, in batches, and cook until browned on all sides. Transfer to a bowl until all the beef has been seared.
3. Return all the beef to the pot and add broth, soup mix, onions, mushrooms, and garlic, stir to combine.
4. Add the lid and set to slow cook on low. Cook 5-6 hours until beef is tender.
5. 30 minutes before the beef tips are done, whisk together the water and cornstarch until smooth and stir into the beef mixture. Stir well before serving over noodles, mashed potatoes or mashed cauliflower to keep it low carb.

Nutrition Info:
- Calories 285,Total Fat 11g,Total Carbs 9g,Protein 40g,Sodium 1178mg.

Maple Glazed Pork Chops

Servings: 4
Cooking Time: 12 Minutes

Ingredients:
- 2 tablespoons choc zero maple syrup
- 4 tablespoons mustard
- 2 tablespoons garlic, minced
- Black pepper and salt to taste
- 4 pork chops
- Cooking spray

Directions:
1. Mix the choc zero maple syrup, mustard, garlic, black pepper and salt in a suitable.
2. Marinate the choc zero maple syruped pork chops in the mixture for 20 minutes.
3. Place the pork chops on the Ninja Foodi basket.
4. Put the basket inside the pot. Seal with the crisping lid.
5. Set it to air crisp. Cook at 350 °F for about 12 minutes, flipping halfway through.

Nutrition Info:
- Calories: 348; Fat: 23.3g; Carbohydrate: 14g; Protein: 21.1g

Beef Sirloin Steak

Servings: 4
Cooking Time: 17 Minutes

Ingredients:
- 3 tablespoons butter
- 1/2 teaspoon garlic powder
- 1-2 pounds beef sirloin steaks
- Black pepper and salt to taste
- 1 garlic clove, minced

Directions:
1. Select "Sauté" mode on your Ninja Foodi and add butter; let the butter melt.
2. Stir in beef sirloin steaks.
3. Sauté for 2 minutes on each side.
4. Add garlic powder, garlic clove, salt, and pepper.
5. Lock and secure the Ninja Foodi's lid and cook on "Medium-High" pressure for 15 minutes.
6. Release pressure naturally over 10 minutes.
7. Transfer prepare Steaks to a serving platter, enjoy.

Nutrition Info:

- Calories: 246; Fat: 13g; Carbohydrates: 2g; Protein: 31g

Bacon Strips

Servings: 2
Cooking Time: 7 Minutes
Ingredients:
- 10 bacon strips
- 1/4 teaspoon chilli flakes
- 1/3 teaspoon salt
- 1/4 teaspoon basil, dried

Directions:
1. Rub the bacon strips with chilli flakes, dried basil, and salt.
2. Turn on your air fryer and place the bacon on the rack.
3. Lower the air fryer lid. Cook the bacon at 400 °F for 5 minutes.
4. Cook for 3 minutes more if the bacon is not fully cooked. Serve and enjoy.

Nutrition Info:
- Calories: 500; Fat: 46g; Carbohydrates: 0g; Protein: 21g

Garlicky Pork Chops

Servings: 2
Cooking Time: 10 Minutes
Ingredients:
- 1 tablespoon coconut butter
- 1 tablespoon coconut oil
- 2 teaspoons cloves garlic, grated
- 2 teaspoons parsley, chopped
- Black pepper and salt to taste
- 4 pork chops, sliced into strips

Directions:
1. Combine all the ingredients except the pork strips. Mix well.
2. Marinate the pork in the mixture for 1 hour. Put the pork on the Ninja Foodi basket.
3. Set it inside the pot. Seal with the crisping lid. Choose air crisp function.
4. Cook at 400 °F For 10 minutes.

Nutrition Info:
- Calories: 388; Fat: 23.3g; Carbohydrate: 0.5g; Protein: 18.1g

Pepper Crusted Tri Tip Roast

Servings: 6
Cooking Time: 45 Minutes
Ingredients:
- 1 tbsp. salt
- 1 tbsp. pepper
- 1 tbsp. garlic powder
- 1 tbsp. onion powder
- 1 tsp cayenne pepper
- 1 tbsp. oregano
- 1 tsp rosemary
- ½ tsp sage
- 3 lb. tri-tip roast
- Nonstick cooking spray

Directions:
1. In a small bowl, combine all the spices until mixed.
2. Place the roast on baking sheet and massage the rub mix into all sides. Cover and let sit 1 hour.
3. Lightly spray the cooking pot with cooking spray. Set to sear.
4. Add the roast and brown all sides. Add the tender-crisp lid and set to roast on 300°F.
5. Cook until meat thermometer reaches desired temperature for doneness, 120°F for a rare roast, 130°F for medium-rare and 140°F for medium, about 20-40 minutes.
6. Remove roast from cooking pot, tent with foil and let rest 10-15 minutes. Slice across the grain and serve.

Nutrition Info:
- Calories 169,Total Fat 8g,Total Carbs 7g,Protein 19g,Sodium 2300mg.

Creole Dirty Rice

Servings: 6
Cooking Time: 15 Minutes
Ingredients:
- 1 tbsp. olive oil
- 1 lb. lean ground beef
- 1 stalk celery, sliced
- ½ green bell pepper, chopped
- 2 tbsp. garlic, chopped fine
- 1 onion, chopped
- 4 tbsp. fresh parsley, chopped
- 2 tbsp. creole seasoning
- 5 cups brown rice, cooked

Directions:
1. Add the oil to the cooking pot and set to sauté on med-high heat.

2. Add the beef, celery, bell pepper, garlic, and onion and cook, breaking up beef with a spatula, until meat is no longer pink and vegetables are tender, about 6-8 minutes.
3. Add the parsley and Creole seasoning and mix well.
4. Add the rice and cook, stirring occasionally, about 5 minutes or until heated through. Serve.

Nutrition Info:
- Calories 386, Total Fat 15g, Total Carbs 43g, Protein 19g, Sodium 57mg.

Beef Lasagna

Servings: 4
Cooking Time: 10-15 Minutes

Ingredients:
- 2 small onions
- 2 garlic cloves, minced
- 1-pound ground beef
- 1 large egg
- 1 and 1/2 cups ricotta cheese
- 1/2 cup parmesan cheese
- 1 jar 25 ounces0 marinara sauce
- 8 ounces mozzarella cheese, sliced

Directions:
1. Select "Sauté" mode on your Ninja Foodi and stir in beef, brown the beef.
2. Add onion and garlic.
3. Add parmesan, ricotta, egg in a small dish and keep it on the side.
4. Stir in sauce to browned meat, reserve half for later.
5. Sprinkle mozzarella and half of ricotta cheese into the browned meat.
6. Top with remaining meat sauce.
7. For the final layer, add more mozzarella cheese and the remaining ricotta.
8. Stir well.
9. Cover with a foil transfer to Ninja Foodi.
10. Lock and secure the Ninja Foodi's lid, then cook on "HIGH" pressure for 8-10 minutes.
11. Quick-release pressure.
12. Drizzle parmesan cheese on top.
13. Enjoy.

Nutrition Info:
- Calories: 365; Fats: 25g; Carbohydrates: 6g; Protein: 25g

Beef In Basil Sauce

Servings: 4
Cooking Time: 15 Minutes

Ingredients:
- 2 tbsp. olive oil
- 2 shallots, sliced thin
- 7 cloves garlic sliced
- 1 tbsp. fresh ginger, peeled & grated
- 1/2 red bell pepper, sliced thin
- 1 lb. lean ground beef
- 2 tsp brown sugar
- 2 tbsp. fish sauce
- 6 tbsp. soy sauce, low sodium
- 3 tsp oyster sauce
- 2 tbsp. Asian garlic chili paste
- ½ cup beef broth, low sodium
- ¼ cup water
- 1 tsp cornstarch
- 1 cup basil leaves, chopped
- Cooked Jasmine rice for serving

Directions:
1. Add the oil to the cooking pot and set to sauté on med-high heat.
2. Add the shallots, garlic, ginger, and bell peppers to the pot and cook, stirring frequently, 3 minutes. Use a slotted spoon to transfer mixture to a bowl.
3. Increase heat to high and add the ground beef, cook, breaking it up with a spoon until beef is no longer pink.
4. In a small bowl, whisk together brown sugar, fish sauce, soy sauce, oyster sauce, cornstarch, broth, and water until smooth.
5. Add the pepper mixture back to the pot and pour the sauce over. Cook, stirring, 2 minutes until sauce has thickened.
6. Stir in basil and cook until wilted, about 2 minutes. Serve over hot rice.

Nutrition Info:
- Calories 359, Total Fat 20g, Total Carbs 10g, Protein 34g, Sodium 1785mg.

Peppercorn Meatloaf

Servings: 8
Cooking Time: 35 Min
Ingredients:
- 4 lb. ground beef /1800g
- 10 whole peppercorns, for garnishing
- 1 onion; diced
- 1 cup breadcrumbs /130g
- 1 tbsp parsley /15g
- 1 tbsp Worcestershire sauce /15ml
- 3 tbsp ketchup /45ml
- 1 tbsp basil /15g
- 1 tbsp oregano /15g
- ½ tsp salt /2.5g
- 1 tsp ground peppercorns /5g

Directions:
1. Place the beef in a large bowl. Add all of the ingredients except the whole peppercorns and the breadcrumbs. Mix with your hand until well combined. Stir in the breadcrumbs.
2. Put the meatloaf on a lined baking dish. Insert in the Foodi, close the crisping lid and cook for 25 minutes on Air Crisp mode at 350 °F or 177°C.
3. Garnish the meatloaf with the whole peppercorns and let cool slightly before serving.

Roasted Pork With Apple Gravy

Servings: 6
Cooking Time: 3 Hours 30 Minutes
Ingredients:
- 1 tbsp. fennel seeds, toasted
- 2 tsp peppercorns
- 2 tbsp. fresh thyme, chopped
- 2 tbsp. fresh rosemary, chopped
- 4 cloves garlic, chopped
- 2 tsp salt
- 4 tbsp. olive oil, divided
- 4-5 lbs. pork shoulder, boneless & fat trimmed
- 4 Fuji apples, peeled, cored & cut in wedges
- 1 onion, cut in 12 wedges
- ½ cup dry white wine
- ½ cup water
- ½ tsp Dijon mustard

Directions:
1. Place fennel seeds, peppercorns, thyme, rosemary, garlic, and 2 teaspoons salt into a spice or coffee grinder and grind to a paste.
2. Transfer to a small bowl and stir in 2 tablespoons olive oil. Rub mixture evenly over the pork. Wrap with plastic wrap and refrigerate overnight.
3. Place the apples and onions in the cooking pot and drizzle with remaining oil, toss to coat. Place the pork on top of the apples and onions.
4. Add the tender-crisp lid and set to roast on 450°F. Cook 30 minutes.
5. Remove the lid and add the wine. Cover roast with foil. Add the tender-crisp lid and reduce heat to 325°F. Cook 2 ½ - 3 hours or until pork falls apart when stuck with a fork.
6. Transfer pork to a serving plate and tent with foil to keep warm.
7. Transfer apples and onions to a blender. Add ½ cup water and the mustard and pulse to puree. Mixture should be the consistency of gravy, if not add more water.
8. Slice the pork and serve topped with gravy.

Nutrition Info:
- Calories 111,Total Fat 3g,Total Carbs 4g,Protein 15g,Sodium 229mg.

Korean Pork Chops

Servings: 4
Cooking Time: 10 Minutes
Ingredients:
- ½ cup soy sauce, low sodium
- 4 tbsp. honey
- 12 cloves garlic, chopped
- 4 tsp ginger
- 2 tsp sesame oil
- 2 tbsp. sweet chili sauce
- 4 top loin pork chops
- 2 tsp olive oil

Directions:
1. In a medium bowl, whisk together soy sauce, honey, garlic, ginger, sesame oil, and chili sauce until smooth. Reserve ½ the marinade for later.
2. Add the pork chops to the bowl and turn to coat. Let sit 10 minutes.
3. Add the olive oil to the cooking pot and set to sauté on med-high heat.
4. Add the pork chops and cook 5 minutes until browned. Turn the chops over and add the reserved marinade to the

pot. Cook another 5 minutes or until chops are cooked through. Let rest 3 minutes before serving.

Nutrition Info:
- Calories 364,Total Fat 8g,Total Carbs 24g,Protein 46g,Sodium 2218mg.

Red Pork And Chickpea Stew

Servings: 6
Cooking Time: 40 Min

Ingredients:
- 1 boneless pork shoulder, trimmed and cubed /1350g
- 15 ounces canned chickpeas, drained and rinsed /435g
- 1½ cups water /375ml
- ½ cup sweet paprika /65g
- 1 bay leaf
- 2 red bell peppers; chopped
- 6 cloves garlic; minced
- 1 white onion; chopped
- 1 tbsp cornstarch /15g
- 1 tbsp olive oil /15ml
- 1 tbsp chilli powder/15g
- 1 tbsp water/ 15ml
- 2 tsp salt /10g

Directions:
1. Set on Sear/Sauté, set to Medium High, and choose Start/Stop to preheat the pot; add pork and oil and allow cooking for 5 minutes until browned.
2. Add in the onion, paprika, bay leaf, salt, water, chickpeas, and chili powder. Seal the pressure lid, choose Pressure, set to High, and set the timer to 8 minutes. Press Start.
3. Do a quick release and discard bay leaf. Remove 1 cup of cooking liquid from the Foodi; add to a blender alongside garlic, water, cornstarch, and red bell peppers; blend well until smooth. Add the blended mixture into the stew and mix well.

Beef & Broccoli Casserole

Servings: 4
Cooking Time: 40 Minutes

Ingredients:
- 12 oz. broccoli florets
- 1 lb. extra lean ground beef
- 14 oz. tomato sauce
- 1 stalk celery, chopped fine
- 1 tsp salt
- 1 tsp garlic powder
- ¼ tsp cayenne pepper
- 1 ¾ cup cheddar cheese, grated, divided
- ¼ cup parmesan cheese

Directions:
1. Add the broccoli to large microwave safe bowl, cover and microwave about 5 minutes until tender. Dump onto paper towel lined baking sheet to drain.
2. Add the beef to the cooking pot and set to sauté on med-high heat. Cook, breaking meat up with a spatula, about 5 minutes or until no longer pink.
3. Add tomato sauce, celery, salt, garlic powder, and cayenne stir well. Simmer 10 minutes or until sauce thickens.
4. Add the broccoli and half the cheddar cheese and stir to combine. Sprinkle remaining cheddar and parmesan over the top.
5. Add the tender-crisp lid and set to bake on 375°F. Bake 20 minutes until hot and bubbling. Let rest 10 minutes before serving.

Nutrition Info:
- Calories 432,Total Fat 25g,Total Carbs 13g,Protein 42g,Sodium 1590mg.

Asian Beef

Servings: 6
Cooking Time: 15 Minutes

Ingredients:
- 1/4 cup soy sauce
- 1/2 cup beef broth
- 1 tablespoon sesame oil
- 1/4 cup brown erythritol, packed
- 4 cloves garlic, minced
- 1 teaspoon hot sauce
- 1 tablespoon rice wine vinegar
- 1 tablespoon ginger, grated
- 1/2 teaspoon onion powder
- 1/2 teaspoon pepper
- 3 lb. boneless beef chuck roast, cubed
- 3 tablespoons corn starch dissolved in 1 teaspoon water

Directions:
1. Mix all the seasonings in a suitable bowl except the chuck roast and corn starch.
2. Pour the mixture into the Ninja Foodi. Stir in the beef. Seal the pot.
3. Select pressure. Cook at "HIGH" pressure for 15 minutes.

4. Do a quick pressure release. Stir in the corn starch.
5. Select sauté setting to thicken the sauce.

Nutrition Info:
- Calories: 482; Fat: 16.6g; Carbohydrate: 8.4g; Protein: 70.1g

Beef Bulgogi

Servings: 4
Cooking Time: 10 Minutes

Ingredients:
- 1 lb. lean ground beef
- 10 cloves garlic, chopped
- 1 onion, chopped fine
- 4 tbsp. soy sauce, low sodium
- 2 tbsp. mirin
- 2 tbsp. sugar
- 1 tbsp. apricot jam
- ½ tsp pepper
- 1 tbsp. olive oil
- 5 green onions, chopped
- 1 tsp sesame seeds
- 1 tsp sesame oil

Directions:
1. In a large bowl, combine beef, garlic, onion, soy sauce, mirin, sugar, jam, and pepper, mix well.
2. Add oil to the cooking pot and set to sauté on med-high heat.
3. Add the beef mixture and cook, breaking up the beef with a spatula, 8-10 minutes until meat is fully cooked and all liquid has evaporated.
4. Stir in the green onions. Turn off the heat and add sesame seeds and sesame oil, toss to distribute and serve immediately.

Nutrition Info:
- Calories 419, Total Fat 28g, Total Carbs 19g, Protein 23g, Sodium 602mg.

Mexican Pot Roast

Servings: 8
Cooking Time: 8 Hours

Ingredients:
- 3 lb. beef chuck roast
- 4 cups lemon-lime soda
- 1 tsp chili powder
- 1 tsp salt
- 3 cloves garlic, chopped
- 2 limes juiced

Directions:
1. Place the roast in the cooking pot and pour the soda over the top. Sprinkle with chili powder, salt, and garlic.
2. Add the lid and set to slow cook on low. Cook 8 hours or until roast is tender.
3. Transfer roast to a large bowl and use 2 forks to shred. Pour the lime juice over the meat and serve hot.

Nutrition Info:
- Calories 367, Total Fat 14g, Total Carbs 14g, Protein 46g, Sodium 449mg.

Chunky Pork Meatloaf With Mashed Potatoes

Servings: 4
Cooking Time: 55 Min

Ingredients:
- 2 pounds potatoes; cut into large chunks /900g
- 12 ounces pork meatloaf /360g
- 2 garlic cloves; minced
- 2 large eggs
- 12 individual saltine crackers. crushed
- 1¾ cups full cream milk; divided /438ml
- 1 cup chopped white onion /130g
- ½ cup heavy cream /125ml
- ¼ cup barbecue sauce /62.5ml
- 1 tbsp olive oil /15ml
- 3 tbsp chopped fresh cilantro /45g
- 3 tbsp unsalted butter /45g
- ¼ tsp dried rosemary /1.25g
- 1 tsp yellow mustard /5g
- 1 tsp Worcestershire sauce /5ml
- 2 tsp salt /10g
- ½ tsp black pepper /2.5g

Directions:
1. Select Sear/Sauté and adjust to Medium. Press Start to preheat the pot for 5 minutes. Heat the olive oil until shimmering and sauté the onion and garlic in the oil. Cook for about 2 minutes until the onion softens. Transfer the onion and garlic to a plate and set aside.
2. In a bowl, crumble the meatloaf mix into small pieces. Sprinkle with 1 tsp of salt, the pepper, cilantro, and thyme. Add the sautéed onion and garlic. Sprinkle the crushed saltine crackers over the meat and seasonings.
3. In a small bowl, beat ¼ cup of milk, the eggs, mustard, and Worcestershire sauce. Pour the mixture on the layered

cracker crumbs and gently mix the ingredients in the bowl with your hands. Shape the meat mixture into an 8-inch round.

4. Cover the reversible rack with aluminum foil and carefully lift the meatloaf into the rack. Pour the remaining 1½ cups of milk and the heavy cream into the inner pot. Add the potatoes, butter, and remaining salt. Place the rack with meatloaf over the potatoes in the upper position in the pot.

5. Seal the pressure lid, choose Pressure; adjust the pressure to High and the cook time to 25 minutes; press Start. After cooking, perform a quick pressure release, and carefully open the pressure lid. Brush the meatloaf with the barbecue sauce.

6. Close the crisping lid; choose Broil and adjust the cook time to 7 minutes. Press Start to begin grilling. When the top has browned, remove the rack, and transfer the meatloaf to a serving platter. Mash the potatoes in the pot. Slice the meatloaf and serve with the mashed potatoes.

Sour And Sweet Pork

Servings: 4
Cooking Time: 40 Min
Ingredients:
- 1 pound pork loin; cut into chunks /450g
- 15 ounces canned peaches /450g
- ¼ cup water /62.5ml
- ¼ cup beef stock /62.5ml
- 2 tbsp sweet chili sauce /30ml
- 2 tbsp soy sauce /30ml
- 2 tbsp cornstarch /30g
- 2 tbsp white wine /30ml
- 2 tbsp honey /30ml

Directions:
1. Into the pot, mix soy sauce, beef stock, white wine, juice from the canned peaches, and sweet chili sauce; stir in pork to coat.
2. Seal the pressure lid, choose Pressure, set to High, and set the timer to 5 minutes. Press Start. Release pressure naturally for 10 minutes, then release the remaining pressure quickly. Remove the pork to a serving plate. Chop the peaches into small pieces.
3. In a bowl, mix water and cornstarch until cornstarch dissolves completely; stir the mixture into the pot. Press Sear/Sauté and cook for 5 more minutes until you obtain the desired thick consistency; add in the chopped peaches and stir well. Serve the pork topped with peach sauce and enjoy.

Pesto Pork Chops & Asparagus

Servings: 4
Cooking Time: 20 Minutes
Ingredients:
- Nonstick cooking spray
- 4 pork chops, bone-in, 1-inch thick
- 1 tsp salt, divided
- 1 tsp pepper, divided
- 1 bunch asparagus, trimmed
- 1 cup cherry tomatoes
- 3 tbsp. extra-virgin olive oil, divided
- ¼ cup pesto
- ¼ cup fresh basil, chopped

Directions:
1. Spray the rack with cooking spray and place it in the cooking pot.
2. Rub chops with 2 tablespoons oil and sprinkle with ½ teaspoon salt and pepper on both sides. Cover and let sit 20 minutes.
3. Place chops on the rack and add the tender-crisp lid. Set to broil. Cook chops 6-8 minutes per side or until they reach desired doneness. Remove to serving plate.
4. Place the asparagus and tomatoes in a large bowl and add remaining oil, salt, and pepper, toss to coat. Place the vegetables on the rack and broil 6-8 minutes until asparagus is tender-crisp and tomatoes start to char, turning vegetables every couple of minutes.
5. Place pork chops and vegetables on serving plates, drizzle with pesto and sprinkle with basil. Serve immediately.

Nutrition Info:
- Calories 332,Total Fat 24g,Total Carbs 4g,Protein 25g,Sodium 647mg.

Bacon & Sauerkraut With Apples

Servings: 6
Cooking Time: 30 Minutes
Ingredients:
- ¼ lb. apple-wood smoked bacon
- 1 onion, chopped fine
- 2 Granny Smith apples, peeled, cored, & grated
- 2 cloves garlic, chopped fine
- 1 tsp caraway seeds, ground
- 3 cups apple juice, unsweetened
- ¼ cup white wine vinegar
- 2 lbs. refrigerated sauerkraut, drained

Directions:
1. Add the bacon to the cooking pot and set to sauté on medium heat. Cook until bacon has browned and fat is rendered. Transfer to paper towel lined plat. Drain all but 1 tablespoon of the fat.
2. Add the onions and apples to the pot and cook 6-7 minutes, until onions are translucent. Add the garlic and caraway and cook 1 minute more.
3. Stir in apple juice and vinegar, increase heat to med-high and bring to a boil. Let boil about 5 minutes until liquid is reduced to a syrup.
4. Chop the bacon and add it and the sauerkraut to the pot, stir to mix. Reduce heat to low and cook 10 minutes until heated through and sauerkraut is tender. Salt and pepper to taste and serve.

Nutrition Info:
- Calories 58, Total Fat 2g, Total Carbs 9g, Protein 1g, Sodium 170mg.

Corned Cabbage Beef

Servings: 4
Cooking Time: 100 Minutes

Ingredients:
- 1 corned beef brisket
- 4 cups of water
- 1 small onion, peeled and quartered
- 3 garlic cloves, smashed and peeled
- 2 bay leaves
- 3 whole black peppercorns
- 1/2 teaspoon allspice berries
- 1 teaspoon dried thyme
- 5 medium carrots
- 1 cabbage, cut into wedges

Directions:
1. Stir in corned beef, onion, garlic cloves, water, allspice, peppercorn, thymes to the Ninja Foodi.
2. Lock up the lid and cook for about 90 minutes at "HIGH" pressure.
3. Allow the pressure to release naturally once done.
4. Open up and transfer the meat to your serving plate.
5. Cover it with tin foil and allow it to cool for 15 minutes.
6. Stir in carrots and cabbage to the lid and let them cook for 10 minutes at "HIGH" pressure.
7. Once done, do a quick release. Take out the prepped veggies and serve with your corned beef.

Nutrition Info:
- Calories: 297; Fats: 17g; Carbohydrates:1g; Protein: 14g

Chorizo Stuffed Yellow Bell Peppers

Servings: 4
Cooking Time: 40 Min

Ingredients:
- ¾ pound chorizo /337.5g
- 1 small onion; diced
- ⅔ cup diced fresh tomatoes /88g
- 1½ cups cooked rice /195g
- 1 cup shredded Mexican blend cheese; divided /130g
- 4 large yellow bell peppers
- 2 tsp olive oil /10ml

Directions:
1. Cut about ¼ to ⅓ inch off the top of each pepper. Cut through the ribs inside the peppers and pull out the core and remove as much of the ribs as possible.
2. On the Foodi, choose Sear/Sauté and adjust to Medium. Press Start to preheat the inner pot for 5 minutes. Heat the oil in the pot until shimmering and cook in the chorizo while breaking the meat with a spatula. Cook until just starting to brown, about 2 minutes.
3. Add the onion and sauté until the vegetables soften and the chorizo has now browned, about 3 minutes.
4. Turn the Foodi off and scoop the chorizo and vegetables into a medium bowl. Add the tomatoes, rice, and ½ cup or 65g of cheese to the bowl. Mix to combine well.
5. Spoon the filling mixture into the bell peppers to the brim. Clean the inner pot with a paper towel and return the pot to the base. Pour 1 cup or 250ml of water into the pot and fix the rack in the pot in the lower position. Put the peppers on the rack and cover the tops loosely with a piece of foil.
6. Lock the pressure lid into place and set to Seal. Choose Pressure; adjust the pressure to High and the time to 12 minutes. Press Start.
7. After cooking, perform a quick pressure release and carefully open the lid. Remove the foil from the top of the peppers and sprinkle the remaining ½ cup or 65g of cheese on the peppers.
8. Close the crisping lid; choose Broil, adjust the time to 5 minutes, and press Start to broil the cheese. After 4 minutes, open the lid and check the peppers. The cheese should have melted and browned a bit. If not, close the lid and continue cooking. Let the peppers cool for several minutes before serving.

Southern-style Lettuce Wraps

Servings: 6
Cooking Time: 30 Minutes
Ingredients:
- 3 pounds boneless pork shoulder, cut into 1- to 2-inch cubes
- 2 cups light beer
- 1 cup brown sugar
- 1 teaspoon chipotle chiles in adobo sauce
- 1 cup barbecue sauce
- 1 head iceberg lettuce, quartered and leaves separated
- 1 cup roasted peanuts, chopped or ground
- Cilantro leaves

Directions:
1. Place the pork, beer, brown sugar, chipotle, and barbecue sauce in the pot. Assemble pressure lid, making sure the pressure release valve is in the SEAL position.
2. Select PRESSURE and set to HI. Set the timer to 30 minutes. Select START/STOP to begin.
3. When pressure cooking is complete, quick release the pressure by turning the pressure release valve to the VENT position. Carefully remove lid when unit has finished releasing pressure.
4. Using a silicone-tipped utensil, shred the pork in the pot. Stir to mix the meat in with the sauce.
5. Place a small amount of pork in a piece of lettuce. Top with peanuts and cilantro to serve.

Nutrition Info:
- Calories: 811, Total Fat: 58g, Sodium: 627mg, Carbohydrates: 22g, Protein: 45g.

Cheesy Ham & Potato Casserole

Servings: 6
Cooking Time: 35 Minutes
Ingredients:
- 1 tbsp. butter
- 1 sweet potato, peeled & chopped
- 1 cup onion, chopped
- 2 cloves garlic, chopped fine
- 8 oz. cream cheese, low fat
- 14 ½ oz. chicken broth, low sodium
- ½ cup sour cream, low fat
- ½ tsp thyme, crushed
- ¼ tsp pepper
- 32 oz. hash brown potatoes, thawed
- 1 ½ cups white cheddar cheese, low fat, grated
- 1 cup ham, chopped
- 1 cup grape tomatoes, sliced
- 2 green onions, sliced

Directions:
1. Add butter to the cooking pot and set to sauté on medium heat. Once the butter has melted, add sweet potato, onion, and garlic and cook 5-8 minutes or until potato is tender.
2. Stir in cream cheese until melted. Add broth, sour cream, thyme, and pepper and mix well.
3. Add hash browns, cheese, and ham and mix until combined. Lay the sliced tomatoes evenly over the top.
4. Add the tender-crisp lid and set to bake on 375°F. Bake 30-35 minutes until hot and bubbly and top is lightly browned. Let rest 5 minutes, then serve garnished with green onions.

Nutrition Info:
- Calories 369, Total Fat 13g, Total Carbs 41g, Protein 21g, Sodium 1541mg.

Ham, Ricotta & Zucchini Fritters

Servings: 4
Cooking Time: 10 Minutes
Ingredients:
- 1 ½ tbsp. butter, unsalted
- 1/3 cup milk
- ½ cup ricotta cheese
- 2 eggs
- 1 ½ tsp baking powder
- ½ tsp salt
- ¼ tsp pepper
- 1 cup flour
- ¼ cup fresh basil, chopped
- 3 oz. ham, cut in strips
- ½ zucchini, cut into matchsticks

Directions:
1. Spray the fryer basket with cooking spray. Place in the cooking pot.
2. Place the butter in a large microwave safe bowl and microwave until melted.
3. Whisk milk and ricotta into melted butter until smooth. Whisk in eggs until combined.
4. Stir in baking powder, salt, and pepper until combined. Stir in flour, until combined.
5. Fold in basil, ham and zucchini until distributed evenly. Drop batter by ¼ cups into fryer basket, these will need to be cooked in batches.

6. Add the tender-crisp lid and set to air fry on 375°F. Cook fritters 4-5 minutes per side until golden brown and cooked through. Serve immediately.

Nutrition Info:
- Calories 180, Total Fat 10g, Total Carbs 15g, Protein 7g, Sodium 451mg.

Hot Dogs With Peppers

Servings: 6
Cooking Time: 15 Min
Ingredients:
- 6 sausages pork sausage links
- 1 green bell pepper; sliced into strips
- 1 red bell pepper; sliced into strips
- 1 yellow bell pepper; sliced into strips
- 2 spring onions; sliced
- 1 ½ cups beer /375ml
- 6 hot dog rolls
- 1 tbsp olive oil /15ml

Directions:
1. Warm oil on Sear/Sauté. Add in sausage links and sear for 5 minutes until browned; set aside on a plate. Into the Foodi, pile peppers. Lay the sausages on top. Add beer into the pot.
2. Seal the pressure lid, choose Pressure, set to High, and set the timer to 5 minutes. Press Start. When ready, release the pressure quickly. Serve sausages in buns topped with onions and peppers.

Zucchini & Beef Lasagna

Servings: 4
Cooking Time: 1 Hour
Ingredients:
- 2 zucchini, cut lengthwise in ½-thick slices
- ½ tsp salt
- Nonstick cooking spray
- 3 tomatoes
- 1 cup onion, chopped
- 2 cloves garlic, chopped fine
- 1 serrano chili, chopped fine
- 1 ½ cups mushrooms, chopped
- 1 lb. lean ground beef
- ½ cube chicken bouillon
- 1 tsp paprika
- 1 tsp thyme
- 1 tsp basil
- ½ tsp salt
- ¼ tsp pepper
- ½ cup mozzarella cheese, grated

Directions:
1. Place zucchini in a large bowl, sprinkle with salt and let sit 10 minutes.
2. Spray the rack with cooking spray and add it to the cooking pot. Pat zucchini dry with paper towels and lay them on the rack, these will need to be done in batches. Add the tender-crisp lid and set to broil, cook zucchini 3 minutes. Transfer to a paper-towel lined baking sheet.
3. Bring a pot of water to a boil. Cut the ends off the tomatoes and make an X insertion on the top. Place in boiling water for 2-3 minutes. Transfer to bowl of ice water and remove the skin. Chop the tomatoes.
4. Spray the cooking pot with cooking spray and set to sauté on med-high heat. Add onion, garlic, and chili and cook 1 minute. Add the tomatoes and mushrooms and cook 3-4 minutes or until almost tender. Transfer to a bowl.
5. Add the beef to the cooking pot and cook, breaking up with a spatula, until no longer pink.
6. Add the vegetables to the beef along with the bouillon and remaining spices. Reduce heat to low and simmer 25 minutes, stirring occasionally.
7. Spray an 8x8-inch baking dish with cooking spray. Lay 1/3 of the zucchini across the bottom. Top with 1/3 of the meat mixture. Repeat layers two more times. Sprinkle cheese evenly over the top.
8. Add the rack back to the cooking pot and place lasagna on it. Add the tender-crisp lid and set to bake on 375°F. Bake 35 minutes. Transfer to cutting board and let rest 10 minutes before serving.

Nutrition Info:
- Calories 309, Total Fat 18g, Total Carbs 9g, Protein 28g, Sodium 775mg.

Caribbean Ropa Vieja

Servings: 6
Cooking Time: 1 Hr 10 Min
Ingredients:
- 2 pounds beef skirt steak /900g
- ¼ cup cheddar cheese, shredded /32.5g
- 1 cup tomato sauce /250ml
- 3½ cups beef stock /875ml
- 1 cup dry red wine /250ml
- ¼ cup minced garlic /32.5g
- ¼ cup olive oil /62.5ml
- 1 green bell pepper, thinly sliced

- 1 red bell pepper, thinly sliced
- 2 bay leaves
- 1 red onion, halved and thinly sliced
- 1 tbsp vinegar /15ml
- 1 tsp dried oregano /5g
- 1 tsp ground cumin 5g
- Salt and ground black pepper to taste

Directions:
1. Season the skirt steak with pepper and salt. Add water into Foodi; mix in bay leaves and flank steak. Seal the pressure lid, choose Pressure, set to High, and set the timer to 35 minutes. Press Start. When ready, release the pressure quickly.
2. Remove skirt steak to a cutting board and allow to sit for about 5 minutes. Press Start. When cooled, shred the beef using two forks. Drain the pressure cooker, and reserve the bay leaves and 1 cup liquid.
3. Warm the oil on Sear/Sauté. Add onion, red bell pepper, cumin, garlic, green bell pepper, and oregano and continue cooking for 5 minutes until vegetables are softened.
4. Stir in reserved liquid, tomato sauce, bay leaves and red wine. Return shredded beef to the pot with vinegar; season with pepper and salt.
5. Seal the pressure lid, choose Pressure, set to High, and set the timer to 15 minutes. Press Start. Release pressure naturally for 10 minutes, then turn steam vent valve to Venting to release the remaining pressure quickly. Serve with shredded cheese.

Pork Sandwiches With Slaw

Servings: 8
Cooking Time: 20 Min
Ingredients:
- 2 lb. chuck roast /900g
- 1 white onion; sliced
- 2 cups beef broth /500ml
- ¼ cup sugar /32.5g
- 1 tsp Spanish paprika /5g
- 1 tsp garlic powder /5g
- 2 tbsp apple cider vinegar /30ml
- Salt to taste
- Assembling:
- 4 Buns, halved
- 1 cup red cabbage, shredded /130g
- 1 cup white cabbage, shredded /130g
- 1 cup white Cheddar cheese, grated /130g
- 4 tbsp mayonnaise /60ml

Directions:

1. Place the pork roast on a clean flat surface and sprinkle with paprika, garlic powder, sugar, and salt. Use your hands to rub the seasoning on the meat.
2. Open the Foodi, add beef broth, onions, pork, and apple cider vinegar. Close the lid, secure the pressure valve, and select Pressure mode on High pressure for 12 minutes. Press Start/Stop.
3. Once the timer has ended, do a quick pressure release. Remove the roast to a cutting board, and use two forks to shred them. Return to the pot, close the crisping lid, and cook for 3 minutes on Air Crisp at 300 °F or 149°C.
4. In the buns, spread the mayo, add the shredded pork, some cooked onions from the pot, and shredded red and white cabbage. Top with the cheese.

Beef And Bell Pepper With Onion Sauce

Servings: 6
Cooking Time: 62 Min
Ingredients:
- 2 lb. round steak pieces, about 6 to 8 pieces /900g
- ½ yellow bell pepper, finely chopped
- 1 yellow onion, finely chopped
- 2 cloves garlic; minced
- ½ green bell pepper, finely chopped
- ½ red bell pepper, finely chopped
- ¼ cup flour /32.5g
- ½ cup water /125ml
- 2 tbsp olive oil /30ml
- Salt and pepper, to taste

Directions:
1. Wrap the steaks in plastic wrap, place on a cutting board, and use a rolling pin to pound flat of about 2-inch thickness. Remove the plastic wrap and season them with salt and pepper. Set aside.
2. Put the chopped peppers, onion, and garlic in a bowl, and mix them evenly. Spoon the bell pepper mixture onto the flattened steaks and roll them to have the peppers inside.
3. Use some toothpicks to secure the beef rolls and dredge the steaks in all-purpose flour while shaking off any excess flour. Place them in a plate.
4. Select Sear/Sauté mode on Foodi and heat the oil. Add the beef rolls and brown them on both sides, for about 6 minutes.
5. Pour the water over the meat, close the lid, secure the pressure valve, and select Pressure mode on High pressure for 20 minutes. Press Start/Stop.

6. Once the timer has stopped, do a natural pressure release for 10 minutes. Close the crisping lid and cook for 10 minutes on Broil mode. When ready, Remove the meat to a plate and spoon the sauce from the pot over. Serve the stuffed meat rolls with a side of steamed veggies.

Pork Chops With Green Beans And Scalloped Potatoes

Servings:2
Cooking Time: 45 Minutes
Ingredients:
- 1½ cups chicken broth
- 2 cups half-and-half
- ¼ cup cornstarch
- 2 teaspoons garlic powder
- Kosher salt
- Freshly ground black pepper
- 4 Russet potatoes, sliced ¼-inch thick
- 4 cups shredded Cheddar cheese, divided
- 2 bone-in pork chops
- ½ pound green beans, ends trimmed
- 1 teaspoon minced garlic
- 1 teaspoon extra-virgin olive oil

Directions:
1. In a medium bowl, whisk together the chicken broth, half-and-half, cornstarch, garlic powder, salt, and pepper. Pour just enough broth mixture to cover the bottom of the pot.
2. Layer half of the sliced potatoes in the bottom of the pot. Cover the potatoes with 1 cup of cheese, then layer the remaining potatoes over the cheese. Cover the second layer of potatoes with 1 cup of cheese, then pour in the remaining broth mixture to cover potatoes. Assemble pressure lid, making sure the pressure release valve is in the SEAL position.
3. Select PRESSURE and set to HI. Set time to 25 minutes. Select START/STOP to begin.
4. When pressure cooking is complete, allow pressure to release naturally for 25 minutes. After 25 minutes, quick release remaining pressure by moving the pressure release valve to the VENT position. Carefully remove lid when unit has finished releasing pressure.
5. Cover the potatoes with remaining 2 cups of cheese. Place the Reversible Rack in the broil position in the pot. Close crisping lid.
6. Select BROIL and set time to 20 minutes. Select START/STOP to begin.
7. Season the pork chops with salt and pepper.
8. After 4 minutes, open lid. Place the pork chops on the rack. Close the lid and continue cooking for another 12 minutes.
9. In a large bowl, toss the green beans with the garlic and oil, and season with salt and pepper.
10. After 12 minutes, open lid and add the green beans to the rack with the pork chops. Close lid and continue cooking for the remaining 4 minutes.
11. When cooking is complete, open lid and serve.

Nutrition Info:
- Calories: 1916,Total Fat: 118g,Sodium: 3116mg,Carbohydrates: 107g,Protein: 105g.

Pork Tenderloin With Ginger And Garlic

Servings: 4
Cooking Time: 23 Min
Ingredients:
- 2 lb. pork tenderloin /900g
- ½ cup water + 2 tbsp water /155ml
- ½ cup soy sauce /125ml
- ¼ cup sugar /32.5g
- 2 cloves garlic; minced
- 3 tbsp grated ginger /45g
- 2 tbsp sesame oil /30ml
- 2 tsp cornstarch /10g
- Chopped scallions to garnish
- Sesame seeds to garnish

Directions:
1. In the Foodi's inner pot, add soy sauce, sugar, half cup of water, ginger, garlic, and sesame oil. Use a spoon to stir them. Then, add the pork. Close the lid, secure the pressure valve, and select Pressure mode on High pressure for 12 minutes. Press Start/Stop.
2. Once the timer has ended, do a quick pressure release, and open the pot. Remove the pork and set aside.
3. In a bowl, mix the cornstarch with the remaining water until smooth and pour it into the pot. Bring back the pork. Close the crisping lid and press Broil.
4. Cook for 5 minutes, until the sauce has thickened. Stir the sauce frequently, every 1-2 minutes, to avoid burning. Once the sauce is ready, serve the pork with a side endive salad or steamed veggies. Spoon the sauce all over it.

Beef Bourguignon

Servings: 6
Cooking Time: 9 Hours

Ingredients:

- 5 slices bacon, chopped fine
- 3 lbs. beef chuck, cut in 1-inch cubes
- 1 cup red cooking wine
- 2 cups beef broth, low sodium
- ½ cup tomato sauce
- ¼ cup soy sauce
- ¼ cup flour
- 3 cloves garlic, chopped fine
- 2 tbsp. thyme, chopped fine
- 5 carrots, sliced
- 1 lb. baby potatoes
- 8 oz. mushrooms, sliced
- 2 tbsp. fresh parsley, chopped

Directions:

1. Add the bacon to the cooking pot and set to sauté on med high. Cook until crisp. Transfer to a bowl.
2. Season the beef with salt and pepper. Add to the pot and brown on all sides. Add to the bacon.
3. Add the wine to the pot and stir to scrape up the brown bits from the bottom of the pot. Simmer 2-3 minutes to reduce.
4. Stir in broth, tomato sauce, and soy sauce. Slowly whisk in flour.
5. Add the beef and bacon back to the pot along with remaining ingredients, except parsley, and stir to mix. Add the lid and set to slow cook on low. Cook 8-10 hours or until beef is tender. Stir and serve garnished with parsley.

Nutrition Info:

- Calories 649,Total Fat 28g,Total Carbs 28g,Protein 69g,Sodium 1344mg.

Short Ribs With Egg Noodles

Servings: 4
Cooking Time: 65 Min

Ingredients:

- 4 pounds bone-in short ribs /1800g
- 1 garlic clove; minced
- 1½ cups panko bread crumbs /195g
- Low-sodium beef broth
- 6 ounces egg noodles /180g
- 3 tbsp melted unsalted butter /45ml
- 2 tbsp prepared horseradish /30g
- 6 tbsp Dijon mustard /90g
- 2½ tsp salt /12.5g
- ½ tsp freshly ground black pepper /2.5g

Directions:

1. Season the short ribs on all sides with 1½ tsp s or 7.5g of salt. Pour 1 cup 250ml of broth into the inner pot. Put the reversible rack in the lower position in the pot, and place the short ribs on top. Seal the pressure lid, choose Pressure; adjust the pressure to High and the time to 25 minutes; press Start. After cooking, perform a natural pressure release for 5 minutes, then a quick pressure release, and carefully open the lid. Remove the rack and short ribs.
2. Pour the cooking liquid into a measuring cup to get 2 cups. If lesser than 2 cups, add more broth and season with salt and pepper.
3. Add the egg noodles and the remaining salt. Stir and submerge the noodles as much as possible. Seal the pressure lid, choose Pressure; adjust the pressure to High and the cook time to 4 minutes; press Start.
4. In a bowl, combine the horseradish, Dijon mustard, garlic, and black pepper. Brush the sauce on all sides of the short ribs and reserve any extra sauce.
5. In a bowl, mix the butter and breadcrumbs. Coat the ribs with the crumbs. Put the ribs back on the rack. After cooking, do a quick pressure release, and carefully open the lid. Stir the noodles, which may not be quite done but will continue cooking.
6. Return the rack and beef to the pot in the upper position.
7. Close the crisping lid and Choose Bake/Roast; adjust the temperature to 400°F or 205°C and the cook time to 15 minutes. Press Start. After 8 minutes, open the lid and turn the ribs over. Close the lid and continue cooking. Serve the beef and noodles, with the extra sauce on the side, if desired.

Fish & Seafood Recipes

Chili Mint Steamed Snapper

Servings: 4
Cooking Time: 20 Minutes
Ingredients:
- 2 lb. whole snapper
- 2 tbsp. white wine
- 2 tbsp. soy sauce
- ¼ cup peanut oil
- 2 tsp ginger, cut in fine matchsticks
- 2 red chilies, sliced
- 1 cup fresh mint, chopped

Directions:
1. Pour water in the cooking pot and add the rack.
2. Place the fish in a baking pan and add to the cooker. Add the lid and set to steam for 15 minutes.
3. Transfer fish carefully to serving plate. Pour out any remaining water in the pot.
4. Add the wine and soy sauce to the pot and set to sauté on medium heat. Cook until hot but not boiling. Pour over fish.
5. Add the oil and let it get hot. Add the ginger and cook until crisp, about 1 minute. Turn off the heat and the chilies. Pour this mixture over the fish and sprinkle with mint. Serve immediately.

Nutrition Info:
- Calories 370,Total Fat 17g,Total Carbs 4g,Protein 48g,Sodium 405mg.

Herb Salmon With Barley Haricot Verts

Servings: 4
Cooking Time: 50 Min
Ingredients:
- 4 salmon fillets
- 8 ounces green beans haricot verts, trimmed /240g
- 2 garlic cloves, minced
- 1 cup pearl barley /130g
- 2 cups water /500ml
- ½ tbsp brown sugar /65g
- ½ tbsp freshly squeezed lemon juice /7.5ml
- 1 tbsp olive oil /15ml
- 4 tbsps melted butter/60ml
- ½ tsp dried thyme /2.5g
- ½ tsp dried rosemary /2.5g
- 1 tsp salt; divided /5g
- 1 tsp freshly ground black pepper; divided /5g

Directions:
1. Pour the barley and water in the pot and mix to combine. Place the reversible rack in the pot. Lay the salmon fillets on the rack. Seal the pressure lid, choose Pressure, set to High and set the time to 2 minutes. Press Start.
2. In a bowl, toss the green beans with olive oil, ½ tsp or 5g of black pepper, and ½ tsp or 2.5g of salt.
3. Then, in another bowl, mix the remaining black pepper and salt, the butter, brown sugar, lemon juice, rosemary, garlic, and rosemary.
4. When done cooking the rice and salmon, perform a quick pressure release. Gently pat the salmon dry with a paper towel, then coat with the buttery herb sauce.
5. Position the haricots vert around the salmon. Close the crisping lid; choose Broil and set the time to 7 minutes; press Start/Stop. When ready, remove the salmon from the rack, and serve with the barley and haricots vert.

Cajun Salmon With Lemon

Servings: 1
Cooking Time: 10 Min
Ingredients:
- 1 salmon fillet
- Juice of ½ lemon
- 2 lemon wedges
- 1 tbsp Cajun seasoning /15g
- 1 tbsp chopped parsley; for garnishing /15g
- ¼ tsp brown sugar /1.25g

Directions:
1. Meanwhile, combine the sugar and lemon and coat the salmon with this mixture thoroughly. Coat the salmon with the Cajun seasoning as well.
2. Place a parchment paper into the Ninja Foodi, close the crisping lid and cook the salmon for 7 minutes on Air Crisp mode at 350 °F or 177°C. If you use a thicker fillet, cook no more than 6 minutes. Serve with lemon wedges and chopped parsley.

Arroz Con Cod

Servings: 4
Cooking Time: 30 Minutes
Ingredients:
- ¼ cup olive oil
- 2 tbsp. garlic, chopped
- ½ cup red onion, chopped
- ½ cup red bell pepper, chopped
- ½ cup green bell pepper, chopped
- 2 cups long grain rice
- 3 tbsp. tomato paste
- 2 tsp turmeric
- 2 tbsp. cumin
- ½ tsp salt
- ¼ tsp pepper
- 4 cups chicken broth
- 1 bay leaf
- 1 lb. cod, cut in bite-size pieces
- ½ cup peas, cooked
- 4 tbsp. pimento, chopped
- 4 tsp cilantro, chopped

Directions:
1. Add the oil to the cooking pot and set to sauté on med-high.
2. Add the garlic, onion, and peppers, and cook, stirring frequently for 2 minutes.
3. Stir in rice, tomato paste, and seasonings, and cook another 2 minutes.
4. Add the broth and bay leaf and bring to a boil. Reduce heat, cover, and let simmer 5 minutes.
5. Add the fish, recover the pot and cook 15-20 minutes until all the liquid is absorbed. Turn off the cooker and let sit for 5 minutes.
6. To serve: spoon onto plates and top with cooked peas, pimento and cilantro.

Nutrition Info:
- Calories 282,Total Fat 15g,Total Carbs 35g,Protein 4g,Sodium 1249mg.

Pistachio Crusted Salmon

Servings: 1
Cooking Time: 15 Min
Ingredients:
- 1 salmon fillet
- 3 tbsp pistachios /45g
- 1 tsp grated Parmesan cheese /5g
- 1 tsp lemon juice /5ml
- 1 tsp mustard /5g
- 1 tsp olive oil /5ml
- Pinch of sea salt
- Pinch of garlic powder
- Pinch of black pepper

Directions:
1. Whisk the mustard and lemon juice together. Season the salmon with salt, pepper, and garlic powder. Brush the olive oil on all sides.
2. Brush the mustard-lemon mixture on top of the salmon. Chop the pistachios finely, and combine them with the Parmesan cheese.
3. Sprinkle them on top of the salmon. Place the salmon in the Ninja Foodi basket with the skin side down.
4. Close the crisping lid and cook for 10 minutes on Air Crisp mode at 350 °F or 177°C.

Citrus Glazed Halibut

Servings: 4
Cooking Time: 10 Minutes
Ingredients:
- Nonstick cooking spray
- 1 onion, chopped
- 1 clove garlic, chopped fine
- 4 halibut steaks
- ½ tsp salt
- ¼ tsp lemon-pepper
- ½ cup fresh orange juice
- 1 tbsp. fresh lemon juice
- 2 tbsp. fresh parsley, chopped fine

Directions:
1. Spray the cooking pot with cooking spray. Set to sauté on medium heat.
2. Add the onion and garlic and cook 2-3 minutes until onion starts to soften.
3. Add the halibut and season with salt and pepper. Drizzle the orange and lemon juices over the fish and sprinkle with parsley.
4. Add the lid and reduce heat to med-low. Cook 10-12 minutes until fish flakes easily with a fork. Serve immediately.

Nutrition Info:
- Calories 131,Total Fat 2g,Total Carbs 6g,Protein 22g,Sodium 370mg.

Paella Señorito

Servings: 5
Cooking Time: 25 Min
Ingredients:
- 1 pound frozen shrimp, peeled and deveined /450g
- 2 garlic cloves, minced
- 1 onion; chopped
- 1 lemon, cut into wedges
- 1 red bell pepper; diced
- 2 cups fish broth /500ml
- ¼ cup olive oil /62.5ml
- 1 cup bomba rice /130g
- ¼ cup frozen green peas /32.5g
- 1 tsp paprika /5g
- 1 tsp turmeric /5g
- salt and ground white pepper to taste
- chopped fresh parsley

Directions:
1. Warm oil on Sear/Sauté. Add in bell pepper and onions and cook for 5 minutes until fragrant. Mix in garlic and cook for one more minute until soft.
2. Add paprika, ground white pepper, salt and turmeric to the vegetables and cook for 1 minute.
3. Stir in fish broth and rice. Add shrimp in the rice mixture. Seal the pressure lid, choose Pressure, set to High, and set the timer to 5 minutes; press Start. When ready, release the pressure quickly.
4. Stir in green peas and let sit for 5 minutes until green peas are heated through. Serve warm garnished with parsley and lemon wedges.

Tuna Salad With Potatoes And Asparagus

Servings: 4
Cooking Time: 60 Minutes
Ingredients:
- 1½ pounds potatoes, quartered /675g
- 8 ounces asparagus, cut into three /240g
- 2 cans tuna, drained
- ½ cup pimento stuffed green olives /65g
- ½ cup coarsely chopped roasted red peppers /65g
- 1 cup water /250ml
- 2 tbsps chopped fresh parsley /30g
- 2 tbsps red wine vinegar; divided /30ml
- 3 tbsps olive oil /45ml
- ¼ tsp freshly ground black pepper /1.25g
- 1 tsp salt; divided, plus more as needed 5g

Directions:
1. Pour the water into the inner pot and set the reversible rack. Place the potatoes on the rack. Lock the pressure lid into place and set to Seal. Choose Pressure; adjust the pressure to High and the cook time to 4 minutes. Press Start/Stop.
2. After pressure cooking, perform a quick pressure release and carefully open the pressure lid. Take out the rack, empty the water in the pot, and return the pot to the base.
3. Arrange the potatoes and asparagus on the Crisping Basket. Drizzle the half of olive oil on them, and season with salt.
4. Place the basket in the pot. Close the crisping lid; choose Air Crisp, adjust the temperature to 375°F or 191°C, and the cook time to 12 minutes. Press Start.
5. After 8 minutes, open the lid, and check the veggies. The asparagus will have started browning and crisping. Gently toss with the potatoes and close the lid. Continue cooking for the remaining 4 minutes.
6. Take out the basket, pour the asparagus and potatoes into a salad bowl. Sprinkle with 1 tbsp of red wine vinegar and mix to coat.
7. In a bowl, pour the remaining oil, remaining vinegar, salt, and pepper. Whisk to combine.
8. To the potatoes and asparagus, add the roasted red peppers, olives, parsley, and tuna. Drizzle the dressing over the salad and mix to coat. Adjust the seasoning and serve immediately.

Pistachio Crusted Mahi Mahi

Servings: 6
Cooking Time: 20 Minutes
Ingredients:
- Nonstick cooking spray
- 6 fresh Mahi Mahi filets
- 2 tbsp. fresh lemon juice
- ½ tsp nutmeg
- ¼ tsp pepper
- ¼ tsp salt
- ½ cup pistachio nuts, chopped
- 2 tbsp. butter, melted

Directions:
1. Place the rack in the cooking pot. Lightly spray a small baking sheet with cooking spray.

2. Place the fish on the prepared pan. Season with lemon juice and spices. Top with pistachios and drizzle melted butter over the tops.
3. Place the pan on the rack and add the tender-crisp lid. Set to bake on 350°F. Cook fish 15-20 minutes or until it flakes easily with a fork. Serve immediately.

Nutrition Info:
- Calories 464,Total Fat 14g,Total Carbs 3g,Protein 77g,Sodium 405mg.

Chorizo And Shrimp Boil

Servings: 4
Cooking Time: 30 Min

Ingredients:
- 4 chorizo sausages; sliced
- 1 pound shrimp, peeled and deveined /450g
- 1 lemon, cut into wedges
- 3 red potatoes
- 3 ears corn, cut into 1½-inch rounds
- ¼ cup butter, melted /62.5ml
- 1 cup white wine /250ml
- 2 cups water /500ml
- 2 tbsp of seafood seasoning /30g
- salt to taste

Directions:
1. To your Foodi add all Ingredients except butter and lemon wedges. Do not stir. Seal the pressure lid, choose Pressure, set to High, and set the timer to 2 minutes; press Start. When ready, release the pressure quickly.
2. Drain the mixture through a colander. Transfer to a serving platter. Serve with melted butter and lemon wedges.

Sweet & Spicy Shrimp

Servings: 4
Cooking Time: 5 Minutes

Ingredients:
- ¾ cup pineapple juice, unsweetened
- 1 red bell pepper, sliced
- 1 ½ cups cauliflower, grated
- ¼ cup dry white wine
- ½ cup water
- 2 tbsp. soy sauce
- 2 tbsp. Thai sweet chili sauce
- 1 tbsp. chili paste
- 1 lb. large shrimp, frozen
- 4 green onions, chopped, white & green separated
- 1 ½ cups pineapple chunks, drained

Directions:
1. Add ¾ cup pineapple juice along with remaining ingredients, except the pineapple chunks and green parts of the onion, to the cooking pot. Stir to mix.
2. Add the lid and set to pressure cook on high. Set timer for 2 minutes. When the timer goes off, release pressure 10 minutes before opening the pot.
3. Add the green parts of the onions and pineapple chunks and stir well. Serve immediately.

Nutrition Info:
- Calories 196,Total Fat 1g,Total Carbs 22g,Protein 26g,Sodium 764mg.

Asian Inspired Halibut

Servings: 4
Cooking Time: 15 Minutes

Ingredients:
- Nonstick cooking spray
- 4 halibut fillets
- 2 tbsp. soy sauce, low sodium
- 1/3 cup dry sherry
- 1 tbsp. brown sugar
- ¾ tsp ginger
- 6 oz. snow peas, thawed
- 15 oz. whole baby corn, drained

Directions:
1. Spray the cooking pot with cooking spray. Set to sauté on med-high heat.
2. Add the fish and cook 3-4 minutes per side until it flakes with a fork. Transfer to a plate and keep warm.
3. In a small bowl, whisk together soy sauce, sherry, sugar, and ginger. Add to the pot and cook, stirring to loosen brown bits from the bottom of the pot for 2 minutes.
4. Add the peas and corn and cook until heated through, stirring frequently. Add the fish back to the pot and coat with sauce.
5. Transfer the fish to serving plates and top with vegetable and sauce. Serve immediately.

Nutrition Info:
- Calories 491,Total Fat 7g,Total Carbs 24g,Protein 80g,Sodium 852mg.

Crab Cakes With Spicy Dipping Sauce

Servings: 4
Cooking Time: 20 Minutes
Ingredients:
- Nonstick cooking spray
- 1/3 cup + ¼ cup mayonnaise, divided
- 1 tbsp. + 2 tsp spicy brown mustard, divided
- 1 tsp hot sauce
- ¼ cup + 1 tbsp. celery, chopped fine, divided
- ¼ cup + 1 tbsp. red bell pepper, chopped fine, divided
- 4 tsp Cajun seasoning, divided
- 2 tbsp. fresh parsley, chopped, divided
- 8 oz. jumbo lump crab meat
- ¼ cup green bell pepper, chopped fine
- 2 tbsp. green onions, chopped fine
- ¼ cup bread crumbs

Directions:
1. Spray the fryer basket with cooking spray.
2. In a small bowl, combine 1/3 cup mayonnaise, 2 teaspoons mustard, hot sauce, 1 tablespoon celery, 1 tablespoon red bell pepper, 2 teaspoons Cajun seasoning, and 1 tablespoon parsley, mix well. Cover and refrigerate until ready to use.
3. In a large bowl, combine all remaining ingredients with the crab, green bell pepper, onions, and bread crumbs, mix well. Form into 8 patties.
4. Place the patties in the fryer basket and add the tender-crisp lid. Set to air fry on 400 °F. Cook 20 minutes, or until golden brown, turning over halfway through cooking time.
5. Serve with prepared sauce for dipping.

Nutrition Info:
- Calories 166,Total Fat 8g,Total Carbs 11g,Protein 11g,Sodium 723mg.

Baked Cod Casserole

Servings: 6
Cooking Time: 20 Minutes
Ingredients:
- Nonstick cooking spray
- 1 lb. mushrooms, chopped
- 1 onion, chopped
- ½ cup fresh parsley, chopped
- ½ tsp salt, divided
- ½ tsp pepper, divided
- 6 cod fillets
- ¾ cup dry white wine
- ¾ cup plain bread crumbs
- 2 tbsp. butter, melted
- 1 cup Swiss cheese, grated

Directions:
1. Spray the cooking pot with cooking spray.
2. In a medium bowl, combine mushrooms, onion, parsley, ¼ teaspoon salt, and ¼ teaspoon pepper and mix well. Spread evenly on the bottom of the cooking pot.
3. Place the fish on top of the mushroom mixture and pour the wine over them.
4. In a separate medium bowl, combine remaining ingredients and mix well. Sprinkle over the fish.
5. Add the tender-crisp lid and set to bake on 450°F. Bake 15-20 minutes or until golden brown and fish flakes easily with a fork. Serve immediately.

Nutrition Info:
- Calories 284,Total Fat 10g,Total Carbs 16g,Protein 27g,Sodium 693mg.

Coconut Cilantro Shrimp

Servings: 4
Cooking Time: 4 ½ Hours
Ingredients:
- 3 ¾ cups coconut milk, unsweetened
- 1 ¾ cups water
- 2 tbsp. red curry paste
- 2 ½ tsp lemon garlic seasoning
- 1 lb. shrimp, peeled & deveined
- ¼ cup cilantro, chopped

Directions:
1. Place all ingredients, except shrimp and cilantro, in the cooking pot and stir to well to mix.
2. Add the lid and set to slow cook on low heat. Cook 4 hours, stirring occasionally.
3. Stir in shrimp and continue cooking another 15-30 minutes until shrimp turn pink and tender.
4. Transfer mixture to a serving plate and garnish with cilantro. Serve immediately.

Nutrition Info:
- Calories 525,Total Fat 46g,Total Carbs 8g,Protein 28g,Sodium 168mg.

Stuffed Cod

Servings: 4
Cooking Time: 40 Minutes
Ingredients:
- ½ cup bread crumbs
- 2 ½ tsp garlic powder, divided
- 1 ½ tsp onion powder, divided
- 1 tbsp. parsley
- ¼ cup parmesan cheese
- ½ tsp salt
- ½ lb. scallops, rinsed & dried
- 7 tbsp. butter, divided
- ½ lb. shrimp, peeled & deveined
- 1 tbsp. flour
- ¾ cup chicken broth, low sodium
- ½ tsp dill
- ½ cup sour cream
- ½ tbsp. lemon juice
- 4 cod filets, patted dry

Directions:
1. Set cooker to bake on 400°F. Place the rack in the cooking pot.
2. In a small bowl, combine bread crumbs, 2 teaspoons garlic powder, 1 teaspoon onion powder, parsley, parmesan cheese, and salt, mix well.
3. Place the scallops in a baking pan and pour 3 tablespoons melted butter over top. Add the bread crumb mixture, and with a spatula mix together so scallops are coated on all sides.
4. Cover with foil and place in the cooking pot. Add the tender-crisp lid and bake 10 minutes.
5. Uncover and add the shrimp and 3 tablespoons butter to the scallops, use the spatula again to coat the shrimp. Recover the dish and bake another 10 minutes. Remove from cooking pot and uncover to cool.
6. In a small saucepan over medium heat, melt the remaining tablespoon of butter. Add the flour and cook, whisking, for 1 minute.
7. Whisk in broth, remaining garlic and onion powder, and dill until combined. Bring mixture just to boil, whisking constantly, and cook until thickened, about 5 minutes. Remove from heat let cool 5 minutes before stirring in sour cream and lemon juice.
8. Pour the scallop mixture onto a cutting board and chop. Add it back to the baking dish.
9. Spoon stuffing mixture onto the wide end of the fish filets and fold in half. Secure with a toothpick. Place on a small baking sheet.
10. Spoon a small amount of the sauce over fish and place on the rack in the cooking pot. Set to bake on 375°F. Add the tender-crisp lid and cook 20 minutes. Transfer to serving plates and top with more sauce. Serve immediately.

Nutrition Info:
- Calories 483,Total Fat 27g,Total Carbs 19g,Protein 41g,Sodium 1459mg.

Crab Cakes

Servings: 4
Cooking Time: 55 Min
Ingredients:
- ½ cup cooked crab meat /65g
- ¼ cup breadcrumbs /32.5g
- ¼ cup chopped celery /32.5g
- ¼ cup chopped red pepper /32.5g
- ¼ cup chopped red onion /32.5g
- Zest of ½ lemon
- 3 tbsp mayonnaise /45mk
- 1 tbsp chopped basil /15g
- 2 tbsp chopped parsley /30g
- Old Bay seasoning, as desired
- Cooking spray

Directions:
1. Place all Ingredients in a large bowl and mix well until thoroughly incorporated. Make 4 large crab cakes from the mixture and place on a lined sheet. Refrigerate for 30 minutes, to set.
2. Spay the air basket with cooking spray and arrange the crab cakes in it.
3. Close the crisping lid and cook for 7 minutes on each side on Air Crisp at 390 °F or 199°C.

Spicy Shrimp Pasta With Vodka Sauce

Servings:6
Cooking Time: 11 Minutes
Ingredients:
- 2 tablespoons extra-virgin olive oil
- 2 tablespoons minced garlic
- 1 teaspoon crushed red pepper flakes
- 1 small red onion, diced
- Kosher salt

- Freshly ground black pepper
- ¾ cup vodka
- 2¾ cups vegetable stock
- 1 can crushed tomatoes
- 1 box penne pasta
- 1 pound frozen shrimp, peeled and deveined
- 1 package cream cheese, cubed
- 4 cups shredded mozzarella cheese

Directions:
1. Select SEAR/SAUTÉ and set to MD:HI. Select START/STOP to begin. Let preheat for 5 minutes.
2. Add the olive oil, garlic, and crushed red pepper flakes. Cook until garlic is golden brown, about 1 minute. Add the onions and season with salt and pepper and cook until translucent, about 2 minutes.
3. Stir in the vodka, vegetable stock, crushed tomatoes, penne pasta, and frozen shrimp. Assemble pressure lid, making sure the pressure release valve is in the SEAL position.
4. Select PRESSURE and set temperature to HI. Set time to 6 minutes. Select START/STOP to begin.
5. When pressure cooking is complete, quick release the pressure by turning the pressure release valve to the VENT position. Carefully remove lid when unit has finished releasing pressure.
6. Stir in the cream cheese until it has melted. Layer the mozzarella on top of the pasta. Close crisping lid.
7. Select AIR CRISP, set temperature to 400°F, and set time to 5 minutes. Select START/STOP to begin.
8. When cooking is complete, open lid and serve.

Nutrition Info:
- Calories: 789,Total Fat: 35g,Sodium: 1302mg,Carbohydrates: 63g,Protein: 47g.

Flounder Veggie Soup

Servings: 10
Cooking Time: 20 Minutes
Ingredients:
- 2 cups water, divided
- 14 oz. chicken broth, low sodium
- 2 lbs. potatoes, peeled & cubed
- 1 onion, chopped
- 2 stalks celery, chopped
- 1 carrot, chopped
- 1 bay leaf
- 2 12 oz. cans evaporated milk, fat free
- 4 tbsp. butter
- 1 lb. flounder filets, cut in 1/2-inch pieces
- ½ tsp thyme
- ¼ tsp salt
- ¼ tsp pepper

Directions:
1. Add 1 ½ cups water, broth, potatoes, onion, celery, carrot, and the bay leaf to the cooking pot. Stir to mix.
2. Add the lid and set to pressure cooker on high. Set the timer for 8 minutes. When the timer goes off, use quick release to remove the lid.
3. Set cooker to sauté on med-low. Stir in milk, butter, fish, thyme, salt and pepper and bring to a boil.
4. In a small bowl, whisk together remaining water and cornstarch until smooth. Add to the soup and cook, stirring, until thickened. Discard the bay leaf and serve.

Nutrition Info:
- Calories 213,Total Fat 6g,Total Carbs 25g,Protein 14g,Sodium 649mg.

Haddock With Sanfaina

Servings: 4
Cooking Time: 40 Min
Ingredients:
- 4 haddock fillets
- 1 can diced tomatoes, drained /435g
- ½ small onion; sliced
- 1 small jalapeño pepper, seeded and minced
- 2 large garlic cloves, minced
- 1 eggplant; cubed
- 1 bell pepper; chopped
- 1 bay leaf
- ⅓ cup sliced green olives /44g
- ¼ cup chopped fresh chervil; divided /32.5g
- 3 tbsps olive oil /45ml
- 3 tbsps capers; divided/45g
- ½ tsp dried basil /2.5g
- ¼ tsp salt /1.25g

Directions:
1. Season the fish on both sides with salt, place in the refrigerator, and make the sauce. Press Sear/Sauté and set to Medium. Press Start. Melt the butter until no longer foaming. Add onion, eggplant, bell pepper, jalapeño, and garlic; sauté for 5 minutes.

2. Stir in the tomatoes, bay leaf, basil, olives, half of the chervil, and half of the capers. Remove the fish from the refrigerator and lay on the vegetables in the pot.

3. Seal the pressure lid, choose Pressure; adjust the pressure to Low and the cook time to 3 minutes; press Start. After cooking, do a quick pressure release and carefully open the lid. Remove and discard the bay leaf.

4. Transfer the fish to a serving platter and spoon the sauce over. Sprinkle with the remaining chervil and capers. Serve.

Cajun Shrimp

Servings: 4
Cooking Time: 7 Minutes

Ingredients:
- 1 ¼ pound shrimp
- 1/4 teaspoon cayenne pepper
- 1/2 teaspoon old bay seasoning
- 1/4 teaspoon smoked paprika
- 1 pinch of salt
- 1 tablespoon olive oil

Directions:
1. Preheat Ninja Foodi by pressing the "AIR CRISP" option and setting it to "390 °F" and timer to 10 minutes.
2. Dip the shrimp into a spice mixture and oil.
3. Transfer the prepared shrimp to your Ninja Foodi Grill cooking basket and cook for 5 minutes.
4. Serve and enjoy.

Nutrition Info:
- Calories: 170; Fat: 2g; Carbohydrates: 5g; Protein: 23g

Seafood Gumbo

Servings: 4
Cooking Time: 90 Min

Ingredients:
- 1 pound jumbo shrimp /450g
- 8 ounces lump crabmeat /240g
- 1 medium onion; chopped
- 2 green onions, finely sliced
- 1 small banana pepper, seeded and minced
- 1 small red bell pepper; chopped (about ⅔ cup)
- 2 celery stalks; chopped
- 2 garlic cloves, minced
- 3 cups chicken broth /750ml
- ¼ cup olive oil, plus 2 tsp s /72.5ml
- ⅓ cup all-purpose flour /44g
- 1 cup jasmine rice /130g
- ¾ cup water /375ml
- 1½ tsp s Cajun Seasoning /7.5g
- 1½ tsp s salt divided /7.5g

Directions:
1. Lay the shrimp in the Crisping Basket. Season with ½ tsp or 2.5g of salt and 2 tsp s or 10ml of olive oil. Toss to coat and fix the basket in the inner pot. Close the crisping lid and Choose Air Crisp; adjust the temperature to 400°F or 205°C and the cook time to 6 minutes. Press Start.

2. After 3 minutes, open the lid and toss the shrimp. Close the lid and resume cooking. When ready, the shrimp should be opaque and pink. Remove the basket and set aside.

3. Choose Sear/Sauté and adjust to High. Press Start. Heat the remaining ¼ cup of olive oil. Whisk in the flour with a wooden spoon and cook the roux that forms for 3 to 5 minutes, stirring constantly, until the roux has the color of peanut butter. Turn the pot off.

4. Stir in the Cajun, onion, bell pepper, celery, garlic, and banana pepper for about 5 minutes until the mixture slightly cools. Add the chicken broth and crabmeat, stir.

5. Put the rice into a heatproof bowl. Add the water and the remaining salt. Cover the bowl with foil. Put the reversible rack in the lower position of the pot and set the bowl in the rack.

6. Seal the pressure lid, choose Pressure; adjust the pressure to High and the cook time to 6 minutes; press Start. After cooking, perform a natural pressure for 8 minutes. Take out the rack and bowl and set aside. Stir the shrimp into the gumbo to heat it up for 3 minutes.

7. Fluff the rice with a fork and divide into the center of four bowls. Spoon the gumbo around the rice and garnish with the green onions.

Clam Fritters

Servings: 4
Cooking Time: 10 Minutes

Ingredients:
- Nonstick cooking spray
- 1 1/3 cups flour
- 2 tsp baking powder
- 1 tsp Old Bay seasoning
- ¼ tsp cayenne pepper
- ¼ tsp salt
- ¼ tsp pepper
- 13 oz. clams, chopped
- 3 tbsp. clam juice
- 1 tbsp. lemon juice

- 2 eggs
- 1 ½ tbsp. chives, chopped
- 2 tbsp. milk

Directions:

1. Spray the fryer basket with cooking spray and add it to the cooking pot.
2. In a large bowl, combine flour, baking powder, Old Bay, cayenne pepper, salt, and pepper, mix well.
3. In a medium bowl, combine clams, clam juice, lemon juice, eggs, chives, and milk, mix well. Add the liquid ingredients to the dry ingredients and mix until combined.
4. Drop by spoonful into the fryer basket, don't over crowd them. Add the tender-crisp lid and set to air fry on 400°F. Cook 8-10 minutes until golden brown, turning over halfway through cooking time.

Nutrition Info:

- Calories 276,Total Fat 4g,Total Carbs 37g,Protein 21g,Sodium 911mg.

Lemon Cod Goujons And Rosemary Chips

Servings: 4
Cooking Time: 100 Min

Ingredients:

- 4 cod fillets, cut into strips
- 2 potatoes, cut into chips
- 4 lemon wedges to serve
- 2 eggs
- 1 cup arrowroot starch /130g
- 1 cup flour /130g
- 2 tbsps olive oil /30ml
- 3 tbsp fresh rosemary; chopped /45g
- 1 tbsp cumin powder /15g
- ½ tbsp cayenne powder /7.5g
- 1 tsp black pepper, plus more for seasoning /5g
- 1 tsp salt, plus more for seasoning /5g
- Zest and juice from 1 lemon
- Cooking spray

Directions:

1. Fix the Crisping Basket in the pot and close the crisping lid. Choose Air Crisp, set the temperature to 375°F or 191°C, and the time to 5 minutes. Choose Start/Stop to preheat the pot.
2. In a bowl, whisk the eggs, lemon zest, and lemon juice. In another bowl, combine the arrowroot starch, flour, cayenne powder, cumin, black pepper, and salt.
3. Coat each cod strip in the egg mixture, and then dredge in the flour mixture, coating well on all sides. Grease the preheated basket with cooking spray. Place the coated fish in the basket and oil with cooking spray.
4. Close the crisping lid. Choose Air Crisp, set the temperature to 375°F or 191°C, and the time to 15 minutes; press Start/Stop. Toss the potatoes with oil and season with salt and pepper.
5. After 15 minutes, check the fish making sure the pieces are as crispy as desired. Remove the fish from the basket.
6. Pour the potatoes in the basket. Close the crisping lid; choose Air Crisp, set the temperature to 400°F or 205°C, and the time to 24 minutes; press Start/Stop.
7. After 12 minutes, open the lid, remove the basket and shake the fries. Return the basket to the pot and close the lid to continue cooking until crispy.
8. When ready, sprinkle with fresh rosemary. Serve the fish with the potatoes and lemon wedges.

Spiced Red Snapper

Servings: 6
Cooking Time: 20 Minutes

Ingredients:

- Nonstick cooking spray
- 1 onion, sliced
- 14 ½ oz. stewed tomatoes, undrained, chopped
- 1/3 cup dry white wine
- 3 tbsp. fresh lemon juice
- 1 tsp cumin
- 1/8 tsp cinnamon
- 6 red snapper fillets

Directions:

1. Spray the cooking pot with cooking spray.
2. Set to sauté on med-high heat and add the onion. Cook, stirring, 3-4 minutes or until onions are soft.
3. Add tomatoes, wine, lemon juice, cumin,, and cinnamon and cook about 5 minutes or until sauce has thickened slightly.
4. Add the fish and spoon sauce over the top. Add the lid and reduce heat to medium. Cook 8-10 minutes until fish flakes with a fork.
5. Transfer fish to serving plates and top with sauce. Serve immediately.

Nutrition Info:

- Calories 155,Total Fat 2g,Total Carbs 8g,Protein 25g,Sodium 201mg.

Mediterranean Cod

Servings: 4
Cooking Time: 20 Min
Ingredients:
- 4 fillets cod
- 1 bunch fresh thyme sprigs
- 1 pound cherry tomatoes, halved /450g
- 1 clove garlic, pressed
- 1 cup white rice /130g
- 2 cups water /500ml
- 1 cup Kalamata olives /130g
- 2 tbsp pickled capers /30g
- 1 tbsp olive oil; divided /15ml
- 1 tsp olive oil /15ml
- 1 pinch ground black pepper
- 3 pinches salt

Directions:
1. Line a parchment paper to the steamer basket of your Foodi. Place about half the tomatoes in a single layer on the paper. Sprinkle with thyme, reserving some for garnish. Arrange cod fillets on the top of tomatoes. Sprinkle with a little bit of olive oil.
2. Spread the garlic, pepper, salt, and remaining tomatoes over the fish. In the pot, mix rice and water. Lay a trivet over the rice and water. Lower steamer basket onto the trivet.
3. Seal the pressure lid, choose Pressure, set to High, and set the timer to 7 minutes. Press Start. When ready, release the pressure quickly.
4. Remove the steamer basket and trivet from the pot. Use a fork to fluff rice. Plate the fish fillets and apply a garnish of olives, reserved thyme, pepper, remaining olive oil, and capers. Serve with rice.

Low Country Boil

Servings: 6
Cooking Time: 10 Minutes
Ingredients:
- 2 pounds Red Bliss potatoes, diced
- 3 ears corn, cut crosswise into thirds
- 1 package smoked sausage or kielbasa, sliced into 1-inch pieces
- 4 cups water
- 2½ tablespoons Creole seasoning
- 1 pound medium shrimp, peeled and deveined

Directions:
1. Place the potatoes, corn, sausage, water, and Creole seasoning into the pot and stir. Assemble pressure lid, making sure the pressure release valve is in the SEAL position.
2. Select PRESSURE and set to HI. Set time to 5 minutes. Select START/STOP to begin.
3. When pressure cooking is complete, quick release the pressure by turning the pressure release valve to the VENT position. Carefully remove lid when unit has finished releasing pressure.
4. Stir in the shrimp.
5. Select SEAR/SAUTÉ and set to MD:LO. Simmer for about 5 minutes, until the shrimp is cooked through.
6. When cooking is complete, serve immediately.

Nutrition Info:
- Calories: 445, Total Fat: 20g, Sodium: 1251mg, Carbohydrates: 40g, Protein: 28g.

Drunken Saffron Mussels

Servings: 4
Cooking Time: 25 Minutes
Ingredients:
- 2 tablespoons vegetable oil
- 2 shallots, sliced
- 3 garlic cloves, minced
- 1 cup cherry tomatoes, halved
- 2 pounds fresh mussels, washed with cold water, strained, scrubbed, and debearded, as needed
- 2 cups white wine (chardonnay or sauvignon blanc)
- 2 cups heavy cream
- 1½ teaspoons cayenne pepper
- 1½ teaspoons freshly ground black pepper
- ½ teaspoon saffron threads
- 1 loaf sourdough bread, cut into slices, for serving

Directions:
1. Select SEAR/SAUTÉ and set the temperature to HI. Select START/STOP to begin and allow to preheat for 5 minutes.
2. Add oil to the pot and allow to heat for 1 minute. Add the shallots, garlic, and cherry tomatoes. Stir to ensure the ingredients are coated and sauté for 5 minutes.
3. Add the mussels, wine, heavy cream, cayenne, black pepper, and saffron threads to the pot.
4. Assemble the pressure lid, making sure the pressure release valve is in the VENT position.
5. Select STEAM and set the temperature to HI. Set the time to 20 minutes. Select START/STOP to begin.

6. When cooking is complete, carefully remove the lid.
7. Transfer the mussels and broth to bowls or eat straight from the pot. Discard any mussels that have not opened.
8. Serve with the bread and enjoy!

Nutrition Info:
- Calories: 882,Total Fat: 54g,Sodium: 769mg,Carbohydrates: 61g,Protein: 20g.

Seared Scallops In Asparagus Sauce

Servings: 2
Cooking Time: 25 Minutes

Ingredients:
- 10 sea scallops
- Salt
- 1 lb. asparagus, trimmed
- ¼ cup chicken broth, low sodium
- 2 tbsp. olive oil
- 2-3 tablespoons butter

Directions:
1. Salt both sides of the scallops and set aside.
2. Fill the cooking pot half full with water. Set to sauté on high heat and bring to a boil.
3. Peel off the outer layer of asparagus spears. Chop into 2-inch pieces. When water is boiling add asparagus and cook 5-8 minutes.
4. Transfer asparagus to a food processor or blender. Add half the broth and process until smooth. Discard the water in the pot.
5. Add oil to the cooking pot and set to med-high heat. Let oil heat for 2 minutes.
6. Pat scallops dry with paper towel and lay in the pot, don't overcrowd them. Let cook 3-4 minutes. When you see a golden brown ring on the bottom edge of the scallop, turn them over. Sear another 1-2 minutes. Transfer to a plate and cover to keep warm.
7. Decrease the heat to med-low and pour the pureed asparagus in the pot. Add the butter and cook, stirring until butter melts, do not let it boil. Add salt to taste.
8. To serve, spoon sauce on the bottom of serving plates and top with scallops. Serve immediately.

Nutrition Info:
- Calories 91,Total Fat 8g,Total Carbs 3g,Protein 3g,Sodium 214mg.

Crab Alfredo

Servings: 4
Cooking Time: 25 Minutes

Ingredients:
- ½ cup butter, unsalted
- ½ red bell pepper, seeded & chopped
- 2 tbsp. cream cheese, low fat
- 2 cups half and half
- ¾ cup parmesan cheese, reduced fat
- 1 tsp garlic powder
- 2 cups penne pasta, cooked & drained
- 6 oz. lump crab meat, cooked

Directions:
1. Add butter to the cooking pot and set to sauté on medium heat.
2. When butter has melted, add bell pepper and cook until it starts to soften, about 3-5 minutes.
3. Add the cream cheese and cook, stirring until it melts.
4. Stir in half and half and parmesan cheese, and garlic powder until smooth. Reduce heat to low and simmer 15 minutes.
5. Stir in cooked penne and crab meat and cook just until heated through. Serve immediately.

Nutrition Info:
- Calories 388,Total Fat 23g,Total Carbs 26g,Protein 19g,Sodium 613mg.

Shrimp And Sausage Paella

Servings: 4
Cooking Time: 70 Min

Ingredients:
- 1 pound andouille sausage; sliced /450g
- 1 pound baby squid, cut into ¼-inch rings /450g
- 1 pound jumbo shrimp, peeled and deveined /450g
- 1 white onion; chopped
- 4 garlic cloves, minced
- 1 red bell pepper; diced
- 2 cups Spanish rice /260g
- 4 cups chicken stock /1000ml
- ½ cup dry white wine /125ml
- 1 tbsp melted butter /15ml
- 1 tsp turmeric powder /5g
- 1½ tsp s sweet paprika /7.5g
- ½ tsp freshly ground black pepper /5g
- ½ tsp salt /5g

Directions:
1. Choose Sear/Sauté on the pot and set to Medium High. Choose Start/Stop to preheat the pot. Melt the butter and add the sausage. Cook until browned on both sides, about 3

minutes while stirring frequently. Remove the sausage to a plate and set aside.

2. Sauté the onion and garlic in the same fat for 3 minutes until fragrant and pour in the wine. Use a wooden spoon to scrape the bottom of the pot of any brown bits and cook for 2 minutes or until the wine reduces by half.

3. Stir in the rice and water. Season with the paprika, turmeric, black pepper, and salt. Seal the pressure lid, choose Pressure and set to High. Set the time to 5 minutes, then Choose Start/Stop. When done cooking, do a quick pressure release and carefully open the lid.

4. Choose Sear/Sauté, set to Medium High, and choose Start/Stop. Add the squid and shrimp to the pot and stir gently without mashing the rice.

5. Seal the pressure lid again and cook for 6 minutes, until the shrimp are pink and opaque. Return the sausage to the pot and mix in the bell pepper. Warm through for 2 minutes. Dish the paella and serve immediately.

Shrimp & Sausage Gumbo

Servings: 8
Cooking Time: 1 Hour 30 Minutes
Ingredients:
- ½ cup peanut oil
- ½ cup flour
- 1 green bell pepper, chopped
- 1 onion, chopped
- 3 stalks celery, chopped
- 4 cloves garlic, chopped fine
- 1 tbsp. Cajun seasoning
- 1 quart chicken broth, low sodium
- 1 cup water
- 2 tsp Worcestershire sauce
- ¼ tsp pepper
- ½ tsp salt
- 12 oz. smoked andouille sausage, sliced ¼-inch thick
- 2 lbs. shrimp, peeled & deveined
- 3 green onions, chopped
- Hot sauce to taste

Directions:
1. Add the oil to the cooking pot and set to sauté on medium heat. Whisk in the flour until smooth. Cook, stirring until roux is a golden brown. Reduce heat to med-low and cook 20-30 minutes until roux is a deep brown.

2. Add the bell pepper, onion, and celery and increase heat to med-high. Cook, stirring frequently about 5 minutes. Add the garlic and cook 2 minutes more. Stir in Cajun seasoning.

3. Stirring constantly, slowly add the broth and water. Bring to a simmer and add the Worcestershire, pepper, and salt. Reduce heat to medium and simmer 30 minutes.

4. Add the sausage and cook until heated through, about 5 minutes. Add the shrimp and cook until they turn pink, about 5 minutes. Serve garnished with green onions and hot sauce to taste over cooked rice.

Nutrition Info:
- Calories 111,Total Fat 7g,Total Carbs 4g,Protein 8g,Sodium 207mg.

Italian Flounder

Servings: 4
Cooking Time: 70 Min
Ingredients:
- 4 flounder fillets
- 3 slices prosciutto; chopped
- 2 bags baby kale /180g
- ½ small red onion; chopped
- ½ cup whipping cream /125ml
- 1 cup panko breadcrumbs /130g
- 2 tbsps chopped fresh parsley /30g
- 3 tbsps unsalted butter, melted and divided /45g
- ¼ tsp fresh ground black pepper /1.25g
- ½ tsp salt; divided /2.5g

Directions:
1. On the Foodi, choose Sear/Sauté and adjust to Medium. Press Start to preheat the inner pot. Add the prosciutto and cook until crispy, about 6 minutes. Stir in the red onions and cook for about 2 minutes or until the onions start to soften. Sprinkle with half of the salt.

2. Fetch the kale into the pot and cook, stirring frequently until wilted and most of the liquid has evaporated, about 4-5 minutes. Mix in the whipping cream.

3. Lay the flounder fillets over the kale in a single layer. Brush 1 tbsp or 15ml of the melted butter over the fillets and sprinkle with the remaining salt and black pepper.

4. Close the crisping lid and choose Bake/Roast. Adjust the temperature to 300°F or 149°C and the cook time to 3 minutes. Press Start.

5. Combine the remaining butter, the parsley and breadcrumbs in a bowl.

6. When done cooking, open the crisping lid. Spoon the breadcrumbs mixture on the fillets.

7. Close the crisping lid and Choose Bake/Roast. Adjust the temperature to 400°F or 205°Cand the cook time to 6 minutes. Press Start.

8. After about 4 minutes, open the lid and check the fish. The breadcrumbs should be golden brown and crisp. If not, close the lid and continue to cook for an additional two minutes.

Stir Fried Scallops & Veggies

Servings: 6
Cooking Time: 15 Minutes
Ingredients:
- 2 tbsp. peanut oil
- 3 cloves garlic, chopped fine
- 1 tsp crushed red pepper flakes
- 1 lb. bay scallops
- 2 tbsp. sesame seeds
- 1 ½ tsp ginger
- 1 head bok choy, trimmed and chopped
- 16 oz. stir-fry vegetables
- 1 tbsp. soy sauce, low sodium

Directions:
1. Add the oil to the cooking pot and set to saute on med-high heat.
2. Add the garlic, red pepper flakes, and scallops and cook until scallops are golden brown and cooked. Transfer scallops to a bowl and keep warm.
3. Add the sesame seeds and ginger and cook, stirring, 1-2 minutes until all the liquid is gone.
4. Add the cabbage and vegetables and cook 4-5 minutes, stirring occasionally.
5. Add the soy sauce and return the scallops to the pot. Cook 1-2 minutes more until heated through. Serve immediately.

Nutrition Info:
- Calories 172,Total Fat 5g,Total Carbs 17g,Protein 15g,Sodium 485mg.

Seafood Minestrone

Servings: 14
Cooking Time: 20 Minutes
Ingredients:
- 3 14 oz. cans beef broth, low sodium
- 28 oz. tomatoes, crushed
- 19 oz. garbanzo beans, undrained
- 15 ¼ oz. red kidney beans, undrained
- 16 oz. pkg. frozen mixed vegetables, thawed
- 16 oz. frozen spinach, thawed, chopped & drained
- 1 onion, chopped
- 1 tsp garlic powder
- ½ tsp pepper
- ½ cup elbow macaroni, uncooked
- 1 lb. cod, cut in 1-inch pieces
- 1 lb. shrimp, peeled & deveined

Directions:
1. Set cooker to sauté on med-high. Add the broth, tomatoes, garbanzo beans, kidney beans, vegetables, spinach, onion, and seasonings to the cooking pot, stir to mix. Bring to a boil.
2. Stir in the macaroni and cook until tender, about 8 minutes.
3. Reduce the heat to med-low and add the fish and shrimp. Cook 5-7 minutes until shrimp turn pink and fish flakes easily. Serve immediately.

Nutrition Info:
- Calories 292,Total Fat 3g,Total Carbs 42g,Protein 25g,Sodium 645mg.

Kung Pao Shrimp

Servings: 4
Cooking Time: 15 Minutes
Ingredients:
- 1 tbsp. olive oil
- 1 red bell pepper, seeded & chopped
- 1 green bell pepper, seeded & chopped
- 3 cloves garlic, chopped fine
- 1 lb. large shrimp, peeled & deveined
- ¼ cup soy sauce
- 1 tsp sesame oil
- 1 tsp brown sugar
- 1 tsp Sriracha
- 1/8 tsp red pepper flakes
- 1 tsp cornstarch
- 1 tbsp. water
- ¼ cup peanuts
- ¼ cup green onions, sliced thin

Directions:
1. Add oil to the cooking pot and set to sauté on med-high heat.
2. Add the bell peppers and garlic and cook, 3-5 minutes, until pepper is almost tender.
3. Add the shrimp and cook until they turn pink, 2-3 minutes.
4. In a small bowl, whisk together soy sauce, sesame oil, brown sugar, Sriracha, and pepper flakes until combined.

5. In a separate small bowl, whisk together cornstarch and water until smooth. Whisk into sauce and pour over shrimp mixture. Add the peanuts.

6. Cook, stirring, until the sauce has thickened, about 2-3 minutes. Serve garnished with green onions.

Nutrition Info:
- Calories 212,Total Fat 11g,Total Carbs 10g,Protein 20g,Sodium 1729mg.

Mackerel En Papillote With Vegetables

Servings: 6
Cooking Time: 25 Min + 2 H For Marinating
Ingredients:
- 3 large whole mackerel, cut into 2 pieces
- 1 pound asparagus, trimmed /450g
- 1 carrot, cut into sticks
- 1 celery stalk, cut into sticks
- 3 cloves garlic, minced
- 2 lemons, cut into wedges
- 6 medium tomatoes, quartered
- 1 large brown onion; sliced thinly
- 1 Orange Bell pepper, seeded and cut into sticks
- ½ cup butter; at room temperature/65g
- 1 ½ cups water /375ml
- 2 ½ tbsp Pernod /37.5g
- Salt and black pepper to taste

Directions:
1. Cut out 6 pieces of parchment paper a little longer and wider than a piece of fish with kitchen scissors. Then, cut out 6 pieces of foil slightly longer than the parchment papers.
2. Lay the foil wraps on a flat surface and place each parchment paper on each aluminium foil.
3. In a bowl, add tomatoes, onions, garlic, bell pepper, pernod, butter, asparagus, carrot, celery, salt, and pepper. Use a spoon to mix them.
4. Place each fish piece on the layer of parchment and foil wraps. Spoon the vegetable mixture on each fish. Then, wrap the fish and place the fish packets in the refrigerator to marinate for 2 hours. Remove the fish to a flat surface.
5. Open the Ninja Foodi, pour the water in, and fit the reversible rack at the bottom of the pot. Put the packets on the trivet.
6. Seal the lid and select Steam mode on High pressure for 3 minutes. Press Start/Stop to start cooking.
7. Once the timer has ended, do a quick pressure release, and open the lid.
8. Remove the trivet with the fish packets onto a flat surface. Carefully open the foil and using a spatula. Return the packets to the pot, on top of the rack.
9. Close the crisping lid and cook on Air Crisp for 3 minutes at 300 °F or 149°C. Then, remove to serving plates. Serve with lemon wedges.

Coconut Curried Mussels

Servings: 4
Cooking Time: 20 Minutes
Ingredients:
- 2 tbsp. water
- ½ cup onion, chopped fine
- ½ cup red bell pepper, seeded & chopped fine
- 3 cloves garlic, chopped fine
- ½ tsp pepper
- 2 tbsp. curry powder
- 1 cup coconut milk, unsweetened
- ½ cup vegetable broth
- 2 lbs. mussels, washed & cleaned
- ¼ cup cilantro, chopped

Directions:
1. Add the water, onion, bell pepper, and garlic to the cooking pot. Set to sauté on medium heat and cook, stirring occasionally until onions are soft, about 5-8 minutes, add more water if needed to prevent vegetables from sticking.
2. Stir in pepper, curry powder, coconut milk, and broth, stir well until smooth. Bring up to a simmer and add the mussels.
3. Add the lid and cook 5-6 minutes, or until all the mussels have opened. Discard any that do not open. Ladle into bowls and garnish with cilantro. Serve.

Nutrition Info:
- Calories 331,Total Fat 18g,Total Carbs 15g,Protein 29g,Sodium 664mg.

Tilapia & Tamari Garlic Mushrooms

Servings: 4
Cooking Time: 10 Minutes
Ingredients:
- 2 tbsp. sesame oil, divided
- 2 cloves garlic, chopped fine
- 2 cups mushrooms, sliced
- 4 tilapia fillets

- ½ tsp salt
- ¼ tsp pepper
- 1 tbsp. fresh lime juice
- 1 tbsp. tamari
- ¼ cup cilantro, chopped

Directions:

1. Add 1 tablespoon oil to the cooking pot and set to sauté on med-high heat.
2. Add the garlic and mushrooms and cook, stirring occasionally, 2-3 minutes.
3. Add the rack to the pot and top with a sheet of foil. Place the fish on the foil and brush with the remaining oil. Season with salt and pepper and drizzle lime juice over the tops.
4. Add the tender-crisp lid and set to roast on 350°F. Cook 5 minutes or until fish flakes with a fork and the liquid from the mushrooms has evaporated.
5. Transfer fish to serving plates. Stir the tamari into the mushrooms and spoon over fish. Garnish with cilantro and serve.

Nutrition Info:

- Calories 298,Total Fat 12g,Total Carbs 2g,Protein 44g,Sodium 610mg.

Succotash With Basil Crusted Fish

Servings: 4
Cooking Time: 65 Min
Ingredients:

- 4 firm white fish fillets; at least 1 inch thick
- 1 large tomato, seeded and chopped
- ½ small onion; chopped
- 1 bay leaf
- 1 garlic clove, minced
- 1 medium red chili, seeded and chopped
- ¼ cup mayonnaise /62.5ml
- 1 ½ cups breadcrumbs /195g
- ¼ cup chicken stock /62.5ml
- ¼ cup chopped fresh basil /32.5g
- 1 cup frozen corn /130g
- 1 cup frozen mixed beans /130g
- 1 cup butternut squash; cubed /130g
- 1 tbsp olive oil /15ml
- 1 tbsp Dijon-style mustard /15g
- ¼ tsp cayenne pepper /1.25g
- ½ tsp Worcestershire sauce /2.5ml
- 1 tsp salt; divided /5g
- Cooking spray

Directions:

1. Press Sear/Sauté and adjust to Medium. Press Start to preheat the pot. Heat the oil and sauté the onion, garlic, and red chili pepper in the oil for 4 minutes or until the vegetables are soft.
2. Stir in the corn, squash, mixed beans, bay leaf, cayenne, chicken stock, Worcestershire sauce, and ½ tsp or 5g salt. Seal the pressure lid, choose Pressure; adjust the pressure to High and the cook time to 5 minutes. Press Start.
3. Season the fish fillets with the remaining salt. In a small bowl, mix the mayonnaise and mustard. Pour the breadcrumbs and basil into another bowl.
4. Use a brush to spread the mayonnaise mixture on all sides of the fish and dredge each piece in the basil breadcrumbs to be properly coated.
5. Once the succotash is ready, perform a quick pressure release and carefully open the pressure lid. Stir in the tomato and remove the bay leaf.
6. Set the reversible rack in the upper position of the pot, line with aluminum foil, and carefully lay the fish in the rack. Oil the top of the fish with cooking spray.
7. Close the crisping lid and Choose Bake/Roast; adjust the temperature to 375°F or 191°C and the cook time to 8 minutes. Press Start.
8. After 4 minutes, open the lid. Use tongs to turn them over and oil the other side with cooking spray. Close the lid and continue cooking. Serve the fillets with the succotash.

Vegan & Vegetable Recipes

Mashed Potatoes With Spinach

Servings: 6
Cooking Time: 30 Min
Ingredients:
- 3 pounds potatoes, peeled and quartered /1350g
- 2 cups spinach; chopped /260g
- ½ cup milk /125ml
- ⅓ cup butter /44g
- 1½ cups water /375ml
- 2 tbsp chopped fresh chives /30g
- ½ tsp salt /2.5g
- fresh black pepper to taste

Directions:
1. In the cooker, mix water, salt and potatoes. Seal the pressure lid, choose Pressure, set to High, and set the timer to 8 minutes. Press Start. When ready, release the pressure quickly. Drain the potatoes, and reserve the liquid in a bowl. In a large bowl, mash the potatoes.
2. Mix with butter and milk; season with pepper and salt. With reserved cooking liquid, thin the potatoes to attain the desired consistency.
3. Put the spinach in the remaining potato liquid and stir until wilted; season with salt and pepper. Drain and serve with potato mash. Garnish with black pepper and chives.

Cheesy Corn Casserole

Servings: 6
Cooking Time: 4 Hours
Ingredients:
- Nonstick cooking spray
- 1 ¾ lbs. corn
- 8 oz. cream cheese, cubed
- 1 cup cheddar cheese, grated
- ¼ cup butter, sliced
- ¼ cup heavy cream
- ½ tsp salt
- ¼ tsp pepper

Directions:
1. Spray the cooking pot with cooking spray.
2. Add all the ingredients to the cooking pot and stir to mix.
3. Add the lid and set to slow cook on low. Cook 3 ½ - 4 hours, stirring occasionally, until all the cheese has melted and casserole is hot. Stir well before serving.

Nutrition Info:
- Calories 420, Total Fat 31g, Total Carbs 29g, Protein 12g, Sodium 540mg.

Veggie Taco Soup

Servings: 6
Cooking Time: 4 Hours
Ingredients:
- Nonstick cooking spray
- 6 corn tortillas, cut in strips
- 3 ½ cups vegetable broth, low sodium
- 14 ½ oz. tomatoes, diced, undrained
- 15 oz. spicy chili beans, undrained
- 4 oz. green chilies, diced & drained
- ¾ cup onions, chopped
- 1 clove garlic, chopped fine
- 2 tsp red wine vinegar
- ¼ tsp crushed red pepper flakes
- ¼ cup cilantro, chopped
- ½ tsp salt

Directions:
1. Spray fryer basket with cooking spray. Add the tortilla strips and spray with cooking spray.
2. Add the tender-crisp lid and set to air fry on 375°F. Cook until crisp, about 5 minutes, turning every couple of minutes. Set aside.
3. Add all ingredients, except cilantro, salt, and tortillas, to the cooking pot, mix well.
4. Add the lid and set to slow cook on high. Cook 3-4 hours, stirring occasionally.
5. Add salt and cilantro and stir well. Ladle into bowls and top with tortilla strips. Serve.

Nutrition Info:
- Calories 172, Total Fat 1g, Total Carbs 33g, Protein 8g, Sodium 617mg.

Tomato Galette

Servings: 4
Cooking Time: 40 Minutes
Ingredients:
- ½ pound mixed tomatoes, cut into ¼-inch slices
- 3 inches of leek, thinly sliced
- 2 garlic cloves, diced
- Kosher salt
- 1 store-bought refrigerated pie crust
- 2 tablespoons bread crumbs
- 4 tablespoons shredded Parmesan cheese, divided
- 4 tablespoons shredded mozzarella, divided
- 1 egg, beaten
- Freshly ground black pepper

Directions:
1. Place the tomatoes, leeks, and garlic into large bowl. Sprinkle with salt and set aside for at least 5 minutes to draw out the juices from the vegetables.
2. Strain the excess juice off the tomato mixture and pat down the vegetables with paper towels.
3. Unroll the pie crust and place it in the Ninja Multi-Purpose Pan or a 1½-quart round ceramic baking dish and form it to the bottom of the pan. Lay the extra dough loosely on the sides of the pan.
4. Sprinkle the bread crumbs in a thin layer on the pie crust bottom, then scatter 3 tablespoons each of Parmesan and mozzarella cheese on top. Place the tomato mixture in a heap in the middle of the dough and top with the remaining 1 tablespoon each of Parmesan and mozzarella cheese.
5. Fold the edges of the crust over the tomatoes and brush with the egg.
6. Close crisping lid. Select BAKE/ROAST, set temperature to 350°F, and set time to 45 minutes. Select START/STOP to begin. Let preheat for 5 minutes.
7. Place pan on the Reversible Rack, making sure the rack is in the lower position. Cover galette loosely with aluminum foil (do not seal the pan).
8. Once unit has preheated, open lid and carefully place the rack with pan in the pot. Close crisping lid.
9. After 20 minutes, open lid and remove the foil. Close lid and continue cooking.
10. When cooking is complete, remove rack with pan and set aside to let cool. Cut into slices, season with pepper, and serve.

Nutrition Info:
- Calories: 288, Total Fat: 15g, Sodium: 409mg, Carbohydrates: 31g, Protein: 9g.

Zucchinis Spinach Fry

Servings: 4
Cooking Time: 17 Minutes
Ingredients:
- 2 zucchinis, sliced
- 1-pound baby spinach
- ½ cup tomato sauce
- Black pepper and salt
- 1 tablespoon avocado oil
- 1 red onion, chopped
- 1 tablespoon sweet paprika
- ½ teaspoon garlic powder
- ½ teaspoon chilli powder

Directions:
1. Set the Foodi on Sauté, stir in the oil, heat it up, add the onion and sauté for 2 minutes.
2. Add the zucchinis, spinach, and the other ingredients Put the Ninja Foodi's lid on and cook on High for 15 minutes.
3. Release the pressure quickly for 5 minutes, divide everything between plates and serve.

Nutrition Info:
- Calories: 130; Fat: 5.5g; Carbohydrates: 3.3g; Protein: 1g

Hawaiian Tofu

Servings: 6
Cooking Time: 3 Hours
Ingredients:
- 1 package extra firm tofu, cubed
- ¼ cup fresh pineapple, cubed
- ¼ cup tamari, low sodium
- 1 tbsp. sesame oil
- 1 tbsp. olive oil
- 1 tbsp. brown rice vinegar
- 2 cloves garlic, chopped
- 2 tsp fresh ginger, chopped
- 4 cups zucchini, chopped
- ¼ cup sesame seeds

Directions:
1. Add the tofu to the cooking pot.
2. Add the pineapple, soy sauce, sesame oil, olive oil, vinegar, garlic, and ginger to a food processor or blender. Process until smooth. Pour over tofu.
3. Add the lid and set to slow cook on low. Cook 3 hours, stirring occasionally.

4. During the last 15 minutes of cooking time, add the zucchini and sesame seeds to the pot and stir to combine. Serve over quinoa or rice.

Nutrition Info:
- Calories 164,Total Fat 13g,Total Carbs 5g,Protein 10g,Sodium 680mg.

Veggie Skewers

Servings: 4
Cooking Time: 20 Min
Ingredients:
- 2 boiled and mashed potatoes
- ¼ cup chopped fresh mint leaves /32.5g
- ⅔ cup canned beans /88g
- ⅓ cup grated carrots /44g
- ½ cup paneer /65g
- 1 green chili
- 1-inch piece of fresh ginger
- 3 garlic cloves
- 2 tbsp corn flour /30g
- ½ tsp garam masala powder /2.5g
- Salt, to taste

Directions:
1. Soak 12 skewers until ready to use. Place the beans, carrots, garlic, ginger, chili, paneer, and mint, in a food processor and process until smooth; transfer to a bowl.
2. Add the mashed potatoes, corn flour, some salt, and garam masala powder to the bowl. Mix until fully incorporated. Divide the mixture into 12 equal pieces.
3. Shape each of the pieces around a skewer. Close the crisping lid and cook the skewers for 10 minutes on Air Crisp mode at 390 °F or 199°C.

Rustic Veggie Tart

Servings: 6
Cooking Time: 40 Minutes
Ingredients:
- 1 tbsp. olive oil
- 3 cups cherry tomatoes
- ½ tsp salt, divided
- 1/8 tsp red pepper flakes
- 1 cup fresh corn kernels
- 1 zucchini, chopped
- 5-6 green onions, sliced thin
- 1 ¼ cups flour
- 8 tbsp. butter, sliced
- ¼ cup sour cream
- 2 tsp fresh lemon juice
- ¼ cup ice water
- ½ cup parmesan cheese
- 1 egg yolk
- 1 tsp water

Directions:
1. In a large bowl, combine flour and ¼ tsp salt. Cut in butter until mixture resembles coarse crumbs.
2. In a small bowl, whisk together sour cream, lemon juice, and water until combined. Add to flour mixture and stir until it forms a soft dough. Form dough into a ball and wrap with plastic wrap, refrigerate at least 1 hour.
3. Add oil to the cooking pot and set to sauté on med-high heat.
4. Add tomatoes, remaining salt, and red pepper flakes, cover and cook until tomatoes burst, turning tomatoes frequently.
5. Reduce heat to medium and add zucchini. Cook 2 minutes until they soften. Add corn and cook 1 minute more. Stir in scallions and turn off the heat. Transfer to a large plate and let cool.
6. Wipe out the cooking pot and add the rack.
7. On a floured surface, roll out dough to a 12-inch circle. Transfer to a piece of parchment paper.
8. Sprinkle vegetables with half the parmesan cheese and spoon into the center of the dough, leaving a 2-inch border. Sprinkle most of the remaining parmesan over the vegetables.
9. Fold edges over the filling, pleating as you go.
10. In a small bowl, beat together egg yolk and teaspoon of water. Brush the crust with egg yolk glaze and sprinkle with the last of the parmesan.
11. Carefully pick up the parchment paper and transfer to the rack in the cooking pot. Add the tender-crisp lid and set to bake on 400°F. Bake 30-40 minutes until golden brown. Transfer to wire rack to cool 5 minutes before serving.

Nutrition Info:
- Calories 159,Total Fat 10g,Total Carbs 14g,Protein 4g,Sodium 170mg.

Beets And Carrots

Servings: 4
Cooking Time: 20 Minutes
Ingredients:
- 1-pound beets, peeled and roughly cubed
- 1-pound baby carrots, peeled
- Black pepper and salt to the taste
- 2 tablespoons olive oil
- 1 tablespoon chives, minced

Directions:
1. In a suitable, mix the beets with the carrots and the other ingredients and toss.
2. Put the beets and carrots in the Foodi's basket.
3. Cook on Air Crisp at 390 °F for 20 minutes, divide between plates and serve.

Nutrition Info:
- Calories: 150; Fat: 4.5g; Carbohydrates: 7.3g; Protein: 3.6g

Roasted Vegetable Salad

Servings: 1
Cooking Time: 25 Min
Ingredients:
- 1 potato, peeled and chopped
- 1 cup cherry tomatoes/130g
- 1 carrot; sliced diagonally
- ½ small beetroot; sliced
- ¼ onion; sliced
- Juice of 1 lemon
- A handful of rocket salad
- A handful of baby spinach
- 2 tbsp olive oil /30ml
- 3 tbsp canned chickpeas /45g
- ½ tsp cumin /2.5g
- ½ tsp turmeric /2.5g
- ¼ tsp sea salt /1.25g
- Parmesan shavings

Directions:
1. Combine the onion, potato, cherry tomatoes, carrot, beetroot, cumin, seas salt, turmeric, and 1 tbsp olive oil, in a bowl. Place in the Ninja Foodi, close the crisping lid and cook for 20 minutes on Air Crisp mode at 370 °F or 188°C; let cool for 2 minutes.
2. Place the rocket, salad, spinach, lemon juice, and 1 tbsp olive oil, into a serving bowl. Mix to combine; stir in the roasted veggies.Top with chickpeas and Parmesan shavings.

Mushroom Risotto With Swiss Chard

Servings: 4
Cooking Time: 60 Min
Ingredients:
- 1 small bunch Swiss chard; chopped
- ½ cup sautéed mushrooms /65g
- ½ cup caramelized onions /65g
- ⅓ cup white wine /88ml
- 2 cups vegetable stock /500ml
- ⅓ cup grated Pecorino Romano cheese /44g
- 1 cup short grain rice /130g
- 3 tbsps ghee; divided /45g
- ½ tsp salt /2.5g

Directions:
1. Press Sear/Sauté and adjust to Medium. Press Start to preheat the inner pot. Melt 2 tbsps of ghee and sauté the Swiss chard for 5 minutes until wilted. Spoon into a bowl and set aside.
2. Use a paper towel to wipe out any remaining liquid in the pot and melt the remaining ghee. Stir in the rice and cook for about 1 minute.
3. Add the white wine and cook for 2 to 3 minutes, with occasional stirring until the wine has evaporated. Add in stock and salt; stir to combine.
4. Seal the pressure lid, choose Pressure; adjust the pressure to High and the cook time to 8 minutes; press Start. When the timer is done reading, perform a quick pressure release and carefully open the lid.
5. Stir in the mushrooms, swiss chard, and onions and let the risotto heat for 1 minute. Mix the cheese into the rice to melt, and adjust the taste with salt.Spoon the risotto into serving bowls and serve immediately.

Pesto With Cheesy Bread

Servings: 4
Cooking Time: 60 Min
Ingredients:
- 1 medium red onion; diced
- 1 celery stalk; diced
- 1 large carrot, peeled and diced
- 1 small yellow squash; diced
- 1 can chopped tomatoes /420g
- 1 can cannellini beans, rinsed and drained /810g
- 1 bay leaf

- 1 cup chopped zucchini /130g
- ¼ cup shredded Pecorino Romano cheese /32.5g
- ⅓ cup olive oil based pesto /88ml
- 3 cups water /750ml
- 1 Pecorino Romano rind
- 1 garlic clove, minced
- 4 slices white bread
- 3 tbsps butter; at room temperature /45g
- 3 tbsps ghee /45g
- 1 tsp mixed herbs /5g
- ¼ tsp cayenne pepper/1.25g
- ½ tsp salt /2.5g

Directions:

1. On your Foodi, choose Sear/Sauté, and adjust to Medium to preheat the inner pot. Press Start. Add the ghee to the pot to melt and sauté the onion, celery, and carrot for 3 minutes or until the vegetables start to soften.
2. Stir in the yellow squash, tomatoes, beans, water, zucchini, bay leaf, mixed herbs, cayenne pepper, salt, and Pecorino Romano rind.
3. Seal the pressure lid, choose Pressure, adjust to High, and set the time to 4 minutes. Press Start. In a bowl, mix the butter, shredded cheese, and garlic. Spread the mixture on the bread slices.
4. After cooking the soup, perform a natural pressure release for 2 minutes, then a quick pressure release and carefully open the lid.
5. Adjust the taste of the soup with salt and black pepper, and remove the bay leaf. Put the reversible rack in the upper position of the pot and lay the bread slices in the rack with the buttered-side up.
6. Close the crisping lid. Choose Broil; adjust the cook time to 5 minutes, and Press Start/Stop to begin broiling.
7. When the bread is crispy, carefully remove the rack, and set aside. Ladle the soup into serving bowls and drizzle the pesto over. Serve with the garlic toasts.

Veggie Loaded Pasta

Servings:8
Cooking Time: 2 Minutes
Ingredients:

- 1 box dry pasta, such as rigatoni or penne
- 4 cups water
- 2 tablespoons extra-virgin olive oil, divided
- 2 teaspoons kosher salt, divided
- 3 avocados
- Juice of 2 limes
- 2 tablespoons minced cilantro
- 1 red onion, chopped
- 1 cup cherry tomatoes, halved
- 4 heaping cups spinach, half an 11-ounce container
- ¼ cup shredded Parmesan cheese, divided
- Freshly ground black pepper, for serving

Directions:

1. Place the pasta, water, 1 tablespoon of olive oil, and 1 teaspoon of salt in the pot. Stir to incorporate. Assemble pressure lid, making sure the pressure release valve is in the SEAL position.
2. Select PRESSURE and set to LO. Set time to 2 minutes. Select START/STOP to begin.
3. While pasta is cooking, place the avocados in a medium-sized mixing bowl and mash well with a wooden spatula until a thick paste forms. Add all remaining ingredients to the bowl and mix well to combine.
4. When pressure cooking is complete, allow pressure to naturally release for 10 minutes. After 10 minutes, quick release remaining pressure by moving the pressure release valve to the VENT position. Carefully remove lid when unit has finished releasing pressure.
5. If necessary, strain pasta to remove any residual water and return pasta to pot. Add avocado mixture to pot and stir.
6. Garnish pasta with Parmesan cheese and black pepper, as desired, then serve.

Nutrition Info:

- Calories: 372,Total Fat: 16g,Sodium: 149mg,Carbohydrates: 49g,Protein: 11g.

Spicy Salmon With Wild Rice

Servings: 4
Cooking Time: 50 Min
Ingredients:

- 1 cup wild rice /130g
- 1 cup vegetable stock /250ml
- 2 limes, juiced
- 2 jalapeño peppers, seeded and diced
- 4 garlic cloves, minced
- 4 skinless salmon fillets
- A bunch of asparagus, trimmed and cut diagonally
- 2 tbsps chopped fresh parsley /30g
- 3 tbsps olive oil; divided /45ml
- 2 tbsps honey /30ml
- 1 tsp sweet paprika /5g

- 1 tsp salt /5g
- 1 tsp freshly ground black pepper /5g

Directions:

1. Pour the brown rice and vegetable stock in the pot; stir to combine. Put the reversible rack in the pot in the higher position and lay the salmon fillets on the rack.
2. Seal the pressure lid, choose Pressure, set to High, and set the time to 2 minutes; press Start. In a bowl, toss the broccoli with 1 tbsp of olive oil and season with the salt and black pepper. In another bowl, evenly combine the remaining oil, the lime juice, honey, paprika, jalapeño, garlic, and parsley.
3. When done cooking, do a quick pressure release, and carefully open the pressure lid.
4. Pat the salmon dry with a paper towel and coat the fish with the honey sauce while reserving a little for garnishing.
5. Arrange the asparagus around the salmon. Close the crisping lid; choose Broil and set the time to 7 minutes. Choose Start/Stop.
6. When ready, remove the salmon from the rack. Dish the salmon with asparagus and rice. Garnish with parsley and remaining sauce. Serve immediately.

Mushroom Poutine

Servings:4
Cooking Time: 46 Minutes

Ingredients:

- 2 tablespoons unsalted butter
- 1 small yellow onion, diced
- 1 garlic clove, minced
- 8 ounces cremini mushrooms, sliced
- ¼ cup red wine
- 3 cups vegetable stock
- ¼ cup all-purpose flour
- Kosher salt
- Freshly ground black pepper
- 1 pound frozen French fries
- 8 ounces Cheddar cheese, cubed

Directions:

1. Select SEAR/SAUTÉ and set to MED. Select START/STOP to begin. Let preheat for 3 minutes.
2. Add the butter, onion, and garlic. Cook, stirring occasionally, for 5 minutes. Add the mushrooms and sauté for 5 minutes. Add the wine and let it simmer and reduce for 3 minutes.
3. In large bowl, slowly whisk together the stock and flour. Whisk this mixture into the vegetables in the pot. Cook the gravy for 10 minutes. Season with salt and pepper. Transfer the gravy to a medium bowl and set aside. Clean out the pot and return to unit.
4. Insert Cook & Crisp Basket and add the French fries. Close crisping lid.
5. Select AIR CRISP, set temperature to 360°F, and set time to 18 minutes. Select START/STOP to begin.
6. Every 5 minutes, open lid and remove and shake basket to ensure even cooking.
7. Once cooking is complete, remove fries from basket and place in the pot. Add the cheese and stir. Cover with the gravy. Close crisping lid.
8. Select AIR CRISP, set temperature to 375°F, and set time 5 minutes. Select START/STOP to begin.
9. When cooking is complete, serve immediately.

Nutrition Info:

- Calories: 550,Total Fat: 32g,Sodium: 941mg,Carbohydrates: 42g,Protein: 20g.

Spicy Kimchi And Tofu Fried Rice

Servings:6
Cooking Time: 30 Minutes

Ingredients:

- 1 cup Texmati brown rice
- 1¼ cups water
- 2 tablespoons canola oil
- 2 garlic cloves, minced
- 1 tablespoon minced fresh ginger
- 8 ounces extra-firm tofu, cut into ½-inch squares
- ½ cup frozen peas and carrots
- 1 large egg, beaten
- ½ cup kimchi, chopped
- 2 scallions, sliced thin
- ¼ cup basil, coarsely chopped
- 1 tablespoon soy sauce
- Kosher salt
- Freshly ground black pepper

Directions:

1. Rinse the rice under cold running water in a fine-mesh strainer.
2. Place the rice and water in the pot. Assemble pressure lid, making sure the pressure release valve is in the SEAL position.
3. Select PRESSURE and set to HI. Set time to 2 minutes. Select START/STOP to begin.
4. When pressure cooking is complete, allow pressure to naturally release for 10 minutes. After 10 minutes, quick

release remaining pressure by moving the pressure release valve to the VENT position. Carefully remove lid when unit has finished releasing pressure.
5. Evenly layer the rice on a sheet pan and refrigerate until cool, preferably overnight.
6. Select SEAR/SAUTÉ and set to HI. Select START/STOP to begin. Add the canola oil and let heat for 5 minutes.
7. Add the garlic and ginger and cook for 1 minute. Add the tofu, rice, and peas and carrots, and cook for 5 minutes, stirring occasionally.
8. Move the rice to one side and add the egg to empty side of pot. Cook 30 seconds, stirring occasionally to scramble it. Add the kimchi, scallions, basil, and soy sauce, and stir. Cook for 5 minutes, stirring frequently.
9. Season with salt, pepper, and more soy sauce, if needed. Serve.

Nutrition Info:
- Calories: 229,Total Fat: 9g,Sodium: 928mg,Carbohydrates: 30g,Protein: 8g.

Balsamic Cabbage With Endives

Servings: 4
Cooking Time: 15 Minutes
Ingredients:
- 1 green cabbage head, shredded
- 2 endives, trimmed and sliced lengthwise
- Black pepper and salt to the taste
- 1 tablespoon olive oil
- 2 shallots, chopped
- ½ cup chicken stock
- 1 tablespoon sweet paprika
- 1 tablespoon balsamic vinegar

Directions:
1. Set the Foodi on Sauté mode, stir in the oil, heat it up, add the shallots and sauté for 2 minutes.
2. Add the cabbage, the endives and the other ingredients.
3. Put the Ninja Foodi's lid on and cook on High for 13 minutes.
4. Release the pressure quickly for 5 minutes, divide the mix between plates and serve.

Nutrition Info:
- Calories: 120; Fat: 2g; Carbohydrates: 3.3g; Protein: 4

Grilled Cheese

Servings: 2
Cooking Time: 40 Minutes

Ingredients:
- 1 small cauliflower, cut in florets
- ½ cup mozzarella cheese, low fat, grated
- 1 egg
- ¼ tsp onion powder
- ¼ tsp pepper
- ½ cup sharp cheddar cheese, low fat, grated
- 1 tbsp. butter, soft, divided

Directions:
1. Place the cauliflower in a food processor and pulsed until finely chopped.
2. Place in a microwave safe bowl and microwave 8-9 minutes or until soft. Place in a strainer and press out any excess water.
3. Add the cauliflower to a large bowl and add mozzarella, egg, onion powder, salt, and pepper and mix well.
4. Add the rack to the cooking pot. Lay out a sheet of parchment paper and spread cauliflower mixture on it. Shape into 4 equal squares.
5. Place the parchment paper on the rack and add the tender-crisp lid. Set to bake on 400°F. Bake 15-20 minutes or until golden brown. Remove from cooking pot.
6. Add 1 teaspoon to the cooking pot and set to sauté on med-low heat.
7. Sprinkle cheese evenly on 2 cauliflower squares and top with remaining squares. Place in the cooking pot and spread remaining butter over top.
8. Cook 2-4 minutes until golden brown, flip and cook another 2-4 minutes until cheese is melted. Serve.

Nutrition Info:
- Calories 394,Total Fat 28g,Total Carbs 9g,Protein 28g,Sodium 696mg.

Zucchini Quinoa Stuffed Red Peppers

Servings: 4
Cooking Time: 40 Min

Ingredients:
- 1 small zucchini; chopped
- 4 red bell peppers
- 2 large tomatoes; chopped
- 1 small onion; chopped
- 2 cloves garlic, minced
- 1 cup quinoa, rinsed /130g
- 1 cup grated Gouda cheese /130g
- ½ cup chopped mushrooms /65g

- 1 ½ cup water /375ml
- 2 cups chicken broth /500ml
- 1 tbsp olive oil /15ml
- ½ tsp smoked paprika /2.5g
- Salt and black pepper to taste

Directions:

1. Select Sear/Sauté mode on High. Once it is ready, add the olive oil to heat and then add the onion and garlic. Sauté for 3 minutes to soften, stirring occasionally.
2. Include the tomatoes, cook for 3 minutes and then add the quinoa, zucchinis, and mushrooms. Season with paprika, salt, and black pepper and stir with a spoon. Cook for 5 to 7 minutes, then, turn the pot off.
3. Use a knife to cut the bell peppers in halves (lengthwise) and remove their seeds and stems.
4. Spoon the quinoa mixture into the bell peppers. Put the peppers in a greased baking dish and pour the broth over.
5. Wipe the pot clean with some paper towels, and pour the water into it. After, fit the steamer rack at the bottom of the pot.
6. Place the baking dish on top of the reversible rack, cover with aluminum foil, close the lid, secure the pressure valve, and select Pressure mode on High pressure for 15 minutes. Press Start/Stop.
7. Once the timer has ended, do a quick pressure release and open the lid. Remove the aluminum foil and sprinkle with the gouda cheese.
8. Close the crisping lid, select Bake/Roast mode and cook for 10 minutes on 375 °F or 191°C. Arrange the stuffed peppers on a serving platter and serve right away or as a side to a meat dish.

Veggie Lasagna

Servings: 4
Cooking Time: 35 Minutes

Ingredients:

- Nonstick cooking spray
- 2 Portobello mushrooms, sliced ¼-inch thick
- 1 eggplant, cut lengthwise in 6 slices
- 1 yellow squash, cut lengthwise in 4 slices
- 1 red bell pepper, cut in ½-inch strips
- ½ tsp garlic powder
- ½ tsp salt
- ½ tsp black pepper
- ½ cup ricotta cheese, fat free, divided
- 2 tbsp. fresh basil, chopped, divided
- ¾ cup mozzarella cheese, grated fine, divided
- ¼ cup tomato sauce

Directions:

1. Spray the cooking pot and rack with cooking spray.
2. Place a single layer of vegetables in the cooking pot. Add the rack and place remaining vegetables on it. Season vegetables with garlic powder, salt, and pepper.
3. Add the tender-crisp lid and set to roast on 425°F. Cook vegetables 15-20 minutes until tender, stirring halfway through cooking time. Transfer to a large plate.
4. Spray an 8x8-inch baking pan with cooking spray.
5. Line the bottom of the pan with 3 slices of eggplant. Spread ¼ cup ricotta cheese, 1 tablespoon basil, and ¼ cup mozzarella over eggplant.
6. Layer with remaining vegetables, then remaining ricotta, basil and ¼ cup mozzarella on top. End with 3 slices of eggplant and pour tomato sauce over then sprinkle remaining cheese over the top.
7. Add the rack back to the cooking pot and place the lasagna on it. Add the tender-crisp lid and set to bake on 350°F. Bake 15-20 minutes until cheese is melted and lasagna is heated through, serve.

Nutrition Info:

- Calories 145,Total Fat 3g,Total Carbs 18g,Protein 14g,Sodium 490mg.

Pasta With Roasted Veggies

Servings: 6
Cooking Time: 25 Min

Ingredients:

- 1 lb. penne, cooked /450g
- 1 acorn squash; sliced
- 4 oz. mushrooms; sliced /120g
- 1 zucchini; sliced
- 1 pepper; sliced
- 1 cup grape tomatoes, halved /130g
- ½ cup kalamata olives, pitted, halved /65g
- ¼ cup olive oil /62.5ml
- 3 tbsp balsamic vinegar /45ml
- 2 tbsp chopped basil /30g
- 1 tsp Italian seasoning /5g
- Salt and pepper, to taste

Directions:

1. Combine the pepper, zucchini, squash, mushrooms, and olive oil, in a large bowl. Season with salt and pepper. Close the crisping lid and cook the veggies for 15 minutes on Air Crisp mode at 380 °F or 194°C.

2. In a large bowl, combine the penne, roasted vegetables, olives, tomatoes, Italian seasoning, and vinegar. Sprinkle basil and serve.

Baked Linguine

Servings: 8
Cooking Time: 30 Minutes
Ingredients:
- 1 tbsp. olive oil
- 1 zucchini, cut in 1-inch pieces
- 1 red bell pepper, cut in 1-inch pieces
- 1 eggplant, cut in 1-inch pieces
- 26 oz. light spaghetti sauce
- 1 cup salsa
- 1 lb. linguine, cooked & drained
- ¾ cup mozzarella cheese, grated

Directions:
1. Add the oil to the cooking pot and set to sauté on med-high heat.
2. Add the zucchini, pepper, and eggplant and cook, stirring occasionally, until tender, about 6-8 minutes.
3. Stir in spaghetti sauce and salsa until combined. Add linguine and mix well. Sprinkle cheese over the top.
4. Add the tender-crisp lid and set to bake on 350°F. Bake 25-30 minutes until cheese is melted and linguine is heated through. Serve.

Nutrition Info:
- Calories 200, Total Fat 4g, Total Carbs 33g, Protein 9g, Sodium 698mg.

Veggie And Quinoa Stuffed Peppers

Servings: 1
Cooking Time: 16 Min
Ingredients:
- ¼ cup cooked quinoa /32.5g
- ½ diced tomato, plus one tomato slice
- 1 bell pepper
- ½ tbsp diced onion /7.5g
- 1 tsp olive oil /5ml
- ¼ tsp smoked paprika/1.25g
- ¼ tsp dried basil /1.25g
- Salt and pepper, to taste

Directions:
1. Core and clean the bell pepper to prepare it for stuffing. Brush the pepper with half of the olive oil on the outside.
2. In a small bowl, combine all of the other Ingredients, except the tomato slice and reserved half-tsp olive oil. Stuff the pepper with the filling. Top with the tomato slice.
3. Brush the tomato slice with the remaining half-tsp of oil and sprinkle with basil. Close the crisping lid and cook for 10 minutes on Air Crisp mode at 350 °F or 177°C.

Green Cream Soup

Servings: 4
Cooking Time: 22 Min
Ingredients:
- ½ lb. kale leaves; chopped /225g
- ½ lb. Swiss chard leaves; chopped /225g
- ½ lb. spinach leaves; chopped /225g
- 1 onion; chopped
- 4 cloves garlic, minced
- 4 cups vegetable broth /1000ml
- 1 ¼ cup heavy cream /312.5ml
- 1 tbsp olive oil /15ml
- 1 ½ tbsp white wine vinegar/ 22.5ml
- Salt and pepper, to taste
- Chopped Peanuts to garnish

Directions:
1. Turn on the Ninja Foodi and select Sear/Sauté mode on Medium. Add the olive oil, once it has heated add the onion and garlic and sauté for 2-3 minutes until soft. Add greens and vegetable broth.
2. Close the lid, secure the pressure valve, and select Pressure mode on High pressure for 10 minutes. Press Start/Stop. Once the timer has ended, do a quick pressure release.
3. Add the white wine vinegar, salt, and pepper. Use a stick blender to puree the Ingredients in the pot. Close the crisping lid and cook for 3 minutes on Broil mode. Stir in the heavy cream. Spoon the soup into bowls, sprinkle with peanuts, and serve.

Red Beans And Rice

Servings: 4
Cooking Time: 1 Hr
Ingredients:
- 1 cup red beans, rinsed and stones removed /130g
- ½ cup rice, rinsed /65g
- 1 ½ cup vegetable broth /375ml
- 1 onion; diced
- 1 red bell pepper; diced

- 1 stalk celery; diced
- 1 tbsp fresh thyme leaves, or to taste /15g
- 2 tbsps olive oil /30ml
- ½ tsp cayenne pepper /2.5g
- water as needed
- salt and freshly ground black pepper to taste

Directions:

1. Into the pot, add beans and water to cover about 1-inch. Seal the pressure lid, choose Pressure, set to High, and set the timer to 1 minute. Press Start. When ready, release the pressure quickly. Drain the beans and set aside. Rinse and pat dry the inner pot.

2. Return inner pot to pressure cooker, add oil to the pot and press Sear/Sauté. Add onion to the oil and cook for 3 minutes until soft. Add celery and pepper and cook for 1 to 2 minutes until fragrant. Add garlic and cook for 30 seconds until soft; add rice.

3. Transfer the beans back into inner pot and top with broth. Stir black pepper, thyme, cayenne pepper, and salt into mixture. Seal the pressure lid, choose Pressure, set to High, and set the timer to 15 minutes. Press Start.

4. When ready, release pressure quickly. Add more thyme, black pepper and salt as desired.

Asparagus With Feta

Servings: 4
Cooking Time: 15 Min

Ingredients:

- 1-pound asparagus spears, ends trimmed /450g
- 1 lemon, cut into wedges
- 1 cup feta cheese; cubed /130g
- 1 cup water /250ml
- 1 tbsp olive oil /15ml
- salt and freshly ground black pepper to taste

Directions:

1. Into the pot, add water and set trivet over the water. Place steamer basket on the trivet. Place the asparagus into the steamer basket. Seal the pressure lid, choose Pressure, set to High, and set the timer to 1 minute. Press Start.

2. When ready, release the pressure quickly. Add olive oil in a bowl and toss in asparagus until well coated; season with pepper and salt. Serve alongside feta cheese and lemon wedges.

Hot & Sour Soup

Servings: 5
Cooking Time: 20 Minutes

Ingredients:

- 3 ½ cups chicken broth, low sodium, divided
- ½ lb. firm tofu, cut in 1-inch cubes
- ¼ lb. mushrooms, sliced
- 3 tbsp. soy sauce, low sodium
- 3 tbsp. vinegar
- 1 tsp ginger
- ½ tsp pepper
- 2 tbsp. cornstarch
- 1 egg, lightly beaten
- ½ cup fresh bean sprouts
- ½ tsp sesame oil

Directions:

1. Add 3 ¼ cups broth, tofu, mushrooms, soy sauce, vinegar, ginger, and pepper to the cooking pot and stir well.

2. Set to sauté on medium heat and bring to a boil.

3. In a small bowl, whisk together remaining broth and cornstarch until smooth. Reduce heat to low and whisk in cornstarch mixture until thickened.

4. Slowly stir in egg to form egg "ribbons". Add bean sprouts and simmer 1-2 minutes or until heated through. Stir in sesame oil and serve immediately.

5. Slowly stir in egg to form egg strands. Add bean sprouts and simmer 1 to 2 minutes, or until heated through, stirring occasionally.

Nutrition Info:

- Calories 123,Total Fat 6g,Total Carbs 8g,Protein 11g,Sodium 978mg.

Italian Spinach & Tomato Soup

Servings: 6
Cooking Time: 4 Hours

Ingredients:

- 1 tsp olive oil
- 1 onion, chopped
- 3 cloves garlic, chopped fine
- 3 large tomatoes, chopped
- 2 tsp Italian seasoning
- 28 oz. vegetable broth, low sodium
- 10 oz. fresh spinach, trimmed
- ½ tsp pepper
- 2 tbsp. parmesan cheese

Directions:

1. Add the oil to the cooking pot and set to sauté on med-high.

2. Add the onion and garlic and cook, stirring occasionally, 5 minutes or until onion starts to brown.

3. Stir in remaining ingredients, except spinach and parmesan, and mix well. Add the lid and set to slow cook on high. Cook 3-4 hours until tomatoes are tender. Stir occasionally.

4. Add the spinach and cook until it wilts. Ladle into bowls and sprinkle with parmesan. Serve.

Nutrition Info:
- Calories 60,Total Fat 2g,Total Carbs 10g,Protein 3g,Sodium 602mg.

Cheesy Squash Tart

Servings: 8
Cooking Time: 45 Minutes
Ingredients:
- 1 spaghetti squash
- 2 tbsp. olive oil
- 2 eggs
- 1/3 cup + 2 tbsp. parmesan cheese, divided
- 1 cup ricotta cheese, fat free
- 1 clove garlic, chopped fine
- 2 tsp Italian seasoning
- ¼ tsp salt
- 1 cup light spaghetti sauce
- ½ cup mozzarella cheese, low fat, grated

Directions:

1. Place enough water in the cooking pot to reach 1-inch up sides. Add the squash, whole. Add the lid and set to pressure cook on high. Set timer for 13 minutes.

2. When timer goes off, use natural release to remove the pressure. Squash should be tender. Transfer to a cutting board and let cool 15-20 minutes.

3. Add the rack to the cooking pot. Spray an 8-inch deep-dish pie plate with cooking spray.

4. In a large bowl, combine oil, eggs, and 1/3 cup parmesan cheese, mix well.

5. Cut the squash in half lengthwise and remove the seeds. Use a fork to scrape out the flesh and add it to the egg mixture, mix well.

6. Pour the squash mixture into the prepared pie dish and press on the bottom and up sides to form a "crust".

7. In a small bowl, combine the ricotta, garlic, Italian seasoning, and salt and mix well. Spread evenly in the crust and top with spaghetti sauce.

8. Place the dish on the rack and add the tender-crisp lid. Set to bake on 325°F. Bake 25 minutes. Open the lid and sprinkle the remaining cheese over the top. Bake another 5 minutes or until the cheese melts. Let tart rest 10 minutes before serving.

Nutrition Info:
- Calories 170,Total Fat 9g,Total Carbs 13g,Protein 10g,Sodium 277mg.

Warming Harvest Soup

Servings: 6
Cooking Time: 20 Minutes
Ingredients:
- 3 tbsp. butter, unsalted
- ½ cup onion, chopped
- 2 sprigs thyme, stems removed
- 2 lb. butternut squash, peeled & cut in 1-inch pieces
- 1 tsp sugar
- ½ tsp salt
- 4 cups water
- 2 tbsp. milk

Directions:

1. Add butter to the cooking pot and set to sauté on medium heat.

2. Once butter has melted, add onion and thyme and cook until onion is soft, about 5 minutes.

3. Add squash, sugar, and salt and cook, stirring occasionally 3 minutes. Stir in water.

4. Add the lid and set to pressure cook on high. Set the timer for 10 minutes. When the timer goes off, use quick release to remove the pressure.

5. Transfer soup to a blender in batches and process until smooth. Return the soup back to the pot.

6. Set back to sauté on medium heat. Stir in milk and cook 3-5 minutes until heated through. Serve.

Nutrition Info:
- Calories 129,Total Fat 6g,Total Carbs 19g,Protein 2g,Sodium 206mg.

Pasta Primavera

Servings: 6
Cooking Time: 18 Minutes
Ingredients:
- ½ red onion, sliced
- 1 carrot, thinly sliced
- 1 head broccoli, cut into florets
- 1 red bell pepper, thinly sliced
- 1 yellow squash, halved lengthwise and sliced into half moons
- 1 zucchini, halved lengthwise and sliced into half moons
- ¼ cup extra-virgin olive oil
- ½ teaspoon dried basil
- ½ teaspoon dried oregano
- ½ teaspoon dried parsley
- ¼ teaspoon dried rosemary
- ¼ teaspoon crushed red pepper flakes
- 1 box penne pasta
- 4 cups water
- 2 tablespoons freshly squeezed lemon juice
- ½ cup grated Parmesan cheese, divided

Directions:
1. Place Cook & Crisp Basket in pot. Close crisping lid. Select AIR CRISP, set temperature to 390°F, and set time to 5 minutes. Select START/STOP to begin preheating.
2. In a large bowl, combine the red onion, carrot, broccoli, bell pepper, yellow squash, zucchini, olive oil, basil, oregano, parsley, rosemary, and red pepper flakes, and toss to combine.
3. Once unit has preheated, add the vegetable mixture to the basket. Close lid.
4. Select AIR CRISP, set temperature to 390°F, and set time to 15 minutes. Select START/STOP to begin.
5. When cooking is complete, remove the vegetables and basket, and set aside.
6. Add the pasta and water. Assemble pressure lid, making sure the pressure release valve is in the SEAL position.
7. Select PRESSURE and set to HI. Set time to 3 minutes. Select START/STOP to begin.
8. When pressure cooking is complete, allow pressure to naturally release for 10 minutes. After 10 minutes, quick release remaining pressure by moving the pressure release valve to the VENT position. Carefully remove lid when unit has finished releasing pressure.
9. Add vegetables to pasta. Add the lemon juice and ¼ cup of Parmesan cheese and stir. Serve and top with remaining cheese.

Nutrition Info:
- Calories: 388, Total Fat: 12g, Sodium: 127mg, Carbohydrates: 60g, Protein: 15g.

Cheesy Corn Pudding

Servings: 6
Cooking Time: 3 Hours
Ingredients:
- 10 oz. corn, thawed & divided
- 1 cup milk
- 2 tbsp. flour
- ½ tsp cumin
- 1 tsp salt
- ¼ tsp pepper
- 3 eggs, lightly beaten
- 2 cups Monterey Jack cheese, grated
- 1 jalapeno pepper, seeded & chopped fine

Directions:
1. Add ¾ cup corn, milk, flour, cumin, salt, and pepper to a food processor or blender. Pulse until smooth.
2. Spray the cooking pot with cooking spray.
3. Pour the corn mixture into the pot then stir in remaining ingredients until combined.
4. Add the lid and set to slow cook on low. Cook 3 hours or until pudding is set. Serve hot.

Nutrition Info:
- Calories 298, Total Fat 18g, Total Carbs 17g, Protein 17g, Sodium 707mg.

Hearty Veggie Soup

Servings: 12
Cooking Time: 15 Minutes
Ingredients:
- 2 cups water
- 3 ½ cups vegetable broth, low sodium
- 15 oz. red kidney beans, drained & rinsed
- 16 oz. cannellini beans, drained & rinsed
- 28 oz. tomatoes, crushed
- 10 oz. spinach, chopped
- 1 onion, chopped
- 10 oz. mixed vegetables, frozen
- 1 tsp garlic powder
- ½ tsp pepper

- 1 cup elbow macaroni

Directions:
1. Set the cooker to sauté on med-high heat.
2. Add all the ingredients, except macaroni, and stir to combine. Bring to a boil.
3. Stir in macaroni. Add the lid and set to pressure cook on high. Set timer for 10 minutes. When timer goes off, use natural release to remove the pressure. Stir well and serve.

Nutrition Info:
- Calories 181,Total Fat 1g,Total Carbs 34g,Protein 10g,Sodium 478mg.

Spanish Rice

Servings: 4
Cooking Time: 50 Min
Ingredients:
- 1 small onion; chopped
- 1 can pinto beans, drained and rinsed /480g
- 2 garlic cloves, minced
- 1 banana pepper, seeded and chopped
- ¼ cup stewed tomatoes /32.5g
- ½ cup vegetable stock /125ml
- 1 cup jasmine rice /130g
- ⅓ cup red salsa /88g
- 3 tbsps ghee /45g
- 1 tbsp chopped fresh parsley /15g
- 1 tsp Mexican Seasoning Mix /5g
- 1 tsp salt /5g

Directions:
1. On your Foodi, choose Sear/Sauté and adjust to Medium. Press Start to preheat the inner pot. Add the ghee to melt until no longer foaming and cook the onion, garlic, and banana pepper in the ghee. Cook for 2 minutes or until fragrant.
2. Stir in the rice, salsa, tomato sauce, vegetable stock, Mexican seasoning, pinto beans, and salt. Seal the pressure lid, choose Pressure and adjust the pressure to High and the cook time to 6 minutes; press Start.
3. After cooking, do a natural pressure release for 10 minutes. Stir in the parsley, dish the rice, and serve.

Southern Pineapple Casserole

Servings: 8
Cooking Time: 35 Minutes
Ingredients:
- Nonstick cooking spray
- 1/3 cup butter, soft
- 1/4 cup Stevia
- 2 eggs
- 2 egg whites
- 1 tsp vanilla
- 2 tbsp. flour
- 20 oz. crushed pineapple in juice, drained; reserve 1 cup liquid
- 5 slices whole-wheat bread, cubed

Directions:
1. Spray the cooking pot with cooking spray.
2. In a large bowl, beat butter and Stevia until smooth and creamy.
3. Beat in eggs, egg whites, and vanilla until combined.
4. Stir in flour, pineapple, and reserved juice and mix well.
5. Add bread and toss to coat. Pour into cooking pot.
6. Add tender-crisp lid and set to bake on 350°F. Bake 30-35 minutes or until a knife inserted in center comes out clean. Serve warm.

Nutrition Info:
- Calories 191,Total Fat 10g,Total Carbs 29g,Protein 5g,Sodium 183mg.

Saucy Kale

Servings: 4
Cooking Time: 15 Minutes
Ingredients:
- 1-pound kale, torn
- 2 leeks, sliced
- 2 tablespoons balsamic vinegar
- 1 tablespoon parsley, chopped
- Black pepper and salt to the taste
- 2 shallots, chopped
- ½ cup tomato sauce

Directions:
1. In your Ninja Foodi, combine the kale with the leeks and the other ingredients.
2. Put the Ninja Foodi's lid on and cook on High for 15 minutes.
3. Release the pressure quickly for 5 minutes, divide the mix between plates and serve.

Nutrition Info:
- Calories: 100; Fat: 2g; Carbohydrates: 3.4g; Protein: 4g

Radish Apples Salad

Servings: 4
Cooking Time: 15 Minutes
Ingredients:
- 1-pound radishes, roughly cubed
- 2 apples, cored and cut into wedges
- ¼ cup chicken stock
- 2 spring onions, chopped
- 3 tablespoons tomato paste
- Juice of 1 lime
- Cooking spray
- 1 tablespoon cilantro, chopped

Directions:
1. In your Ninja Foodi, combine the radishes with the apples and the other ingredients.
2. Put the Ninja Foodi's lid on and cook on High for 15 minutes.
3. Release the pressure quickly for 5 minutes, divide everything between plates and serve.

Nutrition Info:
- Calories: 122; Fat: 5g; Carbohydrates: 4.5g; Protein: 3g

Zucchini Rice Gratin

Servings: 6
Cooking Time: 1 Hour
Ingredients:
- Nonstick cooking spray
- 5 tbsp. olive oil, divided
- 1 onion, chopped fine
- 2 cloves garlic, chopped fine
- ½ cup rice
- ½ tsp salt
- ¼ tsp pepper
- 2 ½ lbs. zucchini, trimmed & grated
- ½ cup vegetable broth, low sodium
- 2/3 cup parmesan cheese, divided

Directions:
1. Spray a 2-qt. baking dish with cooking spray.
2. Add 3 tablespoons of the oil to the cooking pot and set to sauté on medium heat.
3. Add the onions and cook until translucent, about 8-10 minutes. Increase heat to med-high and cook until lightly browned, stirring. Stir in garlic and cook 1 minute more.
4. Add the rice and cook, stirring for 2 minutes. Season with salt and pepper. Add to zucchini in a large bowl and mix well.
5. Stir in broth and all but 2 tablespoons of the cheese. Transfer to prepared dish and cover with foil.
6. Place the rack in the pot and place the dish on it. Add the tender-crisp lid and set to bake on 325°F. Bake 50-60 minutes or until rice is tender.
7. Remove foil and drizzle top with remaining oil and cheese. Set to broil, broil 2-3 minutes until top is golden brown and cheese is melted. Serve.

Nutrition Info:
- Calories 113,Total Fat 8g,Total Carbs 8g,Protein 3g,Sodium 187mg.

Mushroom Leek Soup With Parmesan Croutons

Servings: 4
Cooking Time: 15 Minutes
Ingredients:
- 4 slices brioche bread, cut in ¼-inch cubes
- 2 tbsp. olive oil
- 2 tbsp. parmesan cheese
- 2 tsp pepper
- 3 tbsp. butter
- 4 leeks, trimmed, sliced ½-inch thick
- 4 cups cremini mushrooms, sliced
- ½ cup white wine
- 3 tbsp. flour
- 4 cups chicken broth, low sodium
- 2/3 cup milk
- ½ tsp salt

Directions:
1. In a large bowl, combine bread, olive oil, parmesan, and pepper, toss to coat bread.
2. Set cooker to sauté on medium heat. Add the bread and cook, stirring frequently, until toasted, about 5 minutes. Transfer to a plate.
3. Add the butter to the cooking pot and let it melt. Add the leeks and cook 5 minutes or until translucent. Add the mushrooms and cook another 5 minutes.
4. Stir in wine scraping up any browned bits on the bottom of the pan. Cook just until liquid is almost evaporated then stir in flour for 1 minute.
5. Add the broth, stirring until no lumps remain. Add the milk and salt and let simmer 5 minutes.
6. Use an immersion blender, or transfer to a blender, and process until almost smooth. Ladle into bowls and top with croutons. Serve.

Nutrition Info:

- Calories 94,Total Fat 5g,Total Carbs 8g,Protein 3g,Sodium 61mg.

Pepper And Sweet Potato Skewers

Servings: 1
Cooking Time: 20 Min
Ingredients:
- 1 large sweet potato
- 1 green bell pepper
- 1 beetroot
- 1 tbsp olive oil /15ml
- 1 tsp chili flakes /5g
- ¼ tsp black pepper /1.25g
- ½ tsp turmeric /2.5g
- ¼ tsp garlic powder /2.5g
- ¼ tsp paprika /2.5g

Directions:
1. Soak 3 to 4 skewers until ready to use. Peel the veggies and cut them into bite-sized chunks. Place the chunks in a bowl along with the remaining Ingredients Mix until fully coated. Thread the veggies in this order: potato, pepper, beetroot.
2. Place in the Ninja Foodi, close the crisping lid and cook for 15 minutes on Air Crisp mode at 350 °F or 177°C; flip skewers halfway through.

Desserts Recipes

Peanut Butter Pie

Servings:8
Cooking Time: 30 Minutes
Ingredients:
- 10 peanut butter cookies, crushed
- 3 tablespoons unsalted butter, melted
- 2 packages cream cheese, at room temperature
- ¾ cup granulated sugar
- 2 eggs
- ⅓ cup creamy peanut butter
- 10 chocolate peanut butter cups, chopped
- 2 cups water
- 1 tub whipped cream topping

Directions:
1. In a small bowl, mix together peanut butter cookie crumbs and melted butter. Press the mixture into the bottom of the Ninja Multi-Purpose Pan or 8-inch baking dish.
2. In a medium bowl, use an electric hand mixer to combine the cream cheese, sugar, eggs, and peanut butter. Mix on medium speed for 5 minutes.
3. Place the chopped chocolate peanut butter cups evenly on top of crust in the pan. Pour the batter on top. Cover tightly with aluminum foil.
4. Place the water in the pot. Insert Reversible Rack into pot, making sure it is on the lower position. Place covered multipurpose pan onto rack. Assemble pressure lid, making sure the pressure release valve is in the SEAL position.
5. Select PRESSURE and set to HI. Set time to 25 minutes. Press START/STOP to begin.
6. When pressure cooking is complete, allow pressure to naturally release for 15 minutes. After 15 minutes, quick release remaining pressure by moving the pressure release valve to the VENT position. Carefully remove lid when unit has finished releasing pressure.
7. Remove the pan and chill in the refrigerator for at least 3 hours or overnight before serving topped with whipped cream.

Nutrition Info:
- Calories: 645,Total Fat: 47g,Sodium: 383mg,Carbohydrates: 48g,Protein: 13g.

Sweet And Salty Bars

Servings:12
Cooking Time: 10 Minutes
Ingredients:
- 1 cup light corn syrup
- 1 cup granulated sugar
- 1 teaspoon vanilla extract
- 1 bag mini marshmallows
- 1 cup crunchy peanut butter
- 1 bag potato chips with ridges, slightly crushed

- 1 cup pretzels, slightly crushed
- 1 bag hard-shelled candy-coated chocolates

Directions:
1. Select SEAR/SAUTÉ and set temperature to MD:HI. Select START/STOP to begin. Let preheat for 5 minutes.
2. Add the corn syrup, sugar, and vanilla and stir until the sugar is melted.
3. Add the marshmallows and peanut butter and stir until the marshmallows are melted.
4. Add the potato chips and pretzels and stir until everything is evenly coated in the marshmallow mixture.
5. Pour the mixture into a 9-by-13-inch pan and place the chocolate candies on top, slightly pressing them in. Let cool, then cut into squares and serve.

Nutrition Info:
- Calories: 585,Total Fat: 21g,Sodium: 403mg,Carbohydrates: 96g,Protein: 9g.

Raspberry Lemon Cheesecake

Servings: 8
Cooking Time: 30 Minutes
Ingredients:
- Butter flavored cooking spray
- 8 oz. cream cheese, fat free, soft
- 1/3 cup sugar
- ½ tsp lemon juice
- 1 tsp lemon zest
- ½ tsp vanilla
- ½ cup plain Greek yogurt
- 2 eggs, room temperature
- 2 tbsp. white whole wheat flour
- Fresh raspberries for garnish

Directions:
1. Spray an 8-inch baking dish with cooking spray.
2. In a large bowl, beat cream cheese, sugar, lemon juice, zest, and vanilla until smooth.
3. Add yogurt, eggs, and flour and mix well. Spoon into prepared pan.
4. Place pan in the cooking pot and add the tender-crisp lid. Set to bake on 350°F. Bake 25-30 minutes or until cheesecake passes the toothpick test.
5. Transfer to a wire rack to cool. Cover with plastic wrap and refrigerate 2-3 hours. Serve garnished with fresh raspberries.

Nutrition Info:
- Calories 93,Total Fat 6g,Total Carbs 14g,Protein 5g,Sodium 127mg.

Red Velvet Cheesecake

Servings:8
Cooking Time: 25 Minutes
Ingredients:
- 2 cups Oreo cookie crumbs
- 3 tablespoons unsalted butter, melted
- 2 packages cream cheese, at room temperature
- ½ cup granulated sugar
- ½ cup buttermilk
- 2 tablespoons unsweetened cocoa powder
- 1 teaspoon vanilla extract
- 2 tablespoons red food coloring
- ½ teaspoon white vinegar
- 1 cup water

Directions:
1. In a small bowl, combine the cookie crumbs and butter. Press this mixture into the bottom of the Ninja Multi-Purpose Pan or 8-inch baking pan.
2. In a large bowl, use an electric hand mixer to combine the cream cheese, sugar, buttermilk, cocoa powder, vanilla, food coloring, and vinegar for 3 minutes. Pour this over the cookie crust. Cover the pan tightly with aluminum foil.
3. Place the water in the pot. Insert Reversible Rack into pot, making sure it is in the lower position. Place the covered multi-purpose pan onto the rack. Assemble pressure lid, making sure the pressure release valve is in the SEAL position.
4. Select PRESSURE on HI. Set time to 25 minutes. Press START/STOP to begin.
5. When pressure cooking is complete, allow pressure to naturally release for 15 minutes. After 15 minutes, quick release remaining pressure by moving the pressure release valve to the VENT position. Carefully remove lid when unit has finished releasing pressure.
6. Remove cheesecake from the pot. Refrigerate for 3 hours, or overnight if possible before serving.

Nutrition Info:
- Calories: 437,Total Fat: 31g,Sodium: 338mg,Carbohydrates: 36g,Protein: 7g.

Vanilla Chocolate Spread

Servings: 16
Cooking Time: 25 Min
Ingredients:
- 1 ¼ pounds Hazelnuts, halved /562.5g
- ½ cups icing Sugar, sifted /65g
- ½ cup Cocoa Powder /65g
- 10 ounces Water /300ml
- 1 tsp Vanilla Extract /5ml
- ¼ tsp Cardamom, grated /1.25g
- ¼ tsp Cinnamon powder /1.25g
- ½ tsp grated Nutmeg /2.5g

Directions:
1. Place the hazelnut in a blender and blend until you obtain a paste. Place in the cooker along with the remaining ingredients.
2. Seal the pressure lid, choose Pressure, set to High, and set the time to 15 minutes. Press Start. Once the cooking is over, allow for a natural pressure release, for 10 minutes.

Strawberry Crumble

Servings: 5
Cooking Time: 2 Hours
Ingredients:
- 1 cup almond flour
- 2 tablespoons butter, melted
- 10 drops liquid stevia
- 4 cups fresh strawberries, hulled and sliced
- 1 tablespoon butter, chopped

Directions:
1. Lightly, grease the Ninja Foodi's insert.
2. In a suitable, stir in the flour, melted butter and stevia and mix until a crumbly mixture form.
3. In the pot of the prepared Ninja Foodi, place the strawberry slices and dot with chopped butter.
4. Spread the flour mixture on top evenly
5. Close the Ninja Foodi's lid with a crisping lid and select "Slow Cooker".
6. Set on "Low" for 2 hours.
7. Press the "Start/Stop" button to initiate cooking.
8. Place the pan onto a wire rack to cool slightly.
9. Serve warm.

Nutrition Info:
- Calories: 233; Fats: 19.2g; Carbohydrates: 10.7g; Proteins: 0.7g

Chocolate Brownie Cake

Servings: 6
Cooking Time: 35 Minutes.
Ingredients:
- ½ cup 70% dark chocolate chips
- ½ cup butter
- 3 eggs
- ¼ cup Erythritol
- 1 teaspoon vanilla extract

Directions:
1. In a microwave-safe bowl, stir in the chocolate chips and butter and microwave for about 1 minute, stirring after every 20 seconds.
2. Remove from the microwave and stir well.
3. Set a "Reversible Rack" in the pot of the Ninja Foodi.
4. Close the Ninja Foodi's lid with a crisping lid and select "Air Crisp".
5. Set its cooking temperature to 350 °F for 5 minutes.
6. Press the "Start/Stop" button to initiate preheating.
7. In a suitable, add the eggs, Erythritol and vanilla extract and blend until light and frothy.
8. Slowly add in the chocolate mixture and beat again until well combined.
9. Add the mixture into a lightly greased springform pan.
10. After preheating, Open the Ninja Foodi's lid.
11. Place the springform pan into the "Air Crisp Basket".
12. Close the Ninja Foodi's lid with a crisping lid and select "Air Crisp".
13. Set its cooking temperature to 350 °F for 35 minutes.
14. Press the "Start/Stop" button to initiate cooking.
15. Place the hot pan onto a wire rack to cool for about 10 minutes.
16. Flip the baked and cooled cake onto the wire rack to cool completely.
17. Cut into desired-sized slices and serve.

Nutrition Info:
- Calories: 302; Fats: 28.2g; Carbohydrates: 5.6g; Proteins: 5.6g

Fried Oreos

Servings: 9
Cooking Time: 8 Minutes
Ingredients:
- ½ cup complete pancake mix
- ⅓ cup water
- Cooking spray
- 9 Oreo cookies
- 1 tablespoon confectioners' sugar

Directions:
1. Close crisping lid. Select AIR CRISP, set temperature to 400°F, and set time to 5 minutes. Select START/STOP to begin preheating.
2. In a medium bowl, combine the pancake mix and water until combined.
3. Spray the Cook & Crisp Basket with cooking spray.
4. Dip each cookie into the pancake batter and then arrange them in the basket in a single layer so they are not touching each other. Cook in batches if needed.
5. When unit has preheated, open lid and insert basket into pot. Close crisping lid.
6. Select AIR CRISP, set temperature to 400°F, and set time to 8 minutes. Select START/STOP to begin.
7. After 4 minutes, open lid and flip the cookies. Close lid and continue cooking.
8. When cooking is complete, check for desired crispness. Remove basket and sprinkle the cookies with confectioners' sugar. Serve.

Nutrition Info:
- Calories: 83, Total Fat: 2g, Sodium: 158mg, Carbohydrates: 14g, Protein: 1g.

Almond Banana Dessert

Servings: 1
Cooking Time: 8 Min
Ingredients:
- 1 Banana; sliced
- 2 tbsp Almond Butter /30g
- 1 tbsp Coconut oil /15ml
- ½ tsp Cinnamon /2.5g

Directions:
1. Melt oil on Sear/Sauté mode. Add banana slices and fry them for a couple of minutes, or until golden on both sides. Top the fried bananas with almond butter and sprinkle with cinnamon.

Hot Fudge Brownies

Servings: 16
Cooking Time: 25 Minutes
Ingredients:
- Butter flavored cooking spray
- 2/3 cup flour
- 2/3 cup sugar
- ½ cup cocoa powder, unsweetened
- ¼ cup butter, melted
- 2 tbsp. water
- 1 tbsp. vanilla
- ½ tsp baking powder
- 1/3 cup egg substitute
- ¼ cup hot fudge sauce, fat-free, warmed

Directions:
1. Place the rack in the cooking pot. Spray an 8x8-inch baking pan with cooking spray.
2. In a large bowl, combine all ingredients, except hot fudge sauce, and mix well. Spread ½ the batter evenly in prepared pan. Pour hot fudge sauce evenly over batter then spread remaining batter over the top.
3. Place the pan on the rack and add the tender-crisp lid. Set to bake on 350°F. Bake 20-25 minutes or until brownies pass the toothpick test.
4. Transfer to wire rack to cool before serving.

Nutrition Info:
- Calories 102, Total Fat 4g, Total Carbs 17g, Protein 2g, Sodium 35mg.

Pecan Stuffed Apples

Servings: 6
Cooking Time: 20 Min
Ingredients:
- 3 ½ pounds Apples, cored /1575g
- 1 ¼ cups Red Wine /312.5ml
- ¼ cup Pecans; chopped /32.5g
- ¼ cup Graham Cracker Crumbs/32.5g
- ½ cup dried Apricots; chopped /65g
- ¼ cup Sugar /32.5g
- ½ tsp grated Nutmeg /2.5g
- ½ tsp ground Cinnamon /2.5g
- ¼ tsp Cardamom /1.25g

Directions:
1. Lay the apples at the bottom of your cooker, and pour in the red wine. Combine the other ingredients, except the crumbs.

2. Seal the pressure lid, and cook at High pressure for 15 minutes. Once ready, do a quick pressure release. Top with graham cracker crumbs and serve!

Mixed Berry Cobbler

Servings: 4
Cooking Time: 40 Min
Ingredients:
- 2 bags frozen mixed berries
- 1 cup sugar /130g
- 3 tbsps arrowroot starch /45g
- For the topping
- 1 cup self-rising flour /130g
- ⅔ cup crème fraiche, plus more as needed /177ml
- 1 tbsp melted unsalted butter /15ml
- 1 tbsp whipping cream /15ml
- 5 tbsps powdered sugar; divided /75g
- ¼ tsp cinnamon powder /1.25g

Directions:
1. To make the base, pour the blackberries into the inner pot along with the arrowroot starch and sugar. Mix to combine. Seal the pressure lid, choose Pressure; adjust the pressure to High and the cook time to 3 minutes; press Start. After cooking, perform a quick pressure release and carefully open the lid.
2. To make the topping, in a small bowl, whisk the flour, cinnamon powder, and 3 tbsps of sugar. In a separate small bowl, whisk the crème fraiche with the melted butter.
3. Pour the cream mixture on the dry ingredients and combine evenly. If the mixture is too dry, mix in 1 tbsp of crème fraiche at a time until the mixture is soft.
4. Spoon 2 to 3 tbsps of dough on top over the peaches and spread out slightly on top. Brush the topping with the whipping cream and sprinkle with the remaining sugar.
5. Close the crisping lid and Choose Bake/Roast; adjust the temperature to 325°F or 163°C and the cook time to 12 minutes. Press Start. Check after 8 minutes; if the dough isn't cooking evenly, rotate the pot about 90 , and continue cooking.
6. When ready, the topping should be cooked through and lightly browned. Allow cooling before slicing. Serve warm.

Poached Peaches

Servings: 4
Cooking Time: 15 Min
Ingredients:
- 4 Peaches, peeled, pits removed
- 1 cup Freshly Squeezed Orange Juice /250ml
- ½ cup Black Currants /65g
- 1 Cinnamon Stick

Directions:
1. Place black currants and orange juice in a blender. Blend until the mixture becomes smooth. Pour the mixture in your Foodi, and add the cinnamon stick.
2. Add the peaches to the steamer basket and then insert the basket into the pot. Seal the pressure lid, select Pressure, and set to 5 minutes at High pressure. When done, do a quick pressure release. Serve the peaches drizzled with sauce, to enjoy!

Coconut Milk Crème Caramel

Servings: 4
Cooking Time: 20 Min
Ingredients:
- 7 ounces Condensed Coconut Milk /210ml
- 1 ½ cups Water /375ml
- ½ cup Coconut Milk /125ml
- 2 Eggs
- ½ tsp Vanilla /2.5ml
- 4 tbsp Caramel Syrup /60ml

Directions:
1. Divide the caramel syrup between 4 small ramekins. Pour water in the Foodi and add the reversible rack. In a bowl, beat the rest of the ingredients. Divide them between the ramekins. Cover them with aluminum foil and lower onto the reversible rack.
2. Seal the pressure lid, and choose Pressure, set to High, and set the time to 15 minutes. Press Start. Once cooking is completed, do a quick pressure release. Let cool completely. To unmold the flan, insert a spatula along the ramekin' sides and flip onto a dish.

Sweet Potato Pie

Servings: 10
Cooking Time: 45 Minutes
Ingredients:
- Butter flavored cooking spray
- 4 sweet potatoes, baked & cooled
- ½ cup skim milk
- 1 tbsp. maple syrup, sugar free
- ½ cup brown sugar
- 2 eggs
- 1 tbsp. butter, soft

- 1 tsp cinnamon
- 1 tsp vanilla

Directions:
1. Place the rack in the cooking pot. Spray an 8-inch pie plate with cooking spray.
2. Scoop out the flesh of the potatoes and place in a large bowl.
3. Add remaining ingredients and beat until smooth. Pour into pie plate and place on the rack.
4. Add the tender-crisp lid and set to bake on 400°F. Bake 40-45 minutes or until a knife inserted in center comes out clean.
5. Transfer pie to a wire rack to cool. Cover and refrigerate until ready to serve.

Nutrition Info:
- Calories 157,Total Fat 2g,Total Carbs 31g,Protein 3g,Sodium 73mg.

Pumpkin Crème Brulee

Servings: 4
Cooking Time: 3:00 Hours
Ingredients:
- 1 egg yolk
- 1 egg, lightly beaten
- ¾ cup heavy cream
- 4 tbsp. pumpkin puree
- 1 tsp vanilla
- 4 tbsp. sugar, divided
- ¾ tsp pumpkin pie spice

Directions:
1. In a medium bowl, whisk together egg yolk and beaten egg, mix well.
2. Whisk in cream, slowly until combined.
3. Stir in pumpkin and vanilla and mix until combined.
4. In a small bowl, stir together 2 tablespoons sugar and pie spice. Add to pumpkin mixture and stir to blend.
5. Fill 4 small ramekins with mixture and place in the cooking pot. Carefully pour water around the ramekins, it should reach halfway up the sides.
6. Add the lid and set to slow cooking on low. Cook 2-3 hours or until custard is set.
7. Sprinkle remaining 2 tablespoons over the top of the custards. Add the tender-crisp lid and set to broil on 450°F. Cook another 2-3 minutes or until sugar caramelizes, be careful not to let it burn. Transfer ramekins to wire rack to cool before serving.

Nutrition Info:
- Calories 334,Total Fat 21g,Total Carbs 30g,Protein 6g,Sodium 59mg.

Chocolate Rice Pudding

Servings: 8
Cooking Time: 20 Minutes
Ingredients:
- 2/3 cup brown rice, cooked
- 2 cans coconut milk
- ½ cup Stevia
- ½ tsp cinnamon
- 1/8 tsp salt
- 1 tsp vanilla
- ½ cup dark chocolate chips

Directions:
1. Set cooker to sauté on medium. Add milk, Stevia, cinnamon, and salt and bring to a simmer, stirring frequently.
2. Stir in rice and reduce heat to low. Cook 15 minutes, stirring occasionally, until pudding has thickened.
3. Turn off cooker and stir in vanilla and chocolate chips until chocolate has melted. Serve warm or refrigerate at least one hour and serve it cold.

Nutrition Info:
- Calories 325,Total Fat 22g,Total Carbs 35g,Protein 3g,Sodium 62mg.

Chocolate Soufflé

Servings: 2
Cooking Time: 25 Min
Ingredients:
- 2 eggs, whites and yolks separated
- 3 oz. chocolate, melted /90ml
- ¼ cup butter, melted /32.5ml
- 2 tbsp flour /30g
- 3 tbsp sugar /45g
- ½ tsp vanilla extract /2.5ml

Directions:
1. Beat the yolks along with the sugar and vanilla extract. Stir in butter, chocolate, and flour. Whisk the whites until a stiff peak forms.
2. Working in batches, gently combine the egg whites with the chocolate mixture. Divide the batter between two greased ramekins. Close the crisping lid and cook for 14 minutes on Roast at 330 °F or 166°C.

Chocolate Blackberry Cake

Servings: 10
Cooking Time: 3 Hours
Ingredients:
- 2 cups almond flour
- 1 cup unsweetened coconut, shredded
- ½ cup Erythritol
- ¼ cup unsweetened Protein: powder
- 2 teaspoons baking soda
- ¼ teaspoon salt
- 4 large eggs
- ½ cup heavy cream
- ½ cup unsalted butter, melted
- 1 cup fresh blackberries
- 1/3 cup 70% dark chocolate chips

Directions:
1. Grease the Ninja Foodi's insert.
2. In a suitable, mix together the flour, coconut, Erythritol Protein: powder, baking soda and salt.
3. In another large bowl, stir in the eggs, cream and butter and beat until well combined.
4. Stir in the dry flour mixture and mix until well combined.
5. Fold in the blackberries and chocolate chips.
6. In the prepared Ninja Foodi's insert, add the mixture.
7. Close the Ninja Foodi's lid with a crisping lid and select "Slow Cooker".
8. Set on "Low" for 3 hours.
9. Press the "Start/Stop" button to initiate cooking.
10. Transfer the pan onto a wire rack about 10 minutes.
11. Flip the baked and cooled cake onto the wire rack to cool completely.
12. Cut into desired-sized slices and serve.

Nutrition Info:
- Calories: 305; Fats: 27.5g; Carbohydrates: 7.7g; Proteins: 10.6g

Brownie Bites

Servings:10
Cooking Time: 45 Minutes
Ingredients:
- Cooking spray
- 1 box brownie mix, prepared to package instructions
- Confectioners' sugar, for garnish
- Carmel sauce, for garnish

Directions:
1. Coat a silicone egg mold with nonstick cooking spray and set aside.
2. In a large bowl, prepare the brownie mix according to package instructions. Using a cookie scoop, transfer the batter to the prepared mold.
3. Place 1 cup water in the pot. Place the filled molds onto the Reversible Rack in the lower steam position, and lower into the pot.
4. Assemble the pressure lid, making sure the pressure release valve is in the SEAL position.
5. Select PRESSURE and set to HI. Set the time to 45 minutes. Select START/STOP to begin.
6. When pressure cooking is complete, allow the pressure to naturally release for 10 minutes. After 10 minutes, quick release any remaining pressure by moving the pressure release valve to the VENT position. Carefully remove the lid when the unit has finished releasing pressure.
7. Carefully remove the mold from the cooker and let cool for 5 minutes.
8. Flip the brownie onto a plate and garnish with confectioners' sugar and caramel sauce.

Nutrition Info:
- Calories: 288,Total Fat: 5g,Sodium: 168mg,Carbohydrates: 43g,Protein: 2g.

Chocolate Peanut Butter And Jelly Puffs

Servings:4
Cooking Time: 15 Minutes
Ingredients:
- 1 tube prepared flaky biscuit dough
- 2 milk chocolate bars
- Cooking spray
- 16 teaspoons (about ⅓ cup) creamy peanut butter
- 1 cup confectioners' sugar
- 1 tablespoon whole milk
- ¼ cup raspberry jam

Directions:
1. Remove biscuits from tube. There is a natural width-wise separation in each biscuit. Gently peel each biscuit in half using this separation.
2. Break the chocolate into 16 small pieces.
3. Spray a baking sheet with cooking spray.
4. Using your hands, stretch a biscuit half until it is about 3-inches in diameter. Place a teaspoon of peanut butter in center of each biscuit half, then place piece of chocolate on top. Pull an edge of dough over the top of the chocolate and

pinch together to seal. Continue pulling the dough over the top of the chocolate and pinching until the chocolate is completely covered. The dough is pliable, so gently form it into a ball with your hands. Place on the prepared baking sheet. Repeat this step with the remaining biscuit dough, peanut butter, and chocolate.

5. Place the baking sheet in the refrigerator for 5 minutes.
6. Place Cook & Crisp Basket in pot. Close crisping lid. Select AIR CRISP, set temperature to 360°F, and set time to 20 minutes. Select START/STOP to begin. Let preheat for 5 minutes.
7. Remove the biscuits from the refrigerator and spray the tops with cooking spray. Open lid and spray the basket with cooking spray. Place 5 biscuit balls in the basket. Close lid and cook for 5 minutes.
8. When cooking is complete, remove the biscuit balls from the basket. Repeat step 7 two more times with remaining biscuit balls.
9. Mix together the confectioners' sugar, milk, and jam in a small bowl to make a frosting.
10. When the cooked biscuit balls are cool enough to handle, dunk the top of each into the frosting. As frosting is beginning to set, garnish with any toppings desired, such as sprinkles, crushed toffee or candy, or mini marshmallows.

Nutrition Info:
- Calories: 663,Total Fat: 25g,Sodium: 1094mg,Carbohydrates: 101g,Protein: 14g.

Lemon Cheesecake

Servings: 12
Cooking Time: 4 Hours
Ingredients:
- For Crust:
- 1½ cups almond flour
- 4 tablespoons butter, melted
- 3 tablespoons sugar-free peanut butter
- 3 tablespoons Erythritol
- 1 large egg, beaten
- For Filling:
- 1 cup ricotta cheese
- 24 ounces cream cheese, softened
- 1½ cups Erythritol
- 2 teaspoons liquid stevia
- 1/3 cup heavy cream
- 2 large eggs
- 3 large egg yolks
- 1 tablespoon fresh lemon juice

- 1 tablespoon vanilla extract

Directions:
1. Grease the Ninja Foodi's insert.
2. For crust: in a suitable, add all the ingredients and mix until well combined.
3. In the pot of prepared of Ninja Foodi, place the crust mixture and press to smooth the top surface.
4. With a fork, prick the crust at many places.
5. For filling: in a food processor, stir in the ricotta cheese and pulse until smooth.
6. In a large bowl, add the ricotta, cream cheese, Erythritol and stevia and with an electric mixer, beat over medium speed until smooth.
7. In another bowl, stir in the heavy cream, eggs, egg yolks, lemon juice and vanilla extract and beat until well combined.
8. Stir in the egg mixture into cream cheese mixture and beat over medium speed until just combined.
9. Place the prepared filling mixture over the crust evenly.
10. Close the Ninja Foodi's lid with a crisping lid and select "Slow Cooker".
11. Set on "Low" for 3-4 hours.
12. Press the "Start/Stop" button to initiate cooking.
13. Place the pan onto a wire rack to cool.
14. Refrigerate to chill for at least 6-8 hours before serving.

Nutrition Info:
- Calories: 410; Fats: 37.9g; Carbohydrates: 6.9g; Proteins: 13g

Gingerbread

Servings: 12
Cooking Time: 5 Hours
Ingredients:
- Butter flavored cooking spray
- 1½ cups self-rising flour
- ½ cup flour
- 1 tsp cinnamon
- ½ tsp fresh ginger, grated
- ¼ tsp allspice
- ¼ tsp salt
- 8 tbsp. butter, unsalted, soft
- 2/3 cup light molasses
- ¾ cup brown sugar
- 1 egg, beaten
- ½ cup skim milk
- ½ tsp baking soda

Directions:

1. Place the rack in the cooking pot. Spray and flour an 8-inch springform pan.
2. In a large bowl, combine both flours, spices, and salt.
3. Place butter, molasses, and brown sugar in a microwave safe bowl. Microwave on high until butter has melted, mix well.
4. Add butter mixture to dry ingredients and mix well.
5. Whisk in egg until combined.
6. In a measuring cup or small bowl, whisk together milk and baking soda. Add to batter and mix until blended.
7. Pour into prepared pan and place on the rack. Add the lid and set to slow cooking on high. Set timer for 5 hours. Gingerbread is done when it passes the toothpick test.
8. Carefully remove from cooking pot and let cool before cutting and serving.

Nutrition Info:
- Calories 263,Total Fat 9g,Total Carbs 44g,Protein 3g,Sodium 183mg.

Bacon Blondies

Servings:6
Cooking Time: 35 Minutes
Ingredients:
- 6 slices uncooked bacon, cut into ¼ slices
- 1½ cups unsalted butter, at room temperature, plus additional for greasing
- 1 cup dark brown sugar
- 2 cups all-purpose flour
- Ice cream, for serving

Directions:
1. Grease the Ninja Multi-Purpose Pan with butter.
2. Select SEAR/SAUTÉ and set to HI. Select START/STOP to begin. Let preheat for 5 minutes.
3. Place the bacon in the pot. Cook, stirring frequently, for about 5 minutes, or until the fat is rendered and bacon starts to brown. Transfer the bacon to a paper towel-lined plate to drain. Wipe the pot clean of any remaining fat and return to unit.
4. In a medium bowl, beat the butter and brown sugar with a hand mixer until well incorporated. Slowly add in the flour and continue to beat until the flour is fully combined and a soft dough forms. Next, fold the cooked bacon into the dough.
5. Press the dough into the prepared pan. Place pan on Reversible Rack, ensuring it is in the lower position. Lower rack into pot. Close crisping lid.
6. Select BAKE/ROAST, set temperature to 350°F, and set time to 25 minutes. Select START/STOP to begin.
7. After 20 minutes, open lid and check for doneness by sticking a toothpick through the center of the dough. If it comes out clean, remove rack and pan from unit. If not, close lid and continue cooking.
8. When cooking is complete, remove rack and pan from unit. Let the blondies cool for about 30 minutes before serving with ice cream, if desired.

Nutrition Info:
- Calories: 771,Total Fat: 54g,Sodium: 453mg,Carbohydrates: 60g,Protein: 12g.

Coconut Cream Dessert Bars

Servings: 10
Cooking Time: 2 Hour
Ingredients:
- Butter flavored cooking spray
- 1 cup heavy cream
- ¾ cup powdered Stevia
- 4 eggs
- ½ cup coconut milk, full fat
- ¼ cup butter, melted
- 1 cup coconut, unsweetened, grated
- 3 tbsp. coconut flour
- ½ tsp baking powder
- ½ tsp vanilla
- ½ tsp salt

Directions:
1. Spray cooking pot with cooking spray.
2. Place cream, Stevia, and coconut milk in a food processor or blender. Pulse until combined.
3. Add remaining ingredients and pulse until combined.
4. Pour mixture into cooking pot. Place two paper towels over the top. Add the lid and set to slow cooking on high. Cook 1-3 hours or until center is set.
5. Carefully remove lid so no moisture gets on the bars. Transfer cooking pot to a wire rack and let cool 30 minutes.
6. Refrigerate, uncovered at least 1 hour. Cut into 10 squares or bars and serve.

Nutrition Info:
- Calories 190,Total Fat 17g,Total Carbs 24g,Protein 4g,Sodium 236mg.

Steamed Lemon Pudding

Servings: 6
Cooking Time: 90 Minutes
Ingredients:
- Nonstick cooking spray
- ¾ cup butter, unsalted, soft
- 1 cup caster sugar
- 2 eggs
- 2 cups flour
- 1 tsp baking powder
- Zest & juice from 2 lemons

Directions:
1. Lightly spray a 1 liter oven-safe bowl with cooking spray.
2. Add the butter and sugar to the bowl and beat until light and fluffy.
3. Add the eggs, one at a time, beating well after each addition.
4. Stir in the flour and baking powder until combined.
5. Fold in the lemon zest and juice and mix until smooth. Cover lightly with foil.
6. Pour 1 ½ cups water into the cooking pot and add steamer rack.
7. Place the bowl on the rack, secure the lid. Set to steam on 212°F. Cook 90 minutes, or until pudding is cooked through.
8. Remove the pudding from the cooker and let sit 5 minutes before inverting onto serving plate.

Nutrition Info:
- Calories 446,Total Fat 17g,Total Carbs 66g,Protein 7g,Sodium 33mg.

Spiced Poached Pears

Servings: 4
Cooking Time: 4 Hours
Ingredients:
- 4 ripe pears, peeled
- 2 cups fresh orange juice
- ¼ cup maple syrup
- 5 cardamom pods
- 1 cinnamon stick, broke in 2
- 1-inch piece ginger, peeled & sliced

Directions:
1. Slice off the bottom of the pears so they stand upright. Carefully remove the core with a paring knife. Stand in the cooking pot.
2. In a small bowl, whisk together orange juice and syrup. Pour over pears and add the spices.
3. Add the lid and set to slow cooking on low. Cook 3-4 hours or until pears are soft. Baste the pears every hour or so.
4. Serve garnished with whipped cream and chopped walnuts if you like, or just serve them as they are sprinkled with a little cinnamon.

Nutrition Info:
- Calories 219,Total Fat 1g,Total Carbs 53g,Protein 2g,Sodium 6mg.

Berry Apple Crisps

Servings: 8
Cooking Time: 30 Minutes
Ingredients:
- Butter flavored cooking spray
- 2 cups apples, peeled & chopped
- 2 cups blueberries
- 1 tbsp. lemon zest
- 1 tbsp. lemon juice
- ¼ cup + 1/3 cup honey, divided
- 1 tsp cinnamon
- ¼ tsp nutmeg
- 2 tbsp. cornstarch
- 2 ½ cups oats, divided
- ¼ cup walnuts, chopped
- 2 tbsp. coconut oil, melted

Directions:
1. Place the rack in the cooking pot. Lightly spray 8 ramekins with cooking spray.
2. In a medium bowl, combine apples, berries, zest, lemon juice and ¼ cup honey.
3. In a small bowl, stir together spices and cornstarch and sprinkle over fruit, toss gently to combine. Spoon into ramekins.
4. Add 1 ½ cups oats to a food processor or blender and pulse until they reach the consistency of flour. Pour into a medium bowl.
5. Stir the remaining oats and nuts into the oat flour. Add oil and 1/3 cup honey and mix until crumbly. Sprinkle over the tops of the ramekins.
6. Place ramekins on the rack and add the tender-crisp lid. Set to bake on 375°F. Bake 25-30 minutes until top is golden brown and filling is bubbly. Let cool slightly before serving.

Nutrition Info:

- Calories 280, Total Fat 8g, Total Carbs 38g, Protein 5g, Sodium 167mg.

Carrot Raisin Cookie Bars

Servings: 16
Cooking Time: 15 Minutes
Ingredients:
- Butter flavored cooking spray
- ½ cup brown sugar
- ½ cup sugar
- ½ cup coconut oil, melted
- ½ cup applesauce, unsweetened
- 2 eggs
- 1 tsp vanilla
- ½ cup almond flour
- 1 tsp baking soda
- 1 tsp baking powder
- ¼ tsp salt
- 1 tsp cinnamon
- ½ tsp nutmeg
- ½ tsp ginger
- 2 cups oats
- 1 ½ cups carrots, finely grated
- 1 cup raisins

Directions:
1. Place the rack in the cooking pot. Spray an 8x8-inch pan with cooking spray.
2. In a large bowl, combine sugars, oil, applesauce, eggs, and vanilla, mix well.
3. Stir in dry ingredients until combined. Fold in carrots and raisins. Press evenly in prepared pan.
4. Place the pan on the rack and add the tender-crisp lid. Set to bake on 350°F. Bake 12-15 minutes or until golden brown and cooked through.
5. Remove to wire rack to cool before cutting and serving.

Nutrition Info:
- Calories 115, Total Fat 7g, Total Carbs 19g, Protein 3g, Sodium 56mg.

Classic Custard

Servings: 4
Cooking Time: 30 Minutes
Ingredients:
- Nonstick cooking spray
- 4 eggs
- ½ cup half and half
- 2 cups almond milk, unsweetened
- 1/3 cup Stevia
- 1 tsp vanilla
- ¼ tsp cinnamon

Directions:
1. Spray four ramekins with cooking spray.
2. In a large bowl, whisk all the ingredients together until combined. Pour into prepared ramekins
3. Place the ramekins in the cooking pot and pour enough water around them it comes ½ inch up the sides of the ramekins.
4. Add the tender-crisp lid and set to bake on 350°F. Bake 30 minutes or until custard is set. Transfer to a wire rack and let cool before serving.

Nutrition Info:
- Calories 135, Total Fat 5g, Total Carbs 23g, Protein 11g, Sodium 164mg.

Yogurt Cheesecake

Servings: 8
Cooking Time: 40 Minutes
Ingredients:
- 4 cups plain Greek Yogurt
- 1 cup Erythritol
- ½ teaspoon vanilla extract

Directions:
1. Line a cake pans with Parchment paper.
2. In a suitable, stir in the yogurt and Erythritol and with a hand mixer, mix well.
3. Stir in vanilla extract and mix to combine.
4. Add the mixture into the prepared pan and cover with a paper kitchen towel.
5. Then with a piece of foil, cover the pan tightly.
6. In the Ninja Foodi's insert, place 1 cup of water.
7. Set a "Reversible Rack" in the Ninja Foodi's insert.
8. Place the ramekins over the "Reversible Rack".
9. Close the Ninja Foodi's lid with a pressure lid and place the pressure valve to the "Seal" position.
10. Select "Pressure" mode and set it to "High" for 40 minutes.
11. Press the "Start/Stop" button to initiate cooking.
12. Switch the pressure valve to "Vent" and do a "Quick" release.
13. Place the pan onto a wire rack and remove the foil and paper towel.
14. Again, cover the pan with a new paper towel and refrigerate to cool overnight.

Nutrition Info:
- Calories: 88; Fats: 1.5g; Carbohydrates: 8.7g; Proteins: 7g

Coconut Cake

Servings: 4
Cooking Time: 55 Min
Ingredients:
- 3 Eggs, Yolks and Whites separated
- ½ cup Coconut Sugar /65g
- ¾ cup Coconut Flour /98g
- 1 ½ cups warm Coconut Milk /375ml
- 1 cup Water /250ml
- 2 tbsp Coconut Oil, melted /30ml
- ½ tsp Coconut Extract /2.5

Directions:
1. In a bowl, beat in the egg yolks along with the coconut sugar. In a separate bowl, beat the whites until soft form peaks.
2. Stir in coconut extract and coconut oil. Gently fold in the coconut flour. Line a baking dish and pour the batter inside. Cover with aluminum foil.
3. Pour the water in your Foodi and add a reversible rack. Lower the dish onto the rack.
4. Seal the pressure lid, choose Pressure, set to High, and set the time to 35 minutes. Press Start. Do a quick pressure release, and serve.

Mocha Cake

Servings: 6
Cooking Time: 3 Hours 37 Minutes
Ingredients:
- 2 ounces 70% dark chocolate, chopped
- ¾ cup butter, chopped
- ½ cup heavy cream
- 2 tablespoons instant coffee crystals
- 1 teaspoon vanilla extract
- 1/3 cup almond flour
- ¼ cup unsweetened cacao powder
- 1/8 teaspoon salt
- 5 large eggs
- 2/3 cup Erythritol

Directions:
1. Grease the Ninja Foodi's insert.
2. In a microwave-safe bowl, stir in the chocolate and butter and microwave on High for about 2 minutes or until melted completely, stirring after every 30 seconds.
3. Remove from the microwave and stir well.
4. Set aside to cool.
5. In a small bowl, stir in the heavy cream, coffee crystals, and vanilla extract and beat until well combined.
6. In a suitable bowl, mix the flour, cacao powder and salt.
7. In a large bowl, stir in the eggs and with an electric mixer, beat on high speed until slightly thickened.
8. Slowly, stir in the Erythritol and beat on high speed until thick and pale yellow.
9. Stir in the chocolate mixture and beat on low speed until well combined.
10. Stir in the dry flour mixture and mix until just combined.
11. Slowly stir in the cream mixture and beat on medium speed until well combined.
12. In the prepared Ninja Foodi's insert, add the mixture.
13. Close the Ninja Foodi's lid with a crisping lid and select "Slow Cooker".
14. Set on "Low" for 2½-3½ hours.
15. Press the "Start/Stop" button to initiate cooking.
16. Transfer the pan onto a wire rack for about 10 minutes.
17. Flip the baked and cooled cake onto the wire rack to cool completely.
18. Cut into desired-sized slices and serve.

Nutrition Info:
- Calories: 407; Fats: 39.7g; Carbohydrates: 6.2g; Proteins: 9g

Brown Sugar And Butter Bars

Servings: 6
Cooking Time: 55 Min
Ingredients:
- 1 ½ cups Water /375ml
- 1 cup Oats /130g
- ½ cup Brown Sugar /65g
- ½ cup Sugar /65g
- 1 cup Flour /130g
- ½ cup Peanut Butter, softened /65g
- ½ cup Butter, softened /65g
- 1 Egg
- ½ tsp Baking Soda /2.5g
- ½ tsp Salt /2.5g

Directions:
1. Grease a springform pan and line it with parchment paper. Set aside. Beat together the eggs, peanut butter, butter,

salt, white sugar, and brown sugar. Fold in the oats, flour, and baking soda.

2. Press the batter into the pan. Cover the pan with a paper towel and with a piece of foil. Pour the water into the Foodi and add a reversible rack. Lower the springform pan onto the rack.

3. Seal the pressure lid, choose Pressure, set to High, and set the time to 35 minutes. Press Start. When ready, do a quick release. Wait for 15 minutes before inverting onto a plate and cutting into bars.

Vanilla Pound Cake

Servings: 8
Cooking Time: 45 Minutes
Ingredients:
- Nonstick cooking spray
- 1 cup butter, unsalted, soft
- 1 cup sugar
- 4 eggs
- 2 tsp vanilla
- ½ tsp salt
- 2 cups flour

Directions:
1. Add the rack to the cooking pot. Spray a loaf pan with cooking spray.
2. In a large bowl, on high speed, beat butter and sugar until fluffy.
3. Beat in eggs, one at a time, until combined. Stir in vanilla and salt.
4. Turn mixer to low and add flour a 1/3 at a time. Beat just until combined. Pour into prepared pan.
5. Place the pan on the rack and add the tender-crisp lid. Set to bake on 350°F. Bake 45-50 minutes or until cake passes the toothpick test.
6. Let cool in pan 15 minutes then invert onto a wire rack and let cool completely.

Nutrition Info:
- Calories 389,Total Fat 18g,Total Carbs 49g,Protein 7g,Sodium 192mg.

Apricots With Honey Sauce

Servings: 4
Cooking Time: 15 Min
Ingredients:
- 8 Apricots, pitted and halved
- ¼ cup Honey /62.5ml
- 2 cups Blueberries /260g
- ½ Cinnamon stick
- 1 ¼ cups Water /312.5ml
- ½ Vanilla Bean; sliced lengthwise
- 1 ½ tbsp Cornstarch /22.5g
- ¼ tsp ground Cardamom /1.25g

Directions:
1. Add all ingredients, except for the honey and the cornstarch, to your Foodi. Seal the pressure lid, choose Pressure, set to High, and set the time to s 8 minutes. Press Start. Do a quick pressure release and open the pressure lid.
2. Remove the apricots with a slotted spoon. Choose Sear/Sauté, add the honey and cornstarch, then let simmer until the sauce thickens, for about 5 minutes. Split up the apricots among serving plates and top with the blueberry sauce, to serve.

Chocolate Chip Cheesecake

Servings: 12
Cooking Time: 50 Minutes
Ingredients:
- Butter flavored cooking spray
- 16 oz. cream cheese, fat free, soft
- ½ cup + 1 tbsp. Stevia, divided
- 3 eggs
- 1 tsp vanilla, divided
- ½ tsp fresh lemon juice, divided
- ½ cup mini chocolate chips
- 1 cup sour cream, fat free

Directions:
1. Spray an 8-inch baking pan with cooking spray.
2. In a large bowl, beat cream cheese and ½ cup Stevia until smooth.
3. Beat in eggs, one at a time, beat well after each addition.
4. Add ½ teaspoon vanilla, and ¼ teaspoon lemon juice and stir until combined. Stir in chocolate chips and spoon into prepared pan.
5. Place the pan in the cooking pot and add the tender-crisp lid. Set to bake on 325°F. Bake 40 minutes, or until top starts to brown.
6. In a small bowl, combine sour cream, remaining Stevia, vanilla, and lemon juice, mix well. Spread over top of cheesecake and bake another 10 minutes.
7. Transfer to a wire rack to cool. Cover with plastic wrap and refrigerate at least 4 hours before serving.

Nutrition Info:
- Calories 127,Total Fat 5g,Total Carbs 22g,Protein 8g,Sodium 312mg.

Portuguese Honey Cake

Servings: 8
Cooking Time: 15 Minutes
Ingredients:
- Butter flavored cooking spray
- 3 egg yolks, room temperature
- 2 eggs, room temperature
- 2 tbsp. powdered sugar
- ¼ cup honey
- 4 ½ tbsp. cake flour

Directions:
1. Place the rack in the cooking pot. Spray an 8-inch round baking dish with cooking spray and lightly coat with flour.
2. In a large bowl, beat egg yolks, eggs, and powdered sugar until combined.
3. In a small saucepan over medium heat, heat honey until it starts to simmer. Let simmer 2 minutes.
4. With mixer running, slowly beat in the hot honey. Beat mixture 8-10 minutes until pale and thick and doubled in size. Gently tap the bowl on the counter to remove any air bubbles.
5. Sift flour into mixture and gently fold in to combine. Pour the batter into the pan and tap again to remove air bubbles. Place the cake on the rack.
6. Add the tender-crisp lid and set to bake on 350°F. Bake the cake 15 minutes, center should still be soft.
7. Transfer to a wire rack and let cool in pan 30 minutes. Invert onto serving plate and serve.

Nutrition Info:
- Calories 97,Total Fat 3g,Total Carbs14 g,Protein 3g,Sodium 23mg.

Caramel Pecan Coffee Cake

Servings: 16
Cooking Time: 35 Minutes
Ingredients:
- Butter flavored cooking spray
- 3 cups almond flour, sifted
- 1 tsp baking powder
- 1 tsp baking soda
- ½ teaspoon salt
- ½ cup butter, softened
- ½ cup Stevia
- 3 eggs
- ½ cup almond milk, unsweetened
- 1 tsp vanilla
- ½ cup caramel sauce, sugar free, divided
- ½ cup pecans, chopped, divided

Directions:
1. Place the rack in the cooking pot. Spray a Bundt pan with cooking spray.
2. In a medium bowl, combine flour, baking powder, baking soda, and salt, mix well.
3. In a large bowl, beat butter and Stevia until fluffy.
4. Beat in eggs, milk, and vanilla. Stir in dry ingredients just until combined.
5. Pour half the batter in the prepared pan. Top with half the caramel sauce and half the pecans. Use a butter knife to lightly swirl sauce and nuts into the batter. Top with remaining batter.
6. Place the pan and on the rack and add the tender-crisp lid. Set to air fry on 325 °F. Bake 35-40 minutes or until coffee cake passes the toothpick test.
7. Let cool in pan 15 minutes, then invert onto serving plate. Drizzle with remaining caramel sauce and sprinkle with remaining nut. Serve.

Nutrition Info:
- Calories 119,Total Fat 9g,Total Carbs 15g,Protein 2g,Sodium 250mg.

Mexican Chocolate Walnut Cake

Servings: 8
Cooking Time: 2 ½ Hours
Ingredients:
- Butter flavored cooking spray
- 1½ cups flour
- ½ cup cocoa powder, unsweetened
- 2 tsp baking powder
- 2 tsp ground cinnamon
- ¼ tsp cayenne pepper
- 1/8 tsp salt
- 1 cup sugar
- 3 eggs, beaten
- ¾ cup coconut oil melted
- 2 tsp vanilla
- 2 cups zucchini, grated
- ¾ cup walnuts, chopped, divided

Directions:
1. Spray the cooking pot with cooking spray and line the bottom with parchment paper.
2. In a medium bowl, combine dry ingredients and mix well.
3. In a large bowl, beat sugar and eggs until creamy.
4. Stir in oil, vanilla, zucchini, and ½ cup walnuts until combined. Fold in dry ingredients just until combined.
5. Pour batter into cooking pot and sprinkle remaining nuts over the top. Add the lid and set to slow cooking on high. Cook 2 ½ hours or until cake passes the toothpick test. Transfer cake to a wire rack to cool before serving.

Nutrition Info:
- Calories 452,Total Fat 28g,Total Carbs 48g,Protein 7g,Sodium 189mg.

RECIPES INDEX

A

Almond Banana Dessert 100
Almond Quinoa Porridge 17
Apricot Oatmeal 22
Apricots With Honey Sauce 109
Arroz Con Cod 69
Asian Beef 59
Asian Inspired Halibut 71
Asparagus With Feta 92

B

Bacon & Egg Poppers 19
Bacon & Sauerkraut With Apples 61
Bacon Blondies 105
Bacon Strips 56
Bacon Wrapped Scallops 33
Baked Cod Casserole 72
Baked Eggs In Mushrooms 22
Baked Linguine 91
Balsamic Cabbage With Endives 89
Banana Custard Oatmeal 11
Banana Pancakes 14
Barbeque Chicken Drumettes 49
Bbq Chicken Sandwiches 11
Beef & Broccoli Casserole 59
Beef And Bell Pepper With Onion Sauce 65
Beef Bourguignon 67
Beef Bulgogi 60
Beef Chicken Meatloaf 33
Beef In Basil Sauce 57
Beef Lasagna 57
Beef Mole 53
Beef Sirloin Steak 55
Beef Tips & Mushrooms 55
Beets And Carrots 86
Berry Apple Crisps 106

Blueberry Muffins 18
Braised Chicken With Mushrooms And Brussel Sprouts 51
Breakfast Burritos 11
Breakfast Pies 13
Brie Spread With Cherries & Pistachios 35
Broccoli, Ham, And Cheddar Frittata 10
Brown Sugar And Butter Bars 108
Brownie Bites 103
Brussels Sprouts Bacon Hash 17
Buttermilk Chicken Thighs 45

C

Cajun Chicken & Pasta 44
Cajun Salmon With Lemon 68
Cajun Shrimp 75
Caramel Pecan Coffee Cake 110
Caramelized Cauliflower With Hazelnuts 25
Caribbean Chicken Skewers 26
Caribbean Ropa Vieja 64
Carrot Cake Muffins 13
Carrot Raisin Cookie Bars 107
Cauliflower Gratin 28
Cheesecake French Toast 15
Cheesy Basil Stuffed Chicken 49
Cheesy Cauliflower Tater Tots 31
Cheesy Chicken Dip 24
Cheesy Corn Casserole 83
Cheesy Corn Pudding 94
Cheesy Fried Risotto Balls 27
Cheesy Ham & Potato Casserole 63
Cheesy Shakshuka 18
Cheesy Smashed Sweet Potatoes 36
Cheesy Squash Tart 93
Cheesy Stuffed Mushroom 25
Chicken And Broccoli 41
Chicken Bites 31

Chicken Breasts 39
Chicken Fajitas With Avocado 45
Chicken Pasta With Pesto Sauce 47
Chicken Pot Pie 44
Chicken Thighs With Thyme Carrot Roast 48
Chicken With Bacon And Beans 42
Chicken With Rice And Peas 43
Chili Mint Steamed Snapper 68
Chipotle Raspberry Chicken 46
Chocolate Blackberry Cake 103
Chocolate Brownie Cake 99
Chocolate Chip & Zucchini Snack Bars 29
Chocolate Chip Cheesecake 109
Chocolate Peanut Butter And Jelly Puffs 103
Chocolate Rice Pudding 102
Chocolate Soufflé 102
Chorizo And Shrimp Boil 71
Chorizo Omelet 16
Chorizo Stuffed Yellow Bell Peppers 62
Chunky Pork Meatloaf With Mashed Potatoes 60
Cinnamon Bun Oatmeal 12
Citrus Glazed Halibut 69
Clam Fritters 75
Classic Custard 107
Coconut Cake 108
Coconut Cilantro Shrimp 72
Coconut Cream Dessert Bars 105
Coconut Curried Mussels 81
Coconut Milk Crème Caramel 101
Corned Cabbage Beef 62
Crab Alfredo 78
Crab Cakes 73
Crab Cakes With Spicy Dipping Sauce 72
Crab Rangoon's 30
Cranberry Lemon Quinoa 21
Creamy Chicken Carbonara 45
Creamy Tuscan Chicken Pasta 43
Creole Dirty Rice 56
Crispy Cheesy Straws 23
Crispy Cheesy Zucchini Bites 33
Crispy Chicken With Carrots And Potatoes 44

D
Drunken Saffron Mussels 77

F
Flounder Veggie Soup 74
French Dip Sandwiches 21
Fried Oreos 100

G
Garlicky Pork Chops 56
Garlicky Tomato 36
Ginger Orange Chicken Tenders 38
Gingerbread 104
Glazed Carrots 20
Greek Style Turkey Meatballs 48
Green Cream Soup 91
Grilled Cheese 89

H
Haddock With Sanfaina 74
Ham & Spinach Breakfast Bake 19
Ham, Ricotta & Zucchini Fritters 63
Hassel Back Chicken 49
Hawaiian Tofu 84
Hearty Veggie Soup 94
Herb Roasted Drumsticks 50
Herb Roasted Mixed Nuts 32
Herb Salmon With Barley Haricot Verts 68
Herbed Cauliflower Fritters 37
Herby Fish Skewers 27
Honey Garlic Chicken And Okra 40
Honey Mustard Hot Dogs 30
Hot & Sour Soup 92
Hot Dogs With Peppers 64
Hot Fudge Brownies 100

I
Italian Flounder 79
Italian Spinach & Tomato Soup 92
Italian Turkey & Pasta Soup 41

J

Jerk Chicken Thighs With Sweet Potato And Banana Mash 39

K

Korean Barbecued Satay 52
Korean Pork Chops 58
Kung Pao Shrimp 80

L

Lamb Curry 53
Lamb Tagine 54
Lemon Cheesecake 104
Lemon Cod Goujons And Rosemary Chips 76
Lime Chicken Chili 48
Loaded Potato Skins 35
Low Country Boil 77

M

Mackerel En Papillote With Vegetables 81
Maple Glazed Pork Chops 55
Mashed Potatoes With Spinach 83
Mediterranean Cod 77
Mediterranean Quiche 15
Mexican Chocolate Walnut Cake 110
Mexican Pot Roast 60
Mexican Street Corn 34
Mixed Berry Cobbler 101
Mocha Cake 108
Morning Pancakes 19
Mushroom Leek Soup With Parmesan Croutons 96
Mushroom Poutine 88
Mushroom Risotto With Swiss Chard 86
Mushrooms Stuffed With Veggies 32

N

Nutmeg Pumpkin Porridge 12

P

Paella Señorito 70
Pancetta Hash With Baked Eggs 17
Parmesan Breadsticks 26
Parmesan Butternut Crisps 26
Pasta Primavera 94
Pasta With Roasted Veggies 90
Peaches & Brown Sugar Oatmeal 16
Peanut Butter Pie 97
Pecan Stuffed Apples 100
Pepper And Sweet Potato Skewers 97
Pepper Crusted Tri Tip Roast 56
Peppercorn Meatloaf 58
Pepperoni Omelets 20
Pesto Pork Chops & Asparagus 61
Pesto With Cheesy Bread 86
Pistachio Crusted Mahi Mahi 70
Pistachio Crusted Salmon 69
Pizza Stuffed Chicken 46
Poached Egg Heirloom Tomato 12
Poached Peaches 101
Pork Chops With Green Beans And Scalloped Potatoes 66
Pork Sandwiches With Slaw 65
Pork Tenderloin With Ginger And Garlic 66
Portuguese Honey Cake 110
Potato Samosas 36
Pumpkin Breakfast Bread 16
Pumpkin Crème Brulee 102

Q

Quinoa Protein Bake 23

R

Radish Apples Salad 96
Raspberry Lemon Cheesecake 98
Red Beans And Rice 91
Red Pork And Chickpea Stew 59
Red Velvet Cheesecake 98
Roasted Pork With Apple Gravy 58
Roasted Vegetable Salad 86
Rustic Veggie Tart 85

S

Saucy Chicken Wings 34
Saucy Kale 95
Seafood Gumbo 75
Seafood Minestrone 80
Seared Scallops In Asparagus Sauce 78
Seasoned Parsnip Fries 28
Shallot Pepper Pancakes 29
Short Ribs With Egg Noodles 67
Shredded Chicken Salsa 42
Shrimp & Sausage Gumbo 79
Shrimp And Sausage Paella 78
Smoky Horseradish Spare Ribs 54
Soft-boiled Eggs 16
Sour And Sweet Pork 61
Sour Cream & Cheese Chicken 38
South Of The Border Corn Dip 35
Southern Pineapple Casserole 95
Southern-style Lettuce Wraps 63
Southwest Chicken Bake 50
Spanish Chicken & Olives 41
Spanish Potato And Chorizo Frittata 20
Spanish Rice 95
Speedy Fajitas 52
Spiced Poached Pears 106
Spiced Red Snapper 76
Spicy Black Bean Dip 34
Spicy Chicken Wings. 50
Spicy Glazed Pecans 31
Spicy Kimchi And Tofu Fried Rice 88
Spicy Salmon With Wild Rice 87
Spicy Shrimp Pasta With Vodka Sauce 73
Spicy Turkey Meatballs 30
Spinach Hummus 32
Spinach Turkey Cups 14
Steak And Minty Cheese 23
Steamed Lemon Pudding 106
Stir Fried Scallops & Veggies 80
Strawberry Crumble 99
Stuffed Baked Tomatoes 10
Stuffed Cod 73
Succotash With Basil Crusted Fish 82
Sweet & Spicy Shrimp 71
Sweet And Salty Bars 97

Sweet Bread Pudding 22
Sweet Potato Gratin 24
Sweet Potato Pie 101
Sweet Potato Skins 24

T

Taiwanese Chicken 52
Teriyaki Pork Noodles 53
Tilapia & Tamari Garlic Mushrooms 81
Tomato Galette 84
Tuna Salad With Potatoes And Asparagus 70
Turkey & Cabbage Enchiladas 39
Turkey & Squash Casserole 42
Turkey Croquettes 40
Turkey Enchilada Casserole 38
Turkey Green Chili 47
Turkey Scotch Eggs 28
Tuscany Turkey Soup 51

V

Vanilla Chocolate Spread 99
Vanilla Pound Cake 109
Veggie And Quinoa Stuffed Peppers 91
Veggie Lasagna 90
Veggie Loaded Pasta 87
Veggie Skewers 85
Veggie Taco Soup 83
Very Berry Puffs 20

W

Waffle Bread Pudding With Maple-jam Glaze 14
Walnut Orange Coffee Cake 21
Warming Harvest Soup 93

Y

Yogurt Cheesecake 107

Z

Zucchini & Beef Lasagna 64
Zucchini Egg Tots 25
Zucchini Pancakes 18
Zucchini Quinoa Stuffed Red Peppers 89
Zucchini Rice Gratin 96
Zucchinis Spinach Fry 84

Printed in Great Britain
by Amazon